THE EPISTOLARY NOVEL

THE EPISTOLARY NOVEL

ITS ORIGIN, DEVELOPMENT, DECLINE, AND
RESIDUARY INFLUENCE

GODFREY FRANK SINGER

NEW YORK
RUSSELL & RUSSELL · INC
1963

FIRST PUBLISHED IN 1933
REISSUED, 1963, BY RUSSELL & RUSSELL, INC.
L. C. CATALOG CARD NO: 63—9508

PRINTED IN THE UNITED STATES OF AMERICA

To
J. S. AND L. F. S.
*with heartfelt thanks for their great
generosity and many indulgences*

FOREWORD

THAT the English novel first grew into solid form in the eighteenth century is a fact too well established to need more than passing mention. In the course of that century various types of the novel, various "schools" of writing grew up, some of which have been segregated and described in detail in various critical works. Of utmost importance among these groups, both in achievement and as a "type" of fiction, is the novel cast in letter form. It is the purpose of the following dissertation to present as complete a survey as possible of that form of fiction. That it was of great importance will be seen from a consideration both of its quality and of its quantity. In order to show the continuity of that form and to take cognizance of its periodical mutations, I have used and examined several hundred novels, constituting a majority of the novels in that form now extant. This has not been done with any hope of discovering lost masterpieces. It has, however, revealed many sensible, pleasant, and workmanlike books, which hardly deserve the oblivion into which they have fallen. For the vivid flashes which they not infrequently cast upon the manners of the period alone they would be worthy of attention. Taken together with the great mass of writing in the same form during a period of fully half a century they present to the thoughtful mind an exceedingly interesting spectacle of the working out of a literary cycle according to the laws of nature and to the materials of its own composition.

Much of the survey has been made possible by a possession of the books themselves. It is appropriate, however, to mention at once the palpable indebtedness to the invaluable suggestions found in the works of Dr. Charlotte Morgan and Professor Helen Sard Hughes in the history of fiction before the publication of *Pamela* with the attention which they have given to the forms and movements of seventeenth-century and early eighteenth-century prose. Such hints have been further supplemented by references to the Reviews of the period and have sometimes had additions from the long and curious lists of other books on sale by the publisher, which are occasionally found attached to his several volumes.

This work was undertaken at the suggestion of Professor John C. Mendenhall who, patient and analytic critic that he is, has given the friendly guidance and unflagging assistance necessary to the very existence of this study. To him, to Dr. Ralph B. Allen, for help with proof, to Dr. Beaumont S. Bruestle, for help with the index, to certain members of the Department of English of the University of Pennsylvania who have guided my studies and fostered my appreciation during many years, and to my friends my gratitude can hardly be expressed with adequacy. Without their support this study could never have achieved even such slight merit as it may possess. Let this be in no small measure such praise as may be due; the shortcomings are my own.

G. F. S.

Philadelphia, November 10, 1932.

CONTENTS

I

THE DEVELOPMENT OF THE
LITERARY EPISTLE

IN A PRIMITIVE age, the mysterious art of communicating by
means of symbols would be regarded by ordinary mortals
with suspicion, perhaps even with dislike. Of course, the
psychologists will tell us that human beings generally dis-
trust what they do not understand and that this is a pro-
foundly intrinsic truth to be found in human nature. Let
us remember, in addition, that the transmission of a message
on a tablet of bronze or stone (or, later, on a tablet of wood,
waxed over) seemed no less remarkable to the men of
Homer's day than the radio seems to the inhabitants of
darkest Africa today. But by Cicero's day the letter had become established as one of the indispensable conveniences
of life, and oral communication, once the sole means of delivering a message, remained in abeyance, even through the
Middle Ages, until the nineteenth-century invention of the
telephone revived it.

To say that one must return to the dawn of "recorded
time" to find a letter mentioned for the first time would
perhaps be hyperbole. To say that the letter writing impulse
is among the oldest in the nature of man is more accurate.
We need only turn to a consideration of the cuneiform tablets discovered in the nineteenth century at Tell Amarna in
order to find Egyptian letters that date back as far as the
fifteenth century B.C. Most of these letters are concerned
with matters of state, such as the Hittite invasion of Damas-
cus, the Amorite treachery, the war in Phœnicia, and the

I

wars in Palestine, so that, although there is to be found in them much local color and movement, the epistle is used primarily as a matter of necessary information. Whatever story interest is present is subordinate and incidental.

There is, in the sixth book of Homer's *Iliad* a letter (probably the first to be mentioned in Greek literature) which is used purely to convey a message. It is the story of Bellerophon (in all probability not the same Bellerophon we associate in legend with the winged horse of inspiration) and of King Proctos and his wife Anteia, wherein the said Anteia tells the king, her husband, that Bellerophon lusts for her against her will. Actually, the queen is enraged because the young man has scorned her illicit advances.

Then was the King angry when he heard it; yet to slay him did he forbear, for his soul did shame of such a deed. So he sent him to Lykia and gave him tokens *of woe, writing upon a folded tablet of many deadly things,* and bade him show these to Anteia's father that he might be slain.[1]

This passage further tells us how the young Bellerophon went carrying what he thought was a guest token, but what was really his murder warrant, and how he thus became the victim of treachery. The "sealed tablets of woe" which are referred to in this passage may really have been only devices of a hieroglyphic nature. To what extent writing was known amongst the Greeks in Homeric times is still not clear.

In very much the same manner did King David behave toward Uriah the Hittite in the Second Book of Samuel.[2] David arose and saw a beautiful woman washing herself, and having looked upon her and found her fair he went to find out who she was. She was Bathsheba, the wife of Uriah the Hittite. Then Joab was sent for and he was commanded to send Uriah to David. This he did and Uriah came to Jerusalem.

And it came to pass in the morning that David wrote a letter to Joab, and sent it by the hand of Uriah. And he wrote in the

[1] *Iliad*, Book VI, lines 168-69. Translation by T. A. Budsley.
[2] II Sam., 11:3-15.

letter, saying, Set ye Uriah in the forefront of the hottest battle, and retire ye from him, that he may be smitten and die.[3]

In both of these incidents, it will be noted, the letter is used as a means of revenge, or to serve the purpose of lust or jealousy; but in neither does the letter itself tell any story It is merely a message.

The New Testament offers us a surprisingly large portion of itself in the form of letters. The distinguished letters of St. Paul, which contain not only what is information, to be used for the purpose of delivering a message, but are exhortations and exegeses as well, are particularly worthy examples of the early art of letter writing. Many of them are like formal essays or theological dissertations, but the one that is least like either is the rather terse Epistle to Philemon. This consists of only twenty-five verses and is a very fine and memorable example of restrained eloquence. In later times, the influence of the writing of St. Paul on the ecclesiastical writers, particularly the church letter writers of the Middle Ages, is as great as that of Cicero on the secular letter writers of the Renaissance.

If we are to consider the purely informative letter, or letter of message, as a first group, we find a second group to be composed of those letters which were originally written as messages, but which have come to tell stories or to "construct" personalities for later readers other than their first intended recipients. Prime among these are the letters of that great Latin epistolarian, Marcus Tullius Cicero (106-43 B.C.), a man who stands almost between the two groups in that his letters were, for the most part, so definitely written as means of information, but have become to us an invaluable source of original material concerning the character of the man. Of his voluminous correspondence, about eight hundred letters are now extant. Four hundred of these are addressed to his friend Atticus. To those who know only Cicero the senator, the statesman, the advocate, the lawyer —in a word, the public man—it is a pleasant surprise to turn

[3] II Sam., 11:14-15.

to these letters and find Cicero "at home," as it were. If M. Bernard knew Anatole France *en pantoufles*, these letters allow us to know Cicero much after the same fashion. Cicero's letters are, on the other hand, important and pertinent to us for an entirely different reason, and that is because, as they represent the very best tradition of letter writing in Latin, they are the models upon which the English letter writers of the pre-Elizabethan days patterned their letters.

The extant correspondence of Cicero dates from 68 B.C., when he was thirty-nine years of age and, as we have already said, is, in every sense of the word, a model. There is much more grace in these letters than in any of the orations, with the possible exception of the "Pro Archia Poeta," and more personal philosophy than is in any other Ciceronian work except the "De Amicitia" and the "De Senectute." Indeed, the letters show a definite appreciation on the part of the author of the "wine of life" and they reveal that author to us as one who was a gentleman. The depth of his friendship, the tender concern for his family, the dignity of the feeling of the "antique Roman," his connoisseurship of life and of art, are all here revealed as they are nowhere else in his writings. The letters of Cicero give us a daily catalogue of his thought and his activity such as has been furnished us in so distinguished a fashion by few men in public life. Nor is it this alone that makes these letters so valuable, but also, as has already been intimated, the graceful style of the prose herein contained, gracious in its tone, firm in its logic, expressive of the very thought of the man. To those who know Cicero only through the orations there may be vouchsafed an appreciation of a man who is very definitely an artist in his own particular field; to those who know likewise the letters of Cicero there is unfolded the true personality of the man in such a manner that the title of greatness seems to adhere to him as a natural appurtenance. These are the true Cicero and they give us a lasting picture of the proud, yet pathetic, man who has given the best of himself to the service of his country only to receive, ultimately, the gift of exile when his work was done.

Directed more frequently to a semi-public audience than Cicero's, and not without consideration for their literary effect if published, are the letters of Caius Plinius Caecilius, Pliny the Younger. The letters of Pliny, written in imitation of the letters of Cicero, actually owe much, except in the matter of philosophy, to the inspiration of the great orator. The younger Pliny, nephew to Pliny the Elder, belonged to the latter half of the first century A.D., his dates ranging from 61 A.D. to 115 A.D., a period which is sometimes referred to as the Silver Age, in direct contrast to the preceding and much more famous and glorious Golden Age, of the Roman Empire. Like Cicero, he loved his Rome with a great intensity, and if this love had not in it the public patriotism of the earlier Roman it was no less characterized by the same appreciation of its customs, its aspirations and, above all, its native scenes. Pliny was a statesman, a scholar, a gentleman and, beyond all else, a truly literary figure with a basic feeling for the glorious tradition of Greek and Roman letters that lay behind him, stretched out in a sort of golden sunlight of what the author seemed to realize were ages greater than his own. He was undoubtedly conscious of a certain lesser quality in his own age, and yet he felt it had its own merits which, according to his testimony, should be celebrated. The letters of Pliny have proved to be a source, authentic and fairminded, of much of the history of the age in which he lived, but it is not in their being a storehouse of historic data that we are at this point interested in these letters so much as in their representing the tradition of literary letter writing which was speedily growing up.

It has been noted by critics that the letters of Pliny[4] were written with a definite eye to publication and preservation for the pleasure of posterity. That this is so is undeniable. That it is to be considered detrimental to the letters themselves is a distinct matter for argument. These letters are, it

[4] H. H. Harper, *Epistles of Pliny*, Introduction, p. XII.

must be confessed, conscious efforts. Furthermore, the author himself shows a definite consciousness of the good qualities their writing displayed. On the other hand, the judgment of posterity has proved that Pliny was not wrong in the estimation of his own work, and it may then be concluded that there is nothing unfortunate in the estimation itself since it is so accurate and, considering the literary culture of the man, so inevitable.

What these letters have to offer us, aside from their historical revelations, is rather wide in its embrace. We are given much knowledge of the daily routine of Roman patrician life, and it is knowledge that is the more valuable for its minuteness. There is likewise given a personal revelation of the character of the author, his particular philosophy of life, influenced as it was by both the times in which he lived and the social class of which he was a representative. Beyond this, there is a constant expression of the depth of feeling which the author has for the profession and practice of literature, and the letters themselves are full of excerpts from the classics of his day, especially quotations from the *Iliad*, the *Odyssey*, and from Catullus.

Thus, the letters are full of descriptions of the Roman scene, of Roman landscape, and of Roman architecture, and the scene of the bath is repeated many times during the course of these works. One of the most, if not the most, dramatic descriptions which Pliny has given us in his letters is that of the eruption of Vesuvius, since so frequently celebrated in literature. Upon the whole, the latter of the two letters (Book VI, Letters XVI and XX) written at the request of Cornelius Tacitus concerning Pliny's adventures in Misenum during the eruption and earthquake, is by far the more vivid and palpitating, and describes with a notable tenseness the author's belief that he was witnessing, with the remainder of mankind, the end of creation.

The philosophy of the author as revealed in these letters is that of a patrician and gentleman of noble thought and bearing, and there is about it much of the humanist who has a deep appreciation of the foibles of man, the weaknesses and the beauty of life. Nowhere is this better expressed than in the Eighth Book, Letter XXII, where Pliny writes:

Have you ever observed a sort of people who, though they themselves are under the abject dominion of every vice, shew a kind of jealous resentment against the errors of others. . . . The highest of characters, in my estimation, is his who is ready to pardon the rest of mankind as if he were every day guilty himself; and at the same time as cautious of committing a fault as if he never forgave one.

Certainly no passage from this author expresses more succinctly the breadth of mind and the innate nobility of his nature.

The letters are full, as has already been intimated, of Pliny's appreciation of literature, of his appreciation of what he and his friends have written, and of anxiety concerning his friends' opinions of his own works, opinions he seemed to be always on the lookout to receive and welcomed with a sort of sense of sport in such a give-and-take of friendly criticism. Additionally, it must be noted that Pliny kept a servant to read his works to him, and he expresses, at least once (Book VIII, Letter I), extreme anxiety for the well-being of that reader who, alone, seemed to have been able to do vocal justice to the writings of the master. This expresses the connoisseur as well as the compositeur.

That the letters of Pliny are like the letters of Cicero is, in many ways, undeniable, but may be unfairly emphasized; that they are more diverse, more truly literary in their quality of having been written with an eye to the casual reader, rather than the definite recipient, more vigorous, less uneasy and less complaining in tone, must likewise be most definitely stated.

When we approach the fourth and fifth centuries, we find at least three writers among the letter writers in Latin who require some attention. There is, first of all, Quintus Aurelius Symmachus (c. 345-410). There have been left to us nine books of epistles and two from a tenth book published by his son after the death of the author. These letters are written after the fashion of those of Pliny but do not succeed in capturing the pleasant liveliness, nor the wide range of interests that the epistles they imitate possess. However, they help to carry on toward the Middle Ages the sort of personal letter Cicero wrote and, after him, Pliny. Of distinctly more importance as an epistolarian is Sidonius Apollinaris, a Roman prefect and Christian bishop, known chiefly for his letters and poems written between c. 430-484. Both poems and letters were used at a later period as models of style.[5] The most notable single letter is that addressed to one Domitius, in which is given a long and detailed account and description of life in a villa, written in carefully balanced and graceful sentences. The letter of welcome to Constans is an almost equally notable composition touched with the same quality of careful balance. Of somewhat less literary importance as a letter writer is the monk Cassiodorus (490-575), but he, as well as Sidonius, helped preserve and carry forward the Ciceronian tradition of the epistle.

It must be remembered, of course, that the art of letter writing was of considerable importance in the Middle Ages. Especially is this true of official and ceremonious letters. The art of the letter was developed in classical Latin, and when, in the Middle Ages, the Latin tongue became the language of law and of diplomacy, the Latin letter remained as an ideal and retained its importance throughout the Renaissance. The famous school at Orleans taught, in the thirteenth century, Rhetoric as a training for learning official correspondence and developed a carefully trained faculty for letter writing that rivaled that of Italy.[6] The center for the teaching of Dictamen, which was the model for the official correspondence of Western civilization, the Papal Chancery, was Bo-

[5] Edmond Faral, *Les Arts Poétiques du XIIIè Siècle; Recherches et Documents sur la Technique Littéraire du Moyen Age*, Paris, 1924, p. 102; *also* Edmond Faral, *La Littérature Latine du Moyen Age*, Paris, 1923, p. 21.

[6] J. C. Mendenhall, *Aureate Terms*, Phila., 1920, pp. 19 and 26; *also* H. Rashdall, *The Universities of Europe During the Middle Ages*, Oxford, 1895, II, 136-148.

logna; just as the center for the teaching of Grammatica was Chartres. At Bologna, the *stilus Romanus* was of chief importance. There are not only letter collections that have come down to us from this period, but form letters as well, that have stood for centuries as unimpeachable models. Indeed, the prevalence of medieval letter writing and the drill in style and form definitely kept the letter a literary, rather than a practical, phenomenon although it was not, in any sense of the word, fictional.

Of particular note is the preservation of actual correspondence, like that of Alcuin, prime among those monks who continued the Ciceronian ideal of letter writing. Alcuin (735-804) comes down to us as a man of definite note, Charlemagne's English-born "minister of education." The letters of Alcuin are divided into three groups: (1) those addressed to Charlemagne; (2) those addressed to the friends of the writer; (3) those addressed to the pupils of the writer. The correspondence of Alcuin is, in itself, a document of considerable historical importance as a source of information concerning the age of Charlemagne. This correspondence consists, however, as published, not only of the letters of Alcuin, but also of the replies of such men as Angilbert, Adalhard, Leidrad, Theodulph, Benedict of Aniane, Paulinus, Arno, and the magnificent Charlemagne himself. Therefore, these letters do not reconstruct for us the figure of Alcuin alone, but also of these other notable figures so important to the history of their day, and of their relations with each other. Although Alcuin felt, along with his fellow churchmen, that the classics were not to be studied for themselves, but as an aid to the Scriptures, his letters none the less betray much that is allied to the Ciceronian ideal of the epistle, the result of Alcuin's early study of the classics and their authors.

At least two other men of letters have added to the distinction of the epistle by their use of it in the Middle Ages. The Renaissance poet, Francesco Petrarcha (1304-1374), was a man of note in the world in which he lived and, as such, was acquainted with most of the notable men of his day. He seems to have been on corresponding terms with all of these and, for that reason, the number of letters he wrote is almost legion. Many of these letters he is said to have burned, but a large number have been preserved for us. They are divided into four groups: (1) *De rebus familiaribus;* (2) *Seniles;* (3) *Variae;* (4) *Sine Titulo.* From these letters we know the man, his friends, and his times. But Petrarch also wrote a long series of imaginary letters to Latin and Greek authors, long dead, which have almost the interest of fiction. Such letters to dead authors are a popular form in the eighteenth and nineteenth centuries. Petrarch gave the form interest and importance early. The second author, acting as a link between the humanists of the Latin Renaissance and the men of the later age of Greek scholarship, is Desiderius Erasmus (1466-1536), who represents a vital force in learning and in letters. As such he studied the classics because he loved and felt in entire harmony with them. It is because of this that he transferred to his letters, a collection of almost 3000 pieces and a correspondence of permanent value, this feeling for the classic writers and kept alive in his own work their thoughts and style of writing. The letters of Erasmus present an admirable picture of the period in which he lived, a full portrait of himself as man and author (after the fashion of Pliny), and transmit finally the chief values of the Latin letter writers for the perusal of another age.

It is somewhat earlier than this that we begin to find collections of letters in the English tongue (either largely or entirely) that construct for us a group of people notable in history. Early among collections of letters in English are the Paston Letters (1424-1526), by no means unique as a representative of their form. To the same general period belong the Stonor Letters (1290-1483), a collection of similar tone and almost equal importance, but somewhat less interesting than the Paston Letters because they do not contain the rich excitement of close connection with the political turbulence of the times which the correspondence of the Paston family reveals. The great interest that the Pastons took in the affairs of Sir John Fastolfe involved them in disputes and intrigues with powerful neighbors and names which history has brought vividly down to our knowledge. The elder John Paston closely followed the political events of the day while his sons went to court, where they concerned themselves with affairs and became closely acquainted with many of the men by whom was being made the history of those times. Thus, there is reflected in these letters the characters and activities of a whole host of people.

The primary interest, to those who look to the letter collection as a record of everyday life, that lies in these Paston letters, is not to be found so much in a revelation of political events as it is in their revelation of social life. In this respect, in their portrayal of manners, they point forward to the mid-eighteenth century and its usage of the letter; just as, in their occasional formality of phrasing and in the flowing introductory salutations, they look back to the "stylistic" training in letter writing which was taught in the schools of Dictamen; which instruction, in turn, foreshadows the later formal letter-writer. The Paston letters were never written for the sole purpose of conveying trivial social news from writer to reader or written expressly to convey gossip. But occasional bits of such gossip make what might otherwise be a dry recitation of business or political events sometimes sprightly and even humorous reading. It is the incidental matter which has almost unconsciously slipped into a letter by the writer which gives that particular letter, for us, an interest which it would not otherwise have.

The Paston letters are notably full of citations of the dangers of travel in the period of their writing and the imminence of robbery on the road, seven instances of which are given in the letters themselves. All of the cases prove to have happened in times of exceptional disorder: namely in 1451-52, 1454-55, 1461, and 1471; in addition, common footpads were prevalent long after this period. The number of robberies does not prove any preëminence of such tendencies in the fifteenth century. Indeed, one might almost imagine he was reading of the twentieth century instead of the fifteenth. An even more vivid instance of the troubled life of the times is to be found in the narration of the ransacking of the churches by the soldiers of the period, retainers to warring lords, in Letter 406 (July 18, 1461). The incident described curiously reminds me of a similar ransacking of a church and church images in Goethe's stormy drama of the Netherlands, *Egmont* (Act II, Scene I). We may likewise picture just such action as the cause of Sir Thomas Malory's arrest[7] in that same fifteenth century. Such comparisons rather enhance the vitality of the narrative found in this particular Paston Letter. And the same vitality is to be found in the other letters which vigorously tell of scenes of turbulence in this period.

We must turn, however, to passages in which are stray pieces of gossip in order to realize fully the sort of charm which so many of these letters possess. Thus we note from the younger John Paston; "Sir James is ever chopping at me . . . but when he hath most unfitting words I smile a little and tell him it is good hearing of these old tales." Especially delightful, to the lover of "familiar letters," is the not infrequent revelation of family relations. In one epistle from Margaret Paston to her husband we find a message to the effect that he will be able to procure the stuff for a gown for their child cheapest at one Hay's wife.

An amusing touch, a welcome note when it is present, is found in one of the letters from Margaret Paston to her husband, in which she begins:

Right reverend and worshipful husband, I recommend me to you, desiring heartily to hear of your welfare, thanking you for the token that ye sent me by Edmund Perys, praying you to weet that my mother sent to my father to London for a gown cloth of mustyrdevyllers to make a gown for me; . . .[8]

---

[7] Edward Hicks, *Sir Thomas Malory*, Chapter VIII, pp. 43-51.
[8] Letter 809, December 18, 1477.

She then proceeds to remind him in no uncertain terms that he is not to forget to bring the cloth with him when he comes home. A touch of tenderness, too, is present. Margaret Paston's address to her husband in Letter 183 is, indeed, a model of such display. Much of the family feeling which exists in these letters may be found in those written by Margaret to her husband and by Agnes to her son.

It is this feeling, sometimes tenderly, sometimes so naïvely expressed, which gives so much interest to the collection and which makes it, as a whole, the most distinguished monument of the early letter-as-communication series in England. It gives them a value as peculiarly their own as that of the Montagu Letters, or the Letters of Lord Chesterfield to his Son, or the highly colorful personal recordings of Pepys and Evelyn in their Restoration diaries. All of these writings, of course, are of value chiefly because of the highly informative and interesting material contained in them, and not because of any stylistic qualities which particularly distinguish them. Even the letters of Chesterfield are notable for their matter rather than their form, despite the fact that some of them lay claim to a certain stylistic grace. Thus we may say of the Paston Letters, that it is not because of their intrinsic literary qualities, not because of their record of the political turmoil of their day that they are important to us. It is, on the other hand, that they represent a link in the letter writing impulse; that, out of a collection of purely informative messages, they unconsciously construct stories and personalities; that they represent the recorded hopes and joys, fears and quarrels, affections and ambitions of a single family.

Despite the fact that we have such collections of English letters (published much later than the date of their writing, of course) it is still the example of Cicero that remains the strongest influence upon the earliest of the letter writers in English. The Latin tradition, as has already been said, is a continuous one from Cicero's day down and was transmitted through the Latin classical schools directly, and indirectly through the long line of medieval scholars, who gave direction to English learning. Even in the sixteenth century we find such stalwart letter writers as Roger Ascham and John Lyly putting some of their correspondence into Latin. Roger Ascham (1515-1568), especially, has left a large number of personal letters; we are able to find at present over 295 letters[9] written in Latin and English which serve as a sort of personal commentary and record of his career. Although many of the letters are in Latin, Ascham seems to have endeavored, according to evidence in Letter CL, to write his letters in English. Yet, the Ciceronian ideal long remained a standard in English.[10]

By the time we reach the letters of Edmund Spenser (1552-1599), however, we find a genuine correspondent who wrote all his letters in English. Spenser is the first English letter writer who published his personal epistles as a correspondence, and the host of literary men who have done that, or had it done for them, in the period of somewhat less than 400 years since his time is almost without number.

It is the true literary epistle, however, the epistle written in imitation of those in either of the preceding two groups and composed for artistic pleasure, which forms the third group here, and which is the direct ancestor of the "epistolary" novel. We have already noted the use of the letter in a work of fiction in the *Iliad*, but when we turn to the classic writers who have given us a body of letters of purely fictional intent we find the most important to be that late classic author, Alciphron. We must not, however, forget that, at a considerably earlier period, the poet Ovid gave us a series of fictional letters in verse in the *Heroides* (the most famous of which is the lament of Ariadne). The Ovidian use of the letter is a consistent one in literature, especially since the letter itself has a literary quality, as well as a fictional one. It should be remembered that the verse *Epistles* of Horace

---

[9] v. Giles, ed., *English Works of Roger Ascham*, 1864-65.
[10] Charles Sears Baldwin, *Medieval Rhetoric and Poetic*, p. 226, with references given there.

are not fictional but, rather, critical. Of Alciphron's dates, his place of birth, and his career, very little is known to us.[11] It has been conjectured that he died somewhere about 312 A.D. Alciphron is called the "Atticist" by Eustathius, and his personal writings indicate his acquaintance with Athens and Attica. He is guessed to be a rhetorician and a slightly younger contemporary of Lucian, whom he sometimes seems to imitate after the fashion in which Pliny imitates Cicero. That the two may well have been friends is indicated by the fact that we have a third author, Aristænetus, representing, in his own letters of imaginary incidents, a correspondence between Alciphron and Lucian. This may, however, be a fiction based on no possible shred of fact,[12] except that friendship between the two is a plausible possibility. The letters of Alciphron are divided into two sections—*Letters from the Country* and *Letters from the Town*. The first is redivided into "The Fishermen" and "The Farmers", while the second is divided into "The Parasites" and "The Courtesans." It would be difficult to find anywhere a more terse, crisp, varied set of epistles than are those contained in "The Fishermen." There is beauty in them, there is the tang of the sea (so meaningful a thing to the later English pen), there is a keen knowledge of human nature but, above all, there is humor of the sharpest and most direct variety. Thus, in Letter XI we have a girl telling her mother of her inability to marry a youth of her father's choice because she has seen someone she prefers:

. . . a youth at Athens who was carrying the vine branch in the procession on the day you sent me to the city to watch the festival. He is beautiful, mother; so beautiful and such a darling. . . . When he looks at you his eyes gleam with a dark radiance, even as the ocean gleams beneath the rays of the sun. And his whole face! . . . Either I marry him, or else like Sappho of Lesbos I will fling myself, not from the cliffs of Leucas, but from the piers of the Piræus into the foam.

[11] F. A. Wright, *Alciphron*, Introduction, p. 14.
[12] *Ibid.*

The mother's answer begins—"You are mad," and works up to: "If your father were to hear of it, he will not hesitate or argue; he will throw you into the sea for the fish to devour."[13] Here, of course, we find the method of letter and answer used just as it is so frequently employed in the later letter-writers and the epistolary novel.

This entire series is marked by a sort of bluff, healthy, almost Peacockian humor. In no letter is this quality so obvious in its combination of philosophy and humor as it is in the nineteenth: "I did not ask for something you possess but for something which you had lost. However, since you do not wish anyone else to have it, you can keep your losings." Despite the fact that there is a constant feeling of joy in the wildness and the capriciousness of the sea, one concluded from the body of these letters that it is a far safer thing to wring one's livelihood from the soil. The third letter opens with the lines: "The earth is good and ploughed fields bring no danger: the sea is cruel and navigation is a risky business." —which it might be well to place beside the opening lines from the fourth letter of "The Farmers": "The land makes no return worth my labour and I have decided to give my-self to sea craft and to the sea waves"—both of which together offer a study in the vagaries of human nature. There is more bitterness in these letters from the land than is to be found in the previous group, but there is here the same sort of distinctive humor, short, sharp, and shrewd. Especially is there humor to be found in such letters as those of an irate husband to his wife who has taken herself off to the city and the painting of the women there, concluding with the advice that she wash herself "with soap and water" (Letter VIII), and in the letter of one friend to another concerning a drunken escapade. There is present, however, a new note of unrest that, in these people, seems not to be assuaged by the presence of the always moving sea as is the restlessness of the fishermen.

Far more bitter in tone is that group which is combined

[13] Letter XII.

under the general title of "The Parasites," which hits off
with a painful accuracy that class of people. The fourth
group, "The Courtesans," is notable for its fine creation of
character in the figure of Thaïs. She is drawn as a woman of
considerable charm, of sagacity, and of that peculiar sort of
savoir faire which is so necessary to women of her profession.
We remember the vexation of Thaïs at another courtesan
who has made mocks at her, and her elaborate indifference
toward this, which concludes with her expression of intent
to pay her rival out. As in the other groups, we again find
here the sharp humor so characteristic of Alciphron, as, for
instance, this: "Why worry yourself with long letters? I want
fifty pounds; I do not want words. If you love me—pay up.
If you love your money better—don't bother. Good-bye."[14]

The combined whole of this author's epistolary creation
reveals a distinct talent for the telling of story and the revelation of human emotion and character in the form of the letter, that high power which is to be found expressed with the
most complete distinction in the novels of Samuel Richardson. As an advance toward fiction in the form of the epistle,
the letters of Alciphron represent not only the forward step
that has already been intimated, but also something that is
new and fresh in the field of writing. The letters have charm
and humor to a greater degree than they have any other
single characteristic, but they likewise reveal an ability to
sketch character and to gather together in several letters distinct and separate threads of emotion for the painting of a
single group picture. Furthermore, unlike the epistles of
Ovid, they represent ordinary people and the manners of
daily life.

When we turn to those early writers of the letter in English who used the epistle as a literary or art form we come
first to Bishop Hall (1574-1656), though John Lyly (1553-
1606) used the letter as a literary device in *Euphues* (1578),
in which the hero writes some twenty pages of letters to his
friends. Jules Jusserand has said of these letters that Richard-

[14] Letter XIV.

son borrows their point of view in the creation of his
Pamela.[15] Lyly likewise has some literary epistles incorporated in his *Entertainments* (1590). But Bishop Hall, the author of characters, has made greater use of the epistle as a
literary form. In a preface to his letters, dedicatory to Prince
Henry, he says: ". . . Your Grace shall herein perceive a
new fashion of discourses by epistles, new to our language;
usual to all others . . ." His letters were written out of a desire to try literary divertissement, to inculcate true religion
and virtue; and he was, in this sense, cousin-german to
Samuel Richardson. More important as a factor in the development of English letter writing is James Howell (1594-
1666), whose *Epistolae Ho-Elianae* (1645) carried the
history of the English fictional letter one step further. An Oxford graduate, Howell was not only a business man but something of a journalist as well. The fact that he was a journalist, combined with that of his being a Welshman, makes
his veracity seem a tenuous thing, but adds to the general
liveliness of his writing. The letters of James Howell were
much like the later "familiar letters," for he dates them from
various places at home and abroad. Incidentally, there are
many letters of his of which it might be said that, were one
to remove the opening and closing passages, the bodies of
the letters that remain could well pass for familiar essays.
The letters themselves are written in a style which is the
very embodiment of ease and sprightliness, and much of the
gaiety of nature which the author must have possessed seems
to be incorporated in the very manner in which he writes.
Howell seems to be inordinately fond of presenting court
scandal in his letters, and a large number of their passages
play impishly with the notable names of the day which furnish fertile fields for just such sport. Especially amusing is the
author's description of the evening with Ben Jonson in a
letter to Sir Tho. Hawk, Knight, in which he writes: "One
thing intervened which almost spoiled the relish of the rest,
that B. began to engross all the discourse, to vapor extremely

[15] J. J. Jusserand, *The English Novel in the Time of Shakespeare*, p. 130.

of himself, and by vilifying others to magnify his own muse."[16] Again, in his consideration of the fall of Raleigh, Howell shows a proper appreciation of the qualities of that brilliant courtier. Similarly, Howell shows an ability to present, through the means of writing, a full portrait of a character of the day, as in his letter to Dr. Prichard which describes the last days of Francis Bacon and contains the revelatory passage of: ". . . it hath been the fortune of all poets commonly to die beggars; but for an orator, lawyer and philosopher as he was to die so, 'tis rare."[17] That Howell was, as an epistolarian, most attentive to character is shown in such presentations of contemporary figures as those cited; that he possessed descriptive vigor may be seen in such a passage as that of the murder of the Duke of Buckingham (Section V, Letter VII); that he had literary insight may be seen from the excellence of his style. Beyond a doubt, this author has incorporated into the letter the pristine freshness, the investigative spirit, the desire to understand, and the almost over-freedom of expression which was characteristic of his age. He was motivated, too, by his favorite maxim, *Senesco non segnesco*. It is interesting to remember of Howell that he was a great favorite with Thackeray.[18]

It will be seen, from a consideration of the letters of this third group, the "art" letters, that it is the ideal, stylistically, of such letters to seem artless. This will be brought home with particular clarity to anyone who reads the letters of Alciphron and Howell. Experience and imagination are wedded just as they later are in the epistolary novel and, once wedded, are cast in a mould imitative of the formal letter and of its style.

[16] Section IV, Letter VIII.
[17] Section IV, Letter VIII.
[18] *Roundabout Papers*, "On Two Children in Black," p. 8.

II

THE LETTER-WRITER

ALONG with the tendency of literary men and men about the court to write letters, must be noted another tendency, equally important in the development of the use of the letter as a literary (and, ultimately, fictional) instrument. This is the more or less didactic "letter-writer," which sought to instruct one and all in the way they should go in letter writing. The earliest known English letter-writer is *The Enimie of Idlenesse: Teaching the maner and stile how to endite, compose and write all sorts of Epistles and Letters,* the work of William Fulwood, issued in 1568.

William Fulwood was an author of the mid-sixteenth century, and a member of the Merchant Taylors' Company. Indeed, the author has appended his name to the *Enimie of Idlenesse* as "William Fulwood, Marchant," and the volume itself is dedicated in verse to the "Masters, Wardens, and the Company of Marchant Tayllors." This work became very popular and ran through several editions. It is divided into four parts. The first, part original, part borrowed, contains a group of "necessary instructions" along with a group of models, many of which are translations from Cicero and the ancients. The second part contains "the Copies of sundry mens Letters and Epistles," derived from the classics (from Cicero more particularly), and from certain Italian scholars. The third part contains a series of familiar letters ("familiar" almost in the same sense as the word is used later with reference to the Richardsonian letters) which are divided into two groups: letter and answer. These are thought to be original, but Brian W. Downs, in his introduction to *Familiar Letters on Important Occasions,* by Samuel Richardson, considers them sometimes "concocted for exemplary purposes and, again, almost certainly taken from French and Italian originals." The fourth part is made up of six metrical love letters and a few prose specimens similar to those of the preceding group. In later editions of this work seven metrical love letters are to be found instead of six, and there are also a few additions to the prose group.

A second collection, similar in purpose and execution to the Fulwood collection, is *A Panoplie of Epistles, or, a Looking-Glasse for the Unlearned. Containing a perfecte plattforme of inditing letters of all sorts.* This was released in London in 1576. The author was one Abraham Fleming (1552?-1607),[1] an antiquary and poet, born in London. He was a student of Cambridge and later became chaplain to the Countess of Nottingham after he had taken holy orders. He does not seem to have cut a very distinguished figure as a poet, but acquired the reputation of being a considerable antiquarian. His epistolary work, like Fulwood's *Enimie of Idlenesse,* lacks originality, since it is, admittedly, a translation from the Latin. The letters are preceded by "an Epitome of Precepts," which is presented as a dialogue between master and scholar.

It is to be noticed that these two collections of letters look backward to the classic letter writers not only for their inspiration, but for their material as well. When we turn to the next manual of letters extant, we find that there is in it a note of originality not present in either Fulwood or Fleming. This work, which does not definitely owe anything to translation, is Angel Day's *The English Secretorie, wherein is contayned a perfect method for inditing of all manner of Epistles and familiar letters.* Angel Day, a writer of the latter half of the sixteenth century, is chiefly known to us for his pastoral romance, *Daphnis and Chloe,* a translation, or Elizabethan version, through the French of Jacques Amyot, of a Greek romance by one Longus. *The English Secretorie* is

[1] D. N. B., VII, p. 271.

distinctly less well known. It was first published in 1586 and
was reprinted in 1587, 1592, 1599, 1607, perhaps in 1610,
and in 1614. The contents of this work are rather ingeni-
ously arranged and depend chiefly on the use of a single class
of adjectives, as follows:—

I.

Of epistles meerly Descriptory.
Of epistles Laudatory and vituperatory.
Of epistles deliberative.
Of epistles responsory.
Of epistles Dehortatory and disswasory.
Of epistles conciliatory.
Of epistles Reconciliatory.
Of epistles petitory.
Of epistles commendatory.
Of epistles Monetorie and Reprehensorie.
Of epistles Amatorie.

II.

Of epistles Iudiciall.
    (accusatorie, excusatorie, Purgatorie, Defensorie).
Of epistles expostulatorie.
Of epistles invective.
Of epistles Comemoratorie.
Of epistles Deprecatorie.
Of epistles familiar.
Of epistles remuneratorie.
Of epistles Iocatorie and Gratulatorie.
Of epistles obiurgatorie.
Of epistles Mandatorie.

It is only necessary to peruse the above list of contents to
gather a rather comprehensive idea of how considerable a
variety of subjects was treated in these letters of Angel Day.
Indeed, we do not find a more elastic gamut of subject-matter in the *Familiar Letters on Important Occasions* of Samuel

Richardson, himself the dean and apex of all letter-writers. In Angel Day's work the familiar letters show a large majority over those of a more formal bent, but all of them are couched in a cold and unyielding style. The illustrations are accompanied by much theory, and Day still follows the earlier custom of indicating the figures of rhetoric in the margin for ready recognition. The titles themselves tell us, on the other hand, that the sort of letter to be found here does not change much in substance in the later English letter-writers, and "epistles descriptive, conciliatory, commendatorie, amatorie, invective, mandatorie" and so on, are still to be found in prevailing numbers in even the most modern letter manuals.

The habit of the letter-writer, once established, continued until a late date, even, indeed, to a recent one. In 1603 appeared a letter-writer so far in advance of those already mentioned, so definitely a landmark in many respects that it is to be reserved for more elaborate discussion at another point. This is Nicholas Breton's *Poste with a Packet of Mad Letters*. There are, on the other hand, a considerable number of collections of letters after the time of Breton, but they add nothing in the way of variety or distinction to the types already discussed and are, likewise, of less historical significance than those. We are able to find, however, before 1700, such titles as: *A Speedie Post, With Certaine New Letters. Or, The First Fruits of New Conceits, never yet discovered*, by "I. W.," (?1629) ; *The Secretaries Studie: Containing new familiar Epistles*, by "S. S.," (1652) ; *A Flying Post With a Packet of Choice new Letters and Complements: containing Variety of Examples of witty and delightful Letters, upon all Occasions both of Love and Business*, by "W. P.," (1678) ; *The Lover's Secretary in Four Parts: Being a Collection of Billets Doux, Letters Amorous, Letters Tender, and Letters of Praise, Collected from the Greatest Wits of France* (1692) ; and *The Post-boy Robb'd of his Mail; or, the Pacquet broke open* (1692) , by Charles Gildon.

A consideration of such works as these indicates a progression in a definite direction: toward the exclusion of the more formal letter in favor of the development of the true "familiar" letter. We do not find in any of these later letter-writers so remote a subject as the King of Pouille's decision to erect castles and forts throughout his dominions (v. Fulwood's *Enimie of Idlenesse*), but rather matters that would be more closely allied to the interests of the readers of the day. None the less, the range of subject-matter is of considerable breadth, and the author of *The Secretaries Studie* (1652) divides his letters into those amorous, civil, household, politic, chiding, excusing, requesting, gratulatory, and newsy. Probably the "requesting" form of letter is responsible for the growth of all the other groups and it, along with the love letters and letters of chiding, forms the most important body of compositions to be found in these works. There is little necessity for comment upon the predominance of the love letter in the letter-writer; in this form the genre has extended to the early part of the twentieth century, at least. Eighteenth, nineteenth, and early twentieth-century type love letters all reveal the same unrestrained, yet highly artificial, protestations of love, along with records of the despair of the lover, the joy of the lover, the warning of a friend, and so on. In *The Secretary's Guide* of 1753 there is even printed a type letter for the use of love-smitten Quakers. The chiding letters are, likewise, of considerable importance in the great majority of these letter-writers and indicate a certain tendency toward the inclusion of story interest because of the dramatic nuance which many of them betray. Chief among these are letters of warning from a married man to an unmarried friend who is contemplating matrimony, the former extending some advice on the matter; letters of chiding from father to son, from father to daughter, from neighbor to neighbor. It will be noticed that all of these types survive in that most important of letter-writers, Richardson's *Familiar Letters on Important Occasions*, and are carried down from that very complete work even to our own day.

It might be said, then, that the chief function of the earlier letter-writers, at least from Fulwood to Breton, is to give, in formal, stilted and rhetorical fashion, examples of various sorts of letters—verse, prose, love letters, exemplary models from learned men (such as the classic Cicero), familiar letters, and so on. The existence of such a compendium is of a precarious nature and few have survived the period in and for which they were published. They have little, if any, real value as literary productions. Historically alone they are more worthy of preservation, but it is in the light of further development that they are chiefly memorable. They are but leading steps. They give a definite impulse and direction to the creation of the familiar letter as a form of literature. Even the earliest letter-writers do not entirely escape some slight intimation of familiarity, some slight indication of what might be called, for want of a better phrase, story interest. It is due to the further development of the familiar letter itself, in the fiction of the eighteenth century, that these stiffly formal early letter-writers may seem to have contributed their share to the outburst of epistolary fiction that was to come under the influence of the vigorous and determined guidance of Samuel Richardson in that century. Even in the mere matter of title, it may be noted that Angel Day's *The English Secretorie* has not only undoubtedly suggested *The Lover's Secretary*, a letter-writer largely devoted to type love letters and published in 1692, but likewise the title of the later *The Lover's Secretary; or, the Adventures of Lindamira, a Lady of Quality, a Story in Letters*, of which a second edition, revised by Thomas Brown and published in 1713, is the earliest extant.

In continuance of the series of these compilations, side by side with developing fiction, may be noted: *The Academy of Complements; or, A New Way of Wooing. Wherein is a Variety of Love-Letters, very fit to be read by all young men and maids that desire to learn the true ways of complements* (1685; reappearing in somewhat varying forms in 1705, 1713 and 1715); *Familiar Letters of Love and Gallantry for several occasions by wits of the last and present age, from the*

*originals, together with T. Brown's remains, being letters and
dialogues not printed in his works, 1719.* Finally we are able
to record three letter-writers that date later than the publication of *Pamela.* They are: *The Complete Letter-Writer*
(1755); *Select Collections of Original Letters* (1755); and
Epistolary Correspondence made Familiar and Pleasant
(1759).

It must be remembered, however, that all this while the
letters of the classic writers discussed in Chapter I were by
no means submerged, but appeared constantly in new translations and new editions (such as Conyers Middleton's *The
Epistles of M. T. Cicero to M. Brutus and of Brutus to Cicero,*
published in Latin with English translation, in 1743, and
followed by *Letters to Atticus,* 1752, and *Epistolae ad Fa-
miliares,* 1753), so that we find the two streams of material
running side by side in the publications of the day; the epistles of the aforementioned classics running pace and pace in
the favor of the reading public with the rapidly increasing
new material of contemporary writers of letters.

III

THE VITALIZATION OF THE LETTER

IF WE are to recall, for a moment, the letter-writers discussed in the preceding chapter, it will be seen that these are but skeletal works at their best. It is to two or three distinct and separate works that we must turn in order to find what it was that animated the letter, what vitalized it, what gave it a lively verisimilitude to a degree that it became the substance of a definite form of literature. As has already been intimated, it is to Nicholas Breton and his *Poste with a Packet of Mad Letters* that we must look for the true beginning of such vitalizing of the letter-writer and, beyond that, of the sort of letter that appeared therein. In addition to this, Breton is directly responsible for the popularizing of the letter itself, even if he did not quite succeed in making it entirely familiar.

The first edition of the *Packet of Mad Letters*, an edition consisting of the first part only, is without date. The earliest date attached to these letters, and this again refers to the first part, is 1603. Yet the collection bearing this date was, in all probability, preceded by other editions, since it is described as being "newly inlarged." It is the text of 1637 that is largely adopted as the least erroneous representative of both parts of the *Mad Letters*, although it contains certain errors not to be found in the text of 1603.

The dedication to the reader, which Nicholas Breton has placed at the beginning of the first part of the *Packet of Mad Letters*, warrants recording, since it gives a clear impression of the air of mystery with which the author surrounded his

27

"packet" and the care he took that they should not be thought entirely compositions of his own.

Gentle if you be, be you so, gentle Reader; you shall understand, that I know not when, there came a Poste, I know not whence, was going I know not whither, and carried I know not what: But in this way, I know not how, it was his hap with lack of heed, to let fall a Packet of idle papers, the superscription whereof being only to him that finds it, being my fortune to light on it, seeing no greater style in the direction, fell to opening of the enclosure, in which I found divers Letters written, to whom, or from whom I could not learne. . . .

Thus does Breton attempt to throw an aura of romance about his letters, taking care to add that he has ventured a second part because of the happy fate experienced by the first part at the hands of the public. In his preceding dedication of the letters to the "Right Worshipfull Maximilian Dallison of Hawlin," the author intimates that his own inspiration for this work is to be found in similar epistles from the Latin, French, Italian, and Spanish. Here again we are able to find that long continuous classical influence that has so many times already been touched upon in the consideration of the epistolary impulse.

The entire series of letters in this *Packet* is marked by a gracious air of courtesy and politeness, a consciousness on the part of the author that a letter is not the blunt, hasty thing that is speech. Thus, in the letter of a creditor asking for money, called, incidentally, "A kinde Letter of a Creditor for money," we have the following courtesy of request:

Sir, I pray you take it not unkindly, that I write thus earnestly unto you: for more necessity then will have urged me to it: my money is not so much, as you well able to discharge it: my losses by Sea and ill Creditors by land, make me strain courtesie with my Friends, for their helpe in an extremitie, yet doe I desire nothing but my due; but as I was ready to lend, I would be glad to receive with that fulnesse of good wil, that may continue our kindness.[1]

[1] Letter 43.

The answer, forwarding the money, is couched in the same gentlemanly terms, assuring the creditor of the extreme regret of the debtor, and urging the hope that the relationship between the creditor and debtor may be in no way impaired. Similar expressions of graciousness and patience under stress are to be found in Letter 51 to "an unthankful friend" and in that tender Letter 66 to a lovely lady who is being somewhat less than responsive. There are exceptions, of course, to this tone, and one or two of the letters descend to the practice on the part of the correspondents of calling each other names. It is to be noticed, however, that this descent is to be found chiefly between man and woman, of previous amorous attachment, who have some sort of quarrel to pick with each other. The result, however, adds distinctly to the variety of the letters.

The epistles of Nicholas Breton are likewise characterized by an elaborateness of expression and an opulent usage of words which are, basically, rather a characteristic of the times than of the letters themselves. None the less, they assume this quality of the period with a naturalness which makes it their very own. Especially is this elaborateness of epithet to be discerned in the letters of young lovers to their ladies.

Slang?

The Breton letters seek, in a large measure, to give advice in the ordinary cruxes of life, both to those who ask such advice and to those who do not ask it. It is for this reason that so many of the letters are didactic in tone. Wherever they tender advice they are marked by a solemn dignity, but the too easy presentation of formulae makes this advice more definitely applicable to the general than to the particular. Of such mettle is the letter "admonitory to a gentlewoman living in London" which sagely begins:

It is observable that when a man hath a glasse of a brittle substance and for the worth of great price and value, he is very chary and heedfull thereof, because if by fall it should bee broken, it is impossible to have it repaired. . . .[2]

[2] Part I, Letter 4.

—and then proceeds to apply this to the virtue of his cousin which may easily be assailed in the city of London, a place full of "provocatives to Sinne." Perhaps a more unusual use is made of the letter of advice in the epistle to a friend who has lost his mistress. This betrays a deep tenderness which the author seldom shows, for he prefers, in most instances, to hold in check any revealing emotion and, certainly, to refrain at all times from dwelling upon it at any length. The letter of advice from father to son, so prevalent in all letter-writers, finds several single instances, especially notable being that thirty-third Letter which, along with warnings of the usual sort, includes the amusing admonition—"I have heard you are much given to Alchymistry, it is a great charge to many, and profiteth few, imploy your time so, that you lose not the bargaine."

It is almost inevitable that so much that is advisory in its nature should likewise unearth a turn for the philosophic in the author. Among the several letters of advice from an elder to a younger man we find a philosophic and advisory passage which is notable, not only in itself, but also in the fact that it shows itself directly related to at least two other well-known passages of the period. The letter is one of advice to a young courtier, and proceeds as follows:

. . . keepe your purse warily, and your credit charily, your reputation valiantly, and your honor carefully: for your friends, as you find them use them: for your enemies, feare them not, but looke to them: for your love, let it bee secret in the bestowing, and discreet in the placing . . . if thou hast a favour, be not proud of thy fortune, but thinke it discretion to conceale a contentment: goe neate, but not gay, lest it argue a lightnesse, and take heed of lavish expence, lest it beggar thy state: play little, and lose not much, use exercise, but make no toile of a pleasure: read much, but dull not thy braine, and conferre but with the wise, so thou shalt get understanding. Pride is a kind of coynesse, which is a little too womanish: and common familiarity is too neere the Clown for a Courtier. But carry thyself even, that thou fall on neither side. . . .

It is, of course, impossible to read this text without making mental comment on the similarity it bears to that famous speech of Polonius in his advice to his son, Laertes.[3] Exactly what the relationship may be between these two passages is doubtful. It has been largely determined by critics that *Hamlet* was written about the year 1600; the quartos belong to 1603 (first quarto) ; 1604-05 (second and third quartos) ; and 1613 (fourth quarto). Breton's *Poste with a Packet of Mad Letters* was written in 1603, at the latest; undoubtedly it was composed in some earlier year, and may have appeared in print some time before 1603. To say which of the two, *Hamlet* or the *Packet of Mad Letters*, was borrower from the other, if either, is almost impossible. In addition, critics have determined that the Polonius speech of advice[4] is based on an earlier passage from Lyly's *Euphues*, which contains such bits as "Be not lavish of thy tongue. . . . Every one that shaketh thee by the hand is not joined to thee in heart. . . . Be not quarrelous for every light occasion. . . . . It shall be thrice better to hear what they say, than to speak what thou thinkest." None the less, the passages from Shakespeare and Breton are closer in phrasing to each other than either is to that of Lyly. If the two are not related, at least the similarity

[3] *Polonius.*

> Give thy thoughts no tongue,
> Nor any unproportion'd thought his act.
> Be thou familiar, but by no means vulgar.
> Those friends thou hast, and their adoption tried,
> Grapple them to thy soul with hoops of steel;
> But do not dull thy palm with entertainment
> Of each new-hatch'd, unfledg'd comrade. Beware
> Of entrance to a quarrel, but, being in,
> Bear't that the opposed may beware of thee.
> Give every man thine ear, but few thy voice;
> Take each man's censure, but reserve thy judgment.
> Costly thy habit as thy purse can buy,
> But not express'd in fancy; rich, not gaudy;
>
> . . . .
>
> Neither a borrower nor a lender be;
> For loan oft loses both itself and friend,
> And borrowing dulls the edge of husbandry.
> This above all: to thine own self be true,
> And it must follow, as the night the day,
> Thou canst not then be false to any man.

Hamlet, Act I, Scene III.

[4] v. *Hamlet*, New Variorum Edition, p. 66.

indicates that Breton was of a single tissue with his age and some of its philosophy. Incidentally, it may likewise be noted that Samuel Richardson, in his *Familiar Letters on Important Occasions* presents, in any one of a dozen letters, advice similar to the Breton passage not only in tone, but even in phrasing. Such advice, it may be concluded, is scarcely temporal.

Breton's native philosophy is revealed, again, in such passing phrases as: "The craft of one woman is the confusion of many a man" (Part I, Letter 27); and "follow my counsell, study all the Arts superficially, but chiefly Arithmetick, for it is the assured way to wealth" (Part II, Letter 16). The characteristic of this philosophy is its worldliness, which is borne out by a consideration of most of the letters in this packet, since most of them bear the stamp of a man who has known his way about in the world, beheld its pitfalls and, perhaps, fallen into one or two of them, to the furtherance of his personal wisdom. It is to be remembered that Nicholas Breton (1545?-1626?) was descended from an ancient family of Essex and was himself a poet of good education, of worldly experience, and of true refinement.

The letters are, taken as a whole, rather brief, and it is because of this brevity, coupled with a smoothness of composition, that they flow with so considerable an ease and impress us as being composed of graceful, though somewhat tenuous, prose. All in all, they are of a darkling humor, concerning themselves with the more serious problems of life. Yet they are not devoid of the more light and humorous phases, and Letters 21, 22, 23, and 24 (Part I) are full of a gay capriciousness and even of a more vinegared turn of wit. Nor is the waggish letter absent from this packet, and Letters 44, 45 (Part I), and Letter 7 (Part II) are admirable examples of this type. None the less, it is the more dignified and sober subject which claims chief place in this epistolary work and if the pathetic story revealed in Letter 19 (Part II) should be autobiographical in tendency as it is sometimes thought, then the reason for the deadly seriousness of many of these letters when treating of the problems of life is plainly apparent.

As has already been stated, it was the popular estimation of this *Poste with a Packet of Mad Letters* which helped largely to forward the general popularity of the letter-writer. Breton dispensed with the stilted quality of expression so prevalent in letter-writers up to the time of his work and employed instead the language of his own day, in a dignified but informal style. It is in this respect that he is the direct precursor of Richardson and the "familiar" letter-writer.

There is to be found, likewise, in the eighteenth century that type of private letter imbued with the personal and friendly touch, that is analogous to that which exists fictionally in the sixteenth-century correspondence of Nicholas Breton. This is perhaps best exemplified by the letters of the celebrated Alexander Pope (1688-1744). This correspondence extends from 1704 to 1744, a period of forty years full of rich experience of a successful and envied author. Letters such as these show how the personal letter has been vitalized in exactly the way those of Breton vitalized the letters of the letter-writer. The Pope correspondence consists not only of the letters from Pope to such people of note as Wycherley, Addison, Steele, Congreve, Dr. Atterbury, Gay, the Duke of Buckingham, Lady Mary Wortley Montagu, and Swift, along with an additional host of famous figures, but comprises, likewise, the letters these people sent in reply to Pope.

The keynote to Pope's letters is a conviviality and a familiarity, combined with a brilliant vitality which all serves to animate even the simplest epistle with an almost trenchant liveliness. Certainly, the correspondence with Dr. Atterbury and with Dr. Cromwell shows a more severe dignity than most of the letters, yet even in these may we find that consummate ease of expression which seems to be never failing in the author, and which recalls the classic examples of letter writing in Latin literature. In his own twelfth letter to the Duke of Buckingham Pope implies familiarity with the letters of Pliny in the statement: "Pliny was one of those few authors who had a warm house over his head, nay two houses, as appears by two of his epistles." And it is to Pliny, among the classic letter writers, that the style of Pope's letters most definitely refers us by their grace, their vivacity, their keenness of observation, their sharp wit.

That the letters of Pope show a distinctly philosophical, even a moralizing, tendency may be seen from such quotations as that from the eighth letter to Wycherley (Oct. 26, 1705) : "As a man in love with a mistress desires no conversation but hers, so a man in love with himself (as most men are) may be best pleased with his own." Again, he writes (December 30, 1710) : ". . . those that are my friends I laugh with, and those that are not I laugh at; so I am merry in company, and if ever I am wise, it is by myself."[5] There is a brilliant sally in the seventh letter to Sir W. Trumbull (Dec. 16, 1715) : "When rumours increase, and when there is abundance of noise and clamour, believe the second report": —and, finally, in the fifth letter to Edw. Blount, Esq., we find this penetrating and graceful consideration:

The highest gratification we receive here from company is mirth, which at the best is but a fluttering unquiet motion, that beats about the breast for a few moments, and after leaves it void and empty. . . . What we here call science and study are little better: the greater number of arts to which we apply ourselves are mere groping in the dark; and even the search of our most important concerns in a future being, is but a needless, anxious and uncertain haste to be knowing, sooner than we can, what without all this solicitude we shall know a little later.

Thus, it may be seen that we are able to find in these letters of Pope much the same material of observation and advice that exists in the letter-writer itself and, it may be added, such observation is no less conscious here than in the letter-writer, since Pope himself is nothing if not conscious.

The letters, as has already been stated, are definitely familiar in composition. This familiarity enables us to see the personality of the author with an absolute clearness of por-

[5] To H. Cromwell. Letter XXVII.

traiture. They are graceful and elaborate; they are conscious
even to the point of being sometimes rhetorically so; they are
witty and sprightly, full of a cleverness given to the creation
of maxims and aphoris.ns; they contain a frequent asperity
of speech and an occasional arrogance. All these qualities
serve to reveal to us the man behind the letters. As a familiar
document of a human being the epistles of Alexander Pope
are invaluably alive. Moreover, Pope's rearranging and re-
ascribing of the letters proves that he consciously regarded
them as literature, not simply as actual correspondence.

It has been said above that Samuel Richardson represents
the very apex of the literary letter-writer with his *Familiar
Letters on Important Occasions* (1741). It is old news that
Richardson was commissioned to compose a letter-writer, in
the course of composing which he became so absorbed that
the subject developed beyond him into a work which resulted
in the creation of *Pamela*. Having finished this novel, this
constantly serious and unfailing conscientious worker returned to his original letter-writer and completed that, a
work we now know as *Familiar Letters on Important
Occasions*.

Samuel Richardson is among those writers of whom it may
be said that he never made any attempt to mystify his readers;
on the contrary, he made every conscious effort to clarify his
purposes for those who might read the results. Thus it is
that we are told, in the Preface to the *Familiar Letters*, exactly what the author purposes to do.

Nature, propriety of character, plain sense, and general use,
have been the chief objects of the author's attention in penning
these letters; and as he everywhere aimed to write to the judgment, rather than to the imagination, he would choose, that
they should generally be found more useful than diverting. . . .
He has endeavoured then, in general, throughout the great variety of his subjects, to inculcate the principles of virtue and
benevolence; to describe properly, and recommend strongly, the
social and relative duties; and to place them in such practical

lights, that the letters may serve for rules to think and act by, as well as forms to write after.[6]

It may justly be said that, with some enlargement, what Richardson has written here is applicable to his entire artistic purpose. In consideration of the *Familiar Letters* alone, he has accomplished all he set out to accomplish, and that so perfectly that he seems to have succeeded in doing even more.

Behind the entire creation of these letters is that high morality which the author possessed working out to the last lofty letter, with its conception of worldly virtue. Of the authors of earlier letter-writers, it may be said that they gave their letters as models of form, and any moralizing that may have appeared therein was but an incidental item. Richardson's letters are here not only models of form, but they are, by intent, models of morality as well. We need turn only to that letter from a friend to a young man who is guilty of reprehensible conduct toward his father (Letter LXIV), filled as it is with a stern and dignified indignation, or to that more stinging letter (CXXXVII) from a young woman of little fortune to the man who has proposed that she be his mistress and that he live with her "as a Gallant," in order to gather how strictly the moral purpose is adhered to in this work. It is the moral tone which so often lends the sober color that is to be found in these letters. In Letter LXV "Against too great a Love of Singing and Music," we have an epistle that warns against the acceptance of life with too definite a lightness and warns likewise against the ease with which the graver things of life are pushed aside when lighter matters are by. "For whenever a chearful singer is in company, adieu to all conversation much of an improving or intellectual nature!"[7] Again, we have a letter (LXX) warning a girl against a French lover who is much too gay in his demeanor (a slight revelation of the insularity of Richardson), and a delightful epistle (XC) in which an uncle writes to

[6] Page xxvii.
[7] Letter LXV.

his niece of his offense at her new riding habit which is made so peculiarly that "one cannot easily distinguish your sex by it. For you neither look like a *modest girl* in it, nor an *agreeable boy*." O tempora! O mores!

It is out of this moral purpose that comes much of the sound advice and wholesome philosophy that is to be found in these epistles. Thus such almost separate pieces, one might call them, are revealed,

Twenty-one or twenty-two years of age is full early for a young man to be his own master.[8]

. . . he who has by his own indiscretions undone himself, is much fitter to be set up as a landmark for a prudent mariner to shun his courses, than an example to follow.[9]

. . . make a right use of those periods of life, which may be proper entrances for us into a still more important one than that behind it.[10]

. . . *maids* often mend their circumstances by marriage, *widows* very rarely.[11]

It may be seen from such quotations that Richardson, like most of his age, is given to aphorisms and maxims but, unlike such a man as Pope, whose maxims are characterized by brilliance and asperity, Richardson blends with his philosophy a kindly concern for the soul of the individual being.

Beyond the shadow of a doubt, these letters indicate a definite bias for narrative on the part of the writer. Any number of letters tell us a story and, although the story is usually presented, if not always, for the sake of the moral lesson involved, none the less we are able to perceive that the author himself has an undeniable interest in the story by means of which he is presenting his moral. Perhaps this is unconscious, but it none the less exists. Inevitably, we notice the germ of *Pamela* in one or two of these letters in which there is told the story of the beautiful servant girl who is subjected to the

---

[8] Letter II.
[9] Letter VII.
[10] Letter LXV.
[11] Letter CXLVII.

moral dangers of the city in which she attempts to make a livelihood. One of the most notable of these is Letter LXII, "A Young Woman in Town to Her Sister in the Country, recounting her narrow Escape from a Snare laid for her, on her first Arrival, by a wicked Procuress." The story moves with an absorbing rapidity, and we even find our fears enlisted with the girl that she may not escape, and our hopes that she will. The letter indicates with positive clarity the fact that Richardson was at all times possessed with the narrative impulse, even in this collection of familiar epistles, and an ability to tell a story well even when he was not telling that story for its own sake. There is to be found, likewise, so very different a story as that contained in Letter XLVI which tells of the ruin of a trader because of his persistent indolence and self-indulgence. Again, in Letter LXXVI, "A humorous Epistle of neighborly Occurences and News" which tells of the fates of many of the friends of both writer and reader, there is contained a very human "slice of life," full of narrative interest and character. There are at least a score of such letters in the volume, some of which (such as Letters CLXI to CLXV) are in series, and all serve to reveal not only the story-telling power of Richardson, but likewise the variety of his material as well.

A development to be found in these letters which does not exist in nearly so perfected a form in any preceding letter-writer is that of character. Although we meet most of the characters for the space of a single letter only, yet we remember a character here and there because of the sheer liveliness and vividness with which he or she is made to reveal himself or herself in the course of the writing. Certainly, there are a number of types to be found in these letters: the irate father, the justly censorious friend, the contrite son, the unhappy lover, the outraged lady, the innocent servant girl, the uncertain widow, and the wise neighbor—all these and more. They are, to be sure, portrayed in different letters with little variation and with an unmistakable family resemblance among them. None the less, there are, aside from the dominant types, some of whom do impress us with their individuality, occasional characters we remember more vividly. The facetious young lady remains with us from Letter LXXXIII as a possible prototype of the lighter moments of the later Miss Byron in *Sir Charles Grandison* (1753-54). Again, that poor tenant of Letters CVI, CVIII is memorable. Others occur. Many of Richardson's heroes and heroines, if they may be so called, are of the lowest classes; but an equally large number are of the merchant classes, and some few of a rank higher.

So far as the style of these letters is concerned, it is characterized by that breadth of flow as of a broad river, proceeding with a steady dignity between its banks and ruffled only near those banks where the persistent imperfections of the shore cause the water to bubble and foam in concentric circles that have no entire effect upon the unshattered breadth that is midstream. The dignity and fullness of expression which characterizes the style is really found in the substance of the letters themselves. As has been said, again and again, they are moral in their purpose; but they are likewise, with few exceptions, temperate in their outlook, full of a grave knowledge of the world, deeply concerned with the true seriousness of life, with the worth of things, and with the sense of values that must always guide the life that is to culminate in a peak of personal worthiness. If it is possible for a letter-writer to be literature—and there seems to be no palpable reason why it may not be—this is indeed literature.

IV

THE FICTIONAL OUTPOSTS AND
THE PRE-RICHARDSONIAN
LETTER STORY

IN THE consideration of the letter-writer we have already seen, even in those early letter-writers produced long before the appearance of Samuel Richardson, the tendency to yield to the narrative impulse in order that some sort of human interest may be developed in the letters presented for the entertainment or for the instruction of the reader. It is not at all to be wondered at, then, that this narrative impulse in the form of the letter took upon itself a particular development of its own into what might be called the letter story, in which the letter is used for the purpose of narrating travel, scandal, politics and, above all else, the story of love.

In her admirable essay, "English Epistolary Fiction before *Pamela*,"[1] Helen Sard Hughes of Wellesley College designates certain stock situations by means of which English epistolary fiction before *Pamela* was developed. There are (1) the "rifled" post-bag; (2) the "letters of travel"; (3) the "friendly correspondence"; and (4) the "correspondence of lovers." It is the last three devices which extend most completely into the epistolary fiction of the eighteenth century and, although all four tendencies are undoubtedly present, the first is but lightly felt as a survival from an earlier period. Thus, it is of an earlier century that such collections of the

[1] *The Manly Anniversary Studies in Language and Literature,* University of Chicago Press, 1923.

40

"rifled" post-bag literature as Nicholas Breton's *A Poste with a Packet of Mad Letters* (1603), already discussed; *A Speedie Poste, with Certaine New Letters.* By "I. W. Gent." (1625); and *The Post-Boy Robb'd of His Mail* (vol. I—1692?; vol. II —1693), are actually part. Even those works, derived from such an impulse, which extend over into the eighteenth century are more of the seventeenth in spirit. Thus we have, as late as 1719, a work attributed to Charles Gildon,[2] which is entitled and described as *The Post-Man Robb'd of His Mail: or, the Packet Broke Open. Being a Collection of Miscellaneous Letters, Serious and Comical, Amorous and Gallant. Amongst which are, The Lover's Sighs: or Amours of the Beautiful Stremunia and Alphonso the Wise, King of Castile and Aragon, and Earl of Provence; with her Passionate Letters to the King on his chusing another Mistress. In Five Books. By the best wits of the present Age.*[3] None the less, we see even here that the chief glory of the collection is the story of Stremunia and Alphonso, a love story in letters.

Of the four epistolary stock situations indicated by Miss Hughes in her essay, two are representative not only of situations but of uses of the letter in fiction as well. These are, of course, the letter of travel and the letter between lovers for the purpose of telling the story of their love. The epistolary story of travel does not seem to have developed until the very close of the seventeenth century, and the first notable work of its kind is *The Ladies Travels into Spain* (1692) by Madam Daunois, author of *Memoirs of the Court of France*, which former is, according to its title in entirety, *The Ingenious and Diverting Letters of the Lady—Travels into Spain. Describing the Devotions, Nunneries, Humours, Customs, Laws, Militia, Trade, Diet, and Recreations of that People. Intermixt with Great Variety of Modern Adventures,*

---

[2] *D. N. B.*, VII, p. 1226.

[3] In the same year, 1719, there appeared a new edition of this work called *The Lover's Sighs, or the Letters of the most beautiful Stremunia to Alphonso the Wise, King of Castile, Aragon and Earl of Provence. Translated out of the Provencial tongue into Latin, by Gonsalvo de Mendoza*, a version which further betrays the influence of the prevalent story of love in letters of that particular period.

and Surprising Accidents: being the Truest and Best Re-marks Extant on that Court and Country. It is interesting to note that the "remarks" extend over a space of some two hundred and eighty-eight closely printed pages. The letters are addressed by the writer to "his" "dear cousin" and, when they are signed at all, are signed rather bafflingly, "yours." As the letters proceed, not only does the signature drop, but the "dear cousin" retires to a minor place and, in Letter XII, is not mentioned until the twenty-third line. These are, then, letters in little more than name. As in most works of this sort it is difficult to say whether the author knew the land of which she wrote with any intimacy. Although she writes with a lively appreciation of her scene, she seems to be combining fancy with fact. Such descriptions as that of the Cavalleros riding horseback "like the Turks and Moors, that is, as they call it, a Genita" (Letter XII) and of the measures taken in Spain to ward off the "evil eye" (Letter VII) betray a certain knowledge of the land, undoubtedly. There is present, on the other hand, that degree of fancy, aside from the author's writing as if she were a man, that even in the most pedestrian of these travel-works in letters, allies them to the type of the *voyage imaginaire.*

Mrs. Mary de la Rivière Manley has likewise contributed to the travel letters in her work of 1696, *Letters written by Mrs. Manley. To which is added, by the Honourable Colonel Pack, a Letter from a Supposed Nun in Portugal to a Gentleman in France: in Imitation of the Nun's Five Letters.* In 1725 this was reprinted as *A Stage-Coach Journey to Exeter, Describing the Humours of the Road, with the Characters and Adventures of the Company. In eight letters to a Friend.* The chief interest in the work lies in the lively picture it gives of the journey, the inns, the customs of travel and the characters themselves. In the presentation of the love-ridden beau and the bumptious sea captain and even the author herself, there is a definite step toward the creation of character in the story told in letters. To Mrs. Manley is likewise assigned *The Bath Intrigues. In Four Letters to a Friend in*

London (1724), a book which is a distinct contribution to the large number of literary works which concern themselves with Bath. Whicher, however, attributes the book to Mrs. Eliza Haywood,[4] a writer of considerable power and versatility.

Amongst other notable collections of travel letters that belong to the early part of the eighteenth century is the *Memoirs of the Adventures of a French Lady of Quality, during her late Residence at Venice, sent by her to an English Lady in London; containing a great Variety of Fortune, with many excellent moral reflections. Recommended to the perusal of the Fair Sex* (1705). We are able to see here the influence of the didactic and philosophic trend of the earlier letter-writers which carried on so definitely into the great flowering of the epistolary novel itself.

Again, to the year 1717 belongs a similar work described as: *Letters from a Lady at Paris to a Lady at Avignon. Containing a Particular Account of the City, the Politiks, Intrigues, Gallantry, and Secret History of Persons of the First Quality in France.* It is of particular interest to note the fact that a commentator, in the Preface to the book, writes: "There is not, perhaps, any kind of Writing so difficult as that of Familiar Letters, nor anything so pleasing when it is well perform'd." Undoubtedly, the author has attempted a sort of lively verisimilitude in her work and succeeds rather well in reporting the scandals about a long series of Dukes and Duchesses, Lords and Ladies, and many another of noble designation. The portrait of Madame de Maintenon (herself, like Madame de Sevigné, a prolific letter writer) presented here by the author is by no means a superficial one and in the sixth letter, at least, we are given considerable insight into the subtle practices of that celebrated woman. It is not until the tenth letter, however, that a complete history of this king's favorite is given, in a lively revelation of her rise through extremest difficulties to a place of power in

---

[4] George F. Whicher, *The Life and Romances of Mrs. Eliza Haywood,* New York, 1915, pp. 111-112.

which she was enabled to mould to her own will a great and capricious monarch. The point to be made is, however, that this collection of letters, along with the two previously mentioned, very definitely further the growing practice of telling life stories, or histories, by means of the letter, and both the *Memoirs of the Adventures of a French Lady of Quality* and the *Letters from a Lady at Paris* indicate clearly the influence of the scandal romance and the secret history so popular at the conclusion of the seventeenth century and the beginning of the eighteenth. Both the scandal romance and the secret history were brought over from the French and Spanish and were translated and imitated in English, largely in the work of female authors, among the ranks of whom Mrs. Manley and Mrs. Haywood were particularly notable. That the familiar letter was a distinct aid to the repetition of scandal and of personal histories is obvious because of the lively verisimilitude and the revelatory qualities which that type of letter possesses. It is thus that we are able to find here a growing fictional interest among collections of letters which were made for some other primary reason than that of the story, or stories, they may have happened to tell.

Of particular interest among the travel letters is a pamphlet written in letter form by Daniel Defoe and published in 1719. The title of this work is *The King of the Pirates: being an Account of the Famous Enterprises of Captain Avery, the mock King of Madagascar. With his Rambles and Piracies; where all the sham accounts formerly published of him are detected. In Two Letters from himself; one during his stay at Madagascar and one since his escape from thence.* Defoe departs from the form of an earlier work, *The King of the Pirates* (1709), at least in that he makes his work epistolary, a fact which may probably be indicative that the work in letters was steadily increasing in popularity. Certainly, this would be observed by a man like Defoe, who always seems to have an eye to the tendencies of the times. The author here used the device of the letter to make a picaresque hero a creature of immediate probability by means of a seemingly actual correspondence.

In 1730 we have the translation of C. de Sécondat, Baron de Montesquieu's *Persian Letters* by Mr. Ozell, and in this work we have the formula of an Englishman or Frenchman who visits some foreign country interestingly reversed. *The Persian Letters* present the correspondence of several Persians, among whom Usbek and Rica are the most important, who have left their Persian habitat to visit Europe, and their philosophic comments upon that continent, its manners, customs and personalities, form the bulk of the letters. Although not strictly a part of the English epistolary impulse, the translation of the French work is sufficient to indicate how definitely the authors of the eighteenth century were interested in things of an epistolary nature.

Of the growing use of the letter for fictional purposes, that of its employment for the presentation of a story of lovers is by all means the most important or, if not, at least, the most prevalent. Of chief importance among collections of letters between lovers are the translations and imitations of that French work which is the direct precursor of much that is to follow in the story of English fictional epistles. In 1668 was published in French the first edition of those *Portuguese Letters* which were shortly to make a profound impression on English fiction. Indeed, so great was their success in France that they proved directly responsible for a new kind of literature referred to as that of "les Portugaises."[5] They appeared first in English in 1678 as *Five Love-Letters from a Nun to a Cavalier. Done out of French into English, by R. L'Estrange.* These were reprinted in 1693, but in 1683 there had already appeared *Seven Portuguese Letters; being the second part to the Five Love-Letters from a Nun to a Cavalier.* This, too, was reprinted in 1693. In 1694 was published a little work called *Five Love-Letters written by a Cavalier (the Chevalier Del) in answer to the five Love-Letters written to*

---

[5] Charlotte E. Morgan, *The Rise of the Novel of Manners*, New York, 1911, p. 73 n.

him by a Nun. All three works were then reprinted together in 1716. Of divergent interest is the existence of six metrical versions of these *Portuguese Letters*, published in 1701, 1713, 1716, and 1716, 1718 and 1731. The question of the genuineness of these letters has caused considerable controversy, and it is now believed that only those of the first series possess any semblance of recorded actuality.[6] Whatever the degree of actuality of these letters may have been originally, they must be looked upon now as a definite step forward toward the fulfilling of epistolary fiction and toward the method of Richardson. Of their timeliness Dr. Morgan writes:

. . . the *Letters* came at the high tide of the revulsion of feeling against the visionary ideals and poetic language of the Hotel de Rambouillet on the one hand, and against the high thinking and plain living of the Puritans on the other, in favor of life in the raw—robustness, passion, and at its worst, immoral license in word and deed.[7]

Concerning the letters themselves, it may be said that the first five letters are a long complaint of the Nun for what she calls, after the fashion of the abandoned Ariadne, "my Inconsiderate, Improvident, and most unfortunate Love." Incidentally, the woman berates her lover in good round terms that are occasionally reminiscent of the writing of a man rather than of a woman. Not that there is present any suggestion of indelicacy, but rather that the tone of much of the writing is possessed of a masculine vigor. Perhaps this is due to the fact that the translation is the work of a man, Sir Roger L'Estrange. Certainly, comparison indicates a more graceful touch in the French than is to be found in the English, as:

Bless me! But must this absence last forever? An Absence so Hellish, that Sorrow itself wants words to express it?

Quoi! cette absence, a laquelle ma douleur, toute ingenieuse qu'elle est, ne peut donner un nom assez funeste.[8]

[6] Hughes, *op. cit.*, p. 163.
[7] Morgan, *op. cit.*, p. 72.
[8] *Five Love-Letters from a Nun to a Cavalier, Done out of French into English* by Sir Roger L'Estrange, pp. 2-3 (2nd Ed.).

It is difficult to say with any degree of finality whether the difference between the English and the French versions is that of the writing of man and woman or the natural difference between the more masculine English timbre and the less masculine French. The letters as a whole are full of attack, recrimination, and regrets, but it must likewise be remembered that they present a narrative of love that has cooled only in the person to whom the letters are addressed and, as such, preserve a certain dignity of sorrow, coupled with a just indignation that renders them singularly sustained in composition. The *Seven Portuguese Letters*, described as "one of the most Passionate Pieces that possibly has ever been extant," seem to be considerably less passionate in tone, as a matter of fact. They record nothing at all new that has not already been touched upon in the previous letters, with the possible exception of a vein of malice which lends the work a touch of unbecoming littleness. We might wish to avoid the original Nun as a dangerous individual in her just anger, but there is about her nothing of the spiteful viciousness which expresses itself in the writing of the second group. Both groups of letters, however, attempt to make the characters involved real flesh-and-blood people and, from that point of view, add to the growing epistolary literature that vein of verisimilitude which, in the work of later epistolarians, and especially of Samuel Richardson, becomes so all-pervading a characteristic.

It is interesting to note that, as late as 1726, Mrs. Jane Barker produced a work, called *The Lining of the Patch-Work Screen*, in which she tells, in the most approved hectic fashion after the manner of Spanish tragedy, the further adventures of the Nun and her escape from the nunnery.

It is undoubtedly as a result of these *Letters from a Nun to a Cavalier* that a French paraphrase of the letters of Abelard and Heloise, published in Latin at Paris in 1616, was published in London in 1693. The London publication of the Latin version (1708) was itself translated into English by John Hughes, about 1722. Before the English version of these sentimental letters was produced, however, there were a number of love letters produced in England. As early as 1671, Mrs. Aphra Behn, that "admirable Astrea" who may better have been called the amazing Astrea, composed a work called the *Love-Letters to a Gentleman* which seems to have fallen under the influence of the French *Portuguese Letters*. The letters themselves present the spectacle of a woman attempting to retain the love of an indifferent gallant by means of the revelation of her own passion. It is scarcely necessary to point out the similarity of this device to the theme of the *Letters from a Nun*. The date of Mrs. Behn's work is not certain, but the year 1671 is held probable because of a reference to "my new play."[9] "New," however, may not necessarily mean "first," since the record of the first is 1670.[10] At least, Mrs. Behn was in the vanguard of the new impulse.

The influence of the *Five Love-Letters from a Nun* may be seen not only in the subject-matter but in the titles themselves of numerous other works, such as: *Love-Letters between a Nobleman and his Sister; with the History of their Adventures* (1683), sometimes referred to as *The Amours of Philander and Sylvia; Love Letters between Polydorus and Messalina* (1689); *Letters of Love and Gallantry and several other subjects. With the Adventures of a Young Lady, written by Herself in several Letters to a Gentleman in the Country. All written by Ladies. Translated from the French* (1693); *Love-Letters from King Henry VIII to Anne Boleyn. Some in French and Some in English. To which are added, Translations of those written in French. With an Appendix, containing Two Letters from Anne Boleyn to Cardinal Wolsey; with her last to Henry VIII* (1714); *Love-Letters between a certain Nobleman and the famous Mr. Wilson. Discovering the true History of the Rise and Surprising Grandeur of that Beau* (1723); and *Love-Letters on all Occasions lately passed between persons of distinction* (1730).

Of special interest here are that rather tender story told

[9] Morgan, *op. cit.*, p. 77.
[10] V. Sackville-West, *Aphra Behn, the Incomparable Astrea*, New York, 1928, p. 171.

in the *Love-Letters between a Nobleman and his Sister*, and
the historical romance revealed in the *Love-Letters from
King Henry VIII to Anne Boleyn*. The first story is almost an
epistolary novel in proportions and tells, in three parts, the
love story of a young nobleman and his adopted sister set
against a background of French history of the time of Catherine de Medici and the Huguenot Protestants under the
Prince of Condé. The nobleman is the handsome Philander;
the heroine of this sentimental tale is Sylvia, the sister to
Philander's wife, Myrtilla. Myrtilla herself is in love with
the Prince of Condé and, as the story progresses, another
young gentleman, friend to Philander, one Octavio, falls in
love with Sylvia. The tale itself becomes extremely involved,
after the fashion of the romance. Of particular importance is
the fact that the letters are not confined to those between
Philander and Sylvia, but that there are given, likewise, letters from Sylvia to Octavio and from Octavio to Sylvia, as
well as the letters exchanged by Philander and Octavio. The
letters themselves reveal a somewhat excessive sentimentality,
and the story proceeds in a fashion which borders upon pre-
ciousness. Among these epistolary efforts *The Love-Letters
between a Nobleman and his Sister* is scarcely one of the most
distinguished works, but it presents none the less a definite
step forward toward the epistolary novel itself. Incidentally,
the *Love-Letters* are supposed to present the story of two
actual people and, from this point of view, have much in
common with the scandal romance.

The *Love-Letters from King Henry VIII to Anne Boleyn*
make no attempt to disguise the personages presented but,
after the manner of fiction, present the story of the love of
these two celebrated figures with all possible verisimilitude.
That they are in two languages is notable and it may be sur-
mised that this is done to indicate the learning of the monarch presented. The letters of the King are open revelations
of his brusque, breezy nature and, although they are love letters, are brief and direct. This is especially noticeable in
contrast to the diffuse and circumlocutory nature of most of

the love letters to be found in this group. The last letter of Anne Boleyn to her lord is, rightly, marked by a distinct and commendable dignity and by no little pathos.

Most of the "love-letters" recorded here indicate the influence of the *Five Love-Letters from a Nun to a Cavalier*, and in such a work as *Letters of Love and Gallantry* we have a nun's letter to a monk which recalls the more famous letters of a nun. The story of love is told in epistolary form, however, in many other works of the day which do not bear the title of "love-letters." Thus, we have the following works which are likewise stories of love in letters: *A New Version of the Lady Gr– s (i.e., of Mary, Lady Grey of Werke) concerning her sister, the lady Berkeley. In a Letter to Madame Fan—* (1682), which is an earlier version of the story presented in the *Love-Letters between a Nobleman and his Sister; The Familiar Epistles of Col. Henry Martin found in his Misses Cabinet* (1685); *Love's Poesie: or, a collection of seven and twenty love-letters, both in verse and prose; that lately passed betwixt a gentleman and a very young lady in France* (1686); *The Unhappy Lovers: or, the Timorous Fair One. A novel. Being the loves of Alexander and Mellecinda. In a Letter* (1694); *An Historic Account of the Amours of the Emperor of Morocco* (1702); *The Perfidious P—. Being Letters from a Nobleman to Two Ladies* (1702); *The Double Captive; or, Chains upon chains, containing the amorous poems and letters of a young gentleman, one of the Preston prisoners in Newgate. To which is added the execution dream, with a preface to the ladies and an introductory novel* (1718); *Letters of a Lady of Quality to a Chevalier* (1721-24) ; *The Constant Lovers; being an entertaining history of the Amours and Adventures of Solenus and Perrigonia, Alexis and Sylvia* (1731); *Pylades and Corinna: or, Memoirs of the lives . . . of R. Gwinnett . . . and Mrs. E. Thomas Jun., containing the Letters . . . which passed between them. . . . Published from their original manuscripts* (1731); *The Honourable Lovers, or 2nd Volume of Pylades and Corinna* (1732); *Letters from the Marchioness de*

M . . . , to the Count de R. . . . Translated from the Original French, by Mr. Humphreys (1734).

This group of love tales in letters is much like the preceding in tone and material. They narrate romantic stories of lovers, usually separated by the misfortune of some unhappy chance. They are sentimental and verbose; they owe much in spirit to the original *Letters from a Portuguese Nun*. It is interesting to note that on the title-page of the *Letters from the Marchioness de M . . .* there is reprinted a "blurb" from the *Journal of Literature* of 1734 which runs as follows:—

If any Love-Letters may be rank'd with the celebrated ones of Abelard and Eloisa; those of a Religious Portuguese Lady, and those of the Chevalier de Her—; They are These of the Marchioness de M— to the Count de R—. They have the Fire, the Turn, the Spirit, and easy Air of those we have mention'd: They furnish us besides with this useful lesson, That Guilty Love must expect to meet with unhappy Consequences.

Particularly notable in this criticism, aside from the lofty comparison to the classic love letters of the day, is the indication that here we have a love story in letters behind which there is to be found a moral impulse, something of that same moral impulse later to be found, indeed, in the art of Samuel Richardson. The final letters of this volume are marked by a passionate outpouring of tragic writing which not only tells us of the separation of the lovers forever, the despair of the Marchioness and her weariness of life, but also makes clear the feeling that such are just punishments of illicit love.

A distinct departure from the story of love in letters is to be found, however, in *Pylades and Corinna*. Here the letters themselves are not used as the sole means of telling the story. There is a first part called the "Life of Corinna. Written by Herself," which is a sort of memoir; in this first part are to be found letters as a part of the narrative. The second part consists of the "Letters to Corinna from Pylades," themselves interspersed with considerable verse and, startlingly enough, with "An Abstract of Sir Isaac Newton's Opticks." A third part consists of "Miscellanies by Corinna." In so far as the

letters dominate the work, the book belongs with this particular group. None the less, it definitely indicates a relationship to that group of works in which use is slowly being made
of the letter as one of the natural adjuncts of narrative.

We likewise have, among the outposts of epistolary fiction,
the letter used as a means of portraying manners, characters,
and contemporary politics and, in another vein, as a means of
reporting contemporary scandal. A rather large number of
the publications of the day may be found to belong here.
Among them are:—*Philosophical Letters: or, Modest Reflections upon some Opinions in Natural Philosophy, Maintained by several Famous and Learned Authors of this Age,
Expressed by way of Letters: by the Thrice Noble, Illustrious, and Excellent Princess, the Lady Marchioness of Newcastle* (1664); *The Gentleman Apothecary; Being a Late
and True Story turned out of the French (of J. de Villiers)*
(1670); *Account of the Secret Services of M. de Vernay . . .
to Count Teckeley, as they passed by the way of Letters, etc.
Translated out of the French* (1683); *Comical Description
of a Nunnery* (1700); *The Country Gentleman's Companion
for the Town: In eighteen Letters from a Gentleman in London to his Friend in the Country; representing the Advantages of a Country Life in opposition to the Follies of the
Town; discovering most of the Humours, Tricks, and Cheats
of the Town, which Gentlemen, when Strangers, are exposed
to* (1702); *Adventures of Lindamira, A Lady of Quality.
Written with her own hand to her friend in the Country*
(1702) — (2nd Ed., in 1713, titled *The Lover's Secretary*);
*Court Intrigues, in a collection of original Letters from the
Island of New Atalantis, etc. By the author of Those Memoirs.* By Mary de la Rivière Manley (1711); *Memoirs of
the Dutchess Mazarine, written in her Name by the Abbot of
St. Réal, with a Letter containing the true Character of her
Person and Conversation, etc.* (1713); *Secret History of the
Most Famous Beauties, Ladies of Quality, from fair Rosa-
mund down to this Time.* By Captain Alexander Smith
(1715); *Spy upon the Conjurer* (1724—revised by Mrs. Eliza

Haywood) ; *Letters from the Palace of Fame. Written by the First Minister of the Region of the Air, to an Inhabitant of this World.* By Mrs. Eliza Haywood (1727) ; *The Perplex'd Duchess* (1727) ; *Friendship in Death; in Twenty Letters from the Dead to the Living* (1728) ; and *Letters Moral and Entertaining, In Prose and Verse* (1729-33) , both of which are the work of Mrs. Elizabeth Rowe.

Of these volumes, *The Gentleman Apothecary; The Account of the Secret Services of M. de Vernay; Court Intrigues;* and *The Letters from the Palace of Fame,* incline toward the scandal fiction of the period, while the portrayal of manners and of character is more definitely to be found in *The Country Gentleman's Companion; The Adventures of Lindamira; Friendship in Death;* and *Letters Moral and Entertaining.* There is, however, no hard and fast line of demarcation between that work which concerns itself primarily with the retelling of scandal and that which is devoted to manners as they are exemplified in this group. The letters of the Duchess of Newcastle are placed here because, despite the fact that they are intended by their title to be a sort of philosophic dissertation in letters, they are none the less representative of the foibles and inclinations of mankind by means of the correspondence of two ladies who are friends. The relation of episodes and the presentation of characters in this work are somewhat too brief, and the general tone of the letters as a whole suffers from too insistent moralizing. Again, the letters are completely lacking at times in verisimilitude and when, as in Letter XXXIX, Section I, there is an extended discussion of the physics of "vapour, clouds, wind and rain," it is very difficult to believe the actuality of its having been written by one woman to another. The same adverse criticism applies to Letter XLI, Section III, which concerns itself with the gout, and indeed to a very large number of these letters in general. As a result, the entire work is too heavy for the purposes of entertainment, and too definitely derivative to rank high as an original product. It has, none the less, an excellent basis to which it adheres with continuous optimism.

It is fitting that the two books by Mrs. Elizabeth Rowe, *Friendship in Death* and *Letters Moral and Entertaining*, be placed here. Although *Friendship in Death* is supposed to be a collection of letters written by the dead to their living friends, there is very little that is spiritual or unearthly about them, and most of the letters are filled with advice which, however moral it may be, is none the less imbued with a considerable worldly interest. In almost any one of the twenty letters, whether it be "To my Lord . . . , from Ethelinda," (Letter IV) ; "From Cleander to his brother, endeavoring to reclaim him from his Extravagancies," (Letter XII) ; or "From Theodosius to Varrius, dissuading him from the Pursuit of an Amour with the beautiful Cleora," (Letter XX) , we are able to find a revelation of close human relationship, of passion, ambition, love and, even beyond that, a very earthly interest of the dead in the living. Such a letter as the seventh, from Delia to Emilia, in which is given a description of the celestial regions, with such phrases as:

But how shall I make you sensible of what an angel's flowing song, in all the pomp of heavenly harmony, would not fully describe! In what figures of celestial eloquence shall I relate the loves of immortal spirits; or tell you the height, the extent, the fullness of their bliss!

is a rarity among these epistles. Incidentally, such a passage as this reveals a distinct talent in Mrs. Rowe for rhetoric of the flowing sort. It is the story interest as revealed by the relationship of human beings to one another that seems to be dominant in all these letters, just as it is in that so much larger collection, *Letters Moral and Entertaining*. All these letters, when considered in a single body, suffer from a monotony of story and characterization. There are too many retellings of the story of languishing lovers, reformed rakes and self-sacrificing friends, and the characters that appear in these stories are too much of a single pattern. None the less, they are all definite examples of the epistolary impulse in narrative.

Among these epistolary outposts are at least two notable works in letters which are romantic satires. These are the eight volumes of *Letters writ by a Turkish Spy, who liv'd Five and Forty Years undiscover'd at Paris: Giving an Impartial account to the Divan at Constantinople of the most remarkable Transactions of Europe: and discovering several Intrigues and Secrets of the Christian Courts, (especially of that of France) continued from the Year 1637, to the Year 1682* (1687); and *The London Spy Compleat.* By Edward Ward (1703). It will be seen from the very title of the first of these works, how much of the secret history, the court scandal romance, and the letter of travel is to be found in the inspirational background of the eight volumes. Since the *Turkish Spy* is of so early date it may well be considered responsible for a part of the vogue of the pseudo-letter in fiction and is thus, in its own way, as important a cog in the machinery of the movement as is the *Letters from a Nun to a Cavalier*.[11] It must be remembered that the *Turkish Spy* is a satire of the long romance with its discursive histories and politics, and adds, as such, along with *The London Spy*, the impulse to use the letter as means of satiric expression. That the former was extraordinarily popular is indicated by the fact that there were twenty-six editions by 1770 and in 1718 Daniel Defoe wrote *Continuation of Letters Written by a Turkish Spy at Paris. The London Spy* is important beyond itself in that it is a work written only partly in letters. Such works indicate further development of the epistle.

Important, also, for the present history is the development of the letter as one of the natural adjuncts of narrative, used to add verisimilitude to the story being told, in almost the same manner as dialogue is made use of to add liveliness and closeness to nature to a narrative which might otherwise be lacking in faithfulness of presentation. We have just noted the fact that *The London Spy* is not written entirely in let-

[11] Morgan, *op. cit.*, p. 74.

ters, but contains letters in the natural course of its narrative prose. There have already been mentioned the *Memoirs of the Court of France. Relating to the Amours of the Duke of Maine, and the Marriages of the other Illegitimate Children of the French King with the Princes and the Princesses of the Blood. Written in French by Madam Daunois, the Famous Author of the Letters of Travels into Spain; and done into English by Mr. A. B.* (1697) ; *The Lover's Secretary; or, the Adventures of Lindamira, A Lady of Quality. Written to her Friend in the Country. In XXVI Letters* (1713) ; and *Pylades and Corinna: or, Memoirs of the Lives, Amours, and Writings of Richard Gwinnett Esq; of Great Shurdington in Gloucestershire; and Mrs. Elizabeth Thomas Jun. of Great Russel Street, Bloomsbury. Containing the Letters and other Miscellaneous Pieces, in Prose and Verse, which passed between them during a courtship of above Sixteen Years* (1731). All three of these works are only partly written in letters. The *Memoirs of the Court of France* contain letters written from various characters in the story to each other; letters from Du Maine to Mademoiselle de Condé and from that lady to Du Maine; letters to and from the Countess Brigid; a letter from the Baroness Olida, and so on. *The Lover's Secretary* is composed chiefly of letters, but there are many interlying passages of narrative prose between the letters, explaining intervening action and, particularly, the emotions with which the letters were received. *Pylades and Corinna* contains not only the love letters of the two characters chiefly concerned, but likewise presents the memoirs of Corinna supposed to have been written by herself, and is additionally interspersed with much verse. From these three books, already mentioned, we may see the growing tendency to use the letter, not as an end in fiction in itself, but as a means to some desired end.

This same growing tendency is further indicated by the publication of such works as: *The Spanish Politician: or, Some Account of the Management of Cardinal Alberoni. Done out of French* (1718) ; *The Fatal Amour between a Beautiful Lady and a Young Nobleman* (pub. 1719, as an addition to *The Secret History of the Prince of the Nazarenes and the Two Turks*) ; *Love in Excess; or the Fatal Inquiry: A Novel. In Three Parts.* By Mrs. Eliza Haywood (1721) ; *The Reform'd Coquet; or, Memoirs of Amoranda. A Novel.* By Mrs. Mary Davys, author of *The Humours of York* (1724) ; *The Amorous History of the Gauls, containing the Intrigues and Gallantries of the Court of France, during the Reign of Louis XIV. Written in French by Roger de Rabutin, Count de Bussy, and now Translated into English* (1727) ; *The Secret History of the Present Intrigues of the Court of Caramania.* By Mrs. Eliza Haywood (1727) ; and *The Life of the Countess de Gondez. Written by her own Hand in French, and Dedicated to the Princess De La Roche-Sur-Yon. And now faithfully translated into English.* By Mrs. P. Aubin (1729).

These seven works are likewise partly or largely, but not completely, composed in letters. *The Spanish Politician* has few more than five or six epistles in its entire one hundred and twenty pages, the most notable of these being the Pope's Letter (p. 48), and the Letter of the Marquis de Grimaldo (p. 71), both admirable and sound compositions. Where the letters are used it is with an obvious attempt at verisimilitude. *The Fatal Amour,* like *The Lover's Secretary,* pursues the device of a running prose commentary between the individual letters, in order to indicate the mood of the letter writer or receiver and any chance, intervening circumstance. The letters themselves are in a highly passionate vein, marked chiefly by a tone of sentimental despair. Of especial beauty and dignity, however, is that letter of the "beautiful lady," in which she confesses to the lord that she is unable to resist him any longer and that his love has triumphed over hers. Here is an oasis of sincerity and simplicity. *Love in Excess* is probably the most distinguished of this group, not only in itself, but because it is again the work of Mrs. Eliza Haywood. Its use of the letter is generous, and as the novel proceeds, the use increases rather than diminishes. The novel itself definitely reflects the growth of sentiment and of the appreciation of tragic situation. Mrs. Haywood indulges, almost to excess, in the confused situations, the amorous dilemmas, and the ethical problems in love that were so popular at this time but, as usual, she writes with that unfailing liveliness which adds a degree of interest to her most pedestrian passages. *The Reform'd Coquet,* by Mrs. Davys, makes considerable use of the letter between pairs and among groups of its various characters as it proceeds. It is a brisk little story, full of sentiment and didacticism, in which it resembles the work of Richardson, and it furthermore presents, in the figure of Lord Lofty, one of the first almost too-ideal gentlemen of his kind, of whom Sir Charles Grandison is the standard example. *The Amorous History of the Gauls* is, like the *Secret Memoirs of the Court of France,* very much of a scandal romance, and makes large use of the letter, almost half of the book being occupied by the bulk of the letters presented. Like the *Secret Memoirs* this book is full of keyhole portraits of the great and near great in the court of France and, even in this English version, retains a French quality of piquancy which makes it distinctly palatable. Of this general type, although tempered with a more English sense of ethics, is Mrs. Eliza Haywood's *Secret History of the Court of Caramania.* This has in it something of both the scandal romance and the *voyage imaginaire.* It makes protracted use of the letter and notably of the P.S. which, in at least one case, (p. 56), is almost as long as the letter to which it is attached. The extended use of the postscript in these letters seems to be a distinct innovation in fiction that is more or less strictly epistolary and is a natural advance towards representation of actuality that is not to be overlooked. The work, taken as a whole, is rather definitely pseudo-history, none the less. The *Life of the Countess de Gondez* presents the affecting story of a highly moral young girl who, married to an old count, falls in love with a young man. She retains her virtue, even after the death of her husband and finally, when she discovers that the young man she loves is not worthy of her, marries another and nobler man. This may give some indication of the basically didactic quality of the novel. There is moderate use made here of the letter, and, whenever an epistle occurs, it is part of the warp and woof of the story itself.

We have seen the growth of the fictional epistle in the latest decade of the seventeenth century and the early part of the eighteenth century as an important means of presenting a story. Chief among the various uses of the letter have been indicated the use as a means of presenting a story of travel, a scandal, a history, a psuedo-history, politics, manners and, above all else, a story of lovers. Beyond this, we have seen, however, the growth of the letter as a fictional device so that it might find its proper place in the general narrative in order to add that naturalness that is accomplished alone by presenting the characters in the story by means of their own words, either spoken in dialogue or recorded in epistle. Above all this, however, is the preparation of the letter in these early works for its ultimate use in the hands of the master, Samuel Richardson, who was not to innovate so much as he was to perfect what was already given him, wherein lies the distinction between the novice and the artist. Among these early letter writers in fiction there is no truly great artist, unless it be Daniel Defoe, and he may not be claimed as an early epistolarian on the grounds of one brief work in letters. But there were many admirable and sincere technicians, many thoroughgoing story-tellers, and it is the developmental work of these that gave the letter, even so early, a true literary distinction.

V

SAMUEL RICHARDSON AND HIS

DEVELOPMENT OF THE

EPISTOLARY NOVEL

BEFORE any discussion of the great Richardson—not only the man who chiefly developed the epistolary novel, but the father largely of the modern English novel—is attempted, it is well to say a few summarizing words concerning prose fiction in English as it stood at the time Samuel Richardson began to write.

Not until the eighteenth century was well started had prose fiction been cultivated for its own sake by English authors. The *Utopia* of More; the *Arcadia* of Sir Philip Sidney; Barclay's *Argenis*; Bacon's *New Atlantis*; and the English imitations of the French *roman de longue haleine*,[1] were all prose fiction of a sort, but it is really Defoe who made prose fiction the popular and artistically self-supporting form which we know today, and not one of the earlier men who may have written in prose. The tendency toward the novel and away from the romance was, however, already at work as early as 1660. At this time the desire for some sort of realism began to become strong in the fictional output of the day and the romances were superseded by more realistic stories developed from the French and Spanish *novelle*. The strain of realism may be found to run straight through from Mrs. Behn to Defoe, along with its development of pretended veri-

[1] v. T. P. Haviland, *The Roman de Longue Haleine on English Soil*, Philadelphia, 1931.

similitude, loose morality, and forced gaiety and vivacity.
There had begun to be developed, likewise, the scandal novel
which, in the capable hands of such women as Mrs. Manley
and Mrs. Haywood, had a considerable influence on the
period. Beyond this, there was the group of "Portuguese
letters" which definitely lent the tone of sentiment and sentimentality to the writing of the day and, even more importantly, suggested the high value of personal, psychological
analysis to the writers of fiction. There were, in addition to
all this, as the eighteenth century dawned and began to unfold, the narratives of Defoe and of Swift. Defoe intensified
pretended verisimilitude; Swift, like the authors of the scandal romances, presented well-known figures and events under
a thin disguise, and added thereto a stinging and entirely
conscious satire. But there was also a distinct development of
the character, the letter, and the dialogue in the growing
fiction of the period, exemplified in so remarkable a collection as, for instance, the *Sir Roger de Coverley Papers*, and
the experiences of the Lizard family in *The Guardian*. It was
for a combination of all these elements, however, that literature was waiting and, although this was tended toward in
some of the semi-domestic works of Mrs. Haywood and in
some of the anonymous novels mentioned in the preceding
chapter, it was not done with any real sense of completeness
or developmental finality. Whether any of these works were
actual novels or not is impossible to say. Indeed, there is no
hard and fast line of demarcation between the romance of the
day and the realistic novel in its earliest forms. For that reason it is impossible to point to this or that piece of fictional
work before the novels of Richardson and call it the first
English novel. It may be said, none the less, that the emergence of the novel as the favored form dates from the appearance of the works of Defoe and Richardson, and that there-
after the novel attains to a height of popularity from which
it reigns supreme until the advent of the romance, resurrected
in the last decade of the eighteenth century, with the work

of Mrs. Radcliffe, Matthew Gregory ("Monk") Lewis, and their countless train of followers and imitators.

It has already been definitely stated that Samuel Richardson is the great developer of the epistolary form in the novel. It is necessary to comprehend, then, exactly what there is, epistolary and non-epistolary, that goes into the warp and woof of the three great novels of Richardson, works of almost mammoth proportions. First of all, the novel itself was, at the time Richardson started to write, beginning to be a chief outlet of pent-up emotions. The dignity and worth of the average man, once recognized, put him in readiness to take a stand for what he conceived himself to be: an individual with many rights not heretofore clearly denoted. Before all this had the possibility of coming to pass, the social order had to be changed; ideas then current had to be reorganized, broadened, and envisioned. A fact of importance is that the theatre was losing ground rapidly, until by 1750 or thereabouts its former hold on English life and thought was, to a large extent, gone. People were no longer completely satisfied either to see or to read the then existing dramas. Naturally, new forms of literary expression would be welcomed. The influence of the drama, none the less, persisted, though weakened. As late as 1764, Horace Walpole's *Castle of Otranto* followed the rules of the drama to an extent that made it even more dramatic than the same author's play, *The Mysterious Mother*. Richardson himself called *Clarissa* dramatic narrative and he arranged his characters as if they were the dramatis personae of a play. Thus, as Professor Raleigh so judiciously points out,[2] the novel seemed a play with elaborate stage directions written out and expanded to a considerable length. The framework thereby added, of course, made matters easier for the reader. Furthermore, the highly developed moralizing attitude of the dramatists continued its hold upon the novelists because public taste demanded it, and the homiletic habit present in almost all of the novels of

[2] Sir Walter Raleigh, *The English Novel . . . to the appearance of Waverley*, London, 1894, p. 142.

the eighteenth century was largely due to a pressure exerted upon the writers, for the most part, from the outside. There is no doubt, however, that in the case of Richardson, the moral impulse springs from within; it is of the very fibre of the man. Richardson had the good sense, in the Steeleian phrase, to "make even virtue fashionable." And since the dramas then being written and produced were extremely slow in action, slow in plot development, and full of analysis, it is safe to assume that they were really essays in dramatic form or already sentimental novels. But novels could portray more advanced ideals of life because they themselves were newer and not encumbered with a set of hackneyed conventions such as those that hampered the drama of the day, and could, at the same time, reach a much wider reading public than that public which was accustomed to go to the theatre. Again, the consciousness of the individual, the theory soon to be given such force by Rousseau, that "all men are free and equal," these things that the drama was not giving expression to because it was largely concerned with heroic greatness and with superficial social comedy, were definitely given expression to in the Richardsonian novel.

It is therefore clear that the eighteenth century was a century of beginnings, literary, social, scientific. Amongst these certainly not the least interesting is Richardson's discovery that the letter-writers and guidebooks of an earlier literature might be made into narratives. Just as the Italians strung together their *novelle* with a link story or character, so did Richardson take a very old form of literature and, by giving to it his particular brand of genius, make the exemplary compilation into the novel. He made use, in one way and another, of all the literary material that was ready for him at the time he began to write.

That the popularity of Richardson is in inverse ratio to the greatness of his literary reputation few will today be able to deny. Everyone knows the names of Pamela Andrews, Clarissa Harlowe, and Sir Charles Grandison, but the volumes in which they are described remain for the most part in undisturbed repose, among those books which, in Charles Lamb's phrase, "no gentleman's library should be without." Leslie Stephen says that "a certain soporific aroma exhales from the endless files of fictitious correspondence."[3] And this is not the only paradox involved in the reputation and influence of this man of paradoxes. But enough of such. It has been the habit of some to call Richardson "the little printer." Suffice it to say that, were these same people just in their estimation of the author, they would call him instead the great printer. He is, after Caxton, the greatest "printer" in English literature.

Aside from the vast folds of his personal and avowed correspondence, Richardson has given us three tremendous novels upon which any consideration of the novelist must necessarily be based. They are, according to their full titles:

(1). *Pamela; or, Virtue Rewarded. In a Series of Familiar Letters from a Beautiful Young Damsel to Her Parents: Published in Order to Cultivate Principles of Virtue and Religion in the Youth of Both Sexes. A Narrative which has Its Foundation in Truth; and at the same Time that it agreeably Entertains, by a Variety of Curious and Affecting Incidents, is Entirely divested of All Those Images which, in Too Many Pieces Calculated for Amusement only, tend to inflame the Minds they should Instruct.*

(2). *Clarissa, or, the History of a Young Lady: comprehending the Most Important Concerns of Private Life. And particularly shewing, the Distresses that may attend the Misconduct Both of Parents and Children, in Relation to Marriage. Published by the Editor of Pamela.*

(3). *History of Sir Charles Grandison, In a Series of Letters, Published from the Originals by the Editor of Pamela and Clarissa.*

It is to be noted that, as we proceed through the titles of the three novels, they grow constantly shorter as if, in the first, the author wished to explain everything by his title to

[3] *Hours in a Library,* "Richardson's Novels," I, p. 48, London, 1892.

the reader and then, having felt his way into the mind of his reader with *Pamela*, proceeded to shorten his titles with following books, leaving the works themselves to explain what the titles did not.

It seems almost imperative, along with the full titles of these three works, to present a brief recital of the contents, or plots, of the three Richardson novels, in order to make clear at the very outset, the distinct similarities existent in all three of them, similarities which indubitably mark the novelist's insistence on presenting a definite sort of morality and particular type of moral issue in the stories he is writing, not for their own sake, but for the sake of that moral issue itself.

It must first be noted, concerning *Pamela*, that, although it begins with Letter I, it is, at the outset of the story, not so much a series of letters as a series of recordings in the journal of the heroine, a combination of letter and journal which is later to be found in several novels of the epistolary group, of which Scott's *Redgauntlet* is by no means the least, although that later novel makes use of narrative in addition to letter and journal, and *Pamela* does not. Many of the letters are here written by Pamela with something like a conviction that they will never reach their destination. And yet she writes! The result, then, is the production of something more nearly a diary than a letter or group of letters. Again, many of the letters written by the heroine with an intended destination fall into the hands of Mrs. Jewkes or Mr. B——, for whom they were not intended, a device whereby Richardson adds to the dramatic suspense of the story.

Pamela tells us, in these letters and the diary, her own story of resistance to the unvirtuous advances of her master. She is a serving-girl in the home of a good and elderly lady, who has one son, Mr. B——, the hero of the novel, in the broader sense of the word. At the beginning of the girl's story, her mistress has just died. In the first letter to her parents, Elizabeth and John Andrews, Pamela tells of this death and of the kindness of her master. In an answering letter, the parents of the girl warn her against possible wicked advances on the part of that master. It is soon apparent that the parents were not amiss in giving such advice to their daughter, and it becomes apparent to Pamela herself, a fact she records in Letter X, that Mr. B— desires her. Pamela, however, still feels safe from all harm because of the presence of Mr. B—'s virtuous and kindly housekeeper, Mrs. Jervis, who indicates with considerable clarity that she would not permit anything untoward to happen to the girl at the hands of her master. Mr. B—, none the less, pursues his advantages, to the increasing distress of Pamela. The girl finally decides to leave Mr. B—'s services entirely, but is persuaded by Mrs. Jervis, who has in the meantime been intimidated by her master, to stay somewhat longer and ultimately to leave the house with her. Mr. B— meanwhile gains entrance to Pamela's and Mrs. Jervis' room (with the knowledge of the housekeeper) and Pamela, upon seeing him, falls into the first of a long series of fainting fits which persist, not only through the entire length of this book but even through the entire range of the literature of sentiment of the day. Mr. B— then offers to make Pamela his mistress at a handsome consideration, but the girl courageously refuses him and prepares to leave his house. She leaves for the home of her father and mother in a carriage along with John, another servant of Mr. B—, who treacherously carries her to his master's country seat in Lincolnshire. She is met there by a dragonous old woman, one Mrs. Jewkes, who is to be her keeper, Pamela thereby becoming the literal prisoner of her master, Mr. B—. At the conclusion of Letter XXXII, in which Pamela tells of her arrival in Lincolnshire, the heroine begins her Journal. It must be remembered, however, that the Journal itself is full of letters, some of which, as has already been intimated, are written with the intent that they be delivered. The Journal begins a long recital of the indignities heaped upon the girl by Mrs. Jewkes, who even proceeds so far as to steal her small savings from her. In addition, a certain Mr. Williams, a young parson, offers her marriage as a means of escape from her predicament, but Pamela refuses this, fearing that she might thereby involve Williams in the distress that has fallen upon her. Her fears are borne out by the fact that Williams is attacked and finally arrested for debt at the instigation of Mr. B—. Pamela's case proceeds from bad to worse, and she is finally tempted to drown herself in a garden pond. She resists the temptation, however, (and this is the dramatic high point of the story) but, on being discovered, is subjected to worse cruelty on the part of Mrs. Jewkes than she suffered before. Mr. B— himself then comes to the Lincolnshire estate, which step further terrifies Pamela. He discovers her Journal, with its record of suicidal intent, and relents of his severity, deciding to permit the persecuted girl to leave. He sends her off with a trusted servant, but on the road they are overtaken by another servant who bears a message from Mr. B—, in which the master declares that he cannot live without his Pamela. Pamela, who has all this while been falling in love with the undisciplined Mr. B—, now finds herself unable to resist his appeal and decides to return. Her master is overjoyed at the girl's return and offers her honorable marriage. Pamela accepts and is later married to Mr. B—, who receives her father with the utmost kindness and proves himself to be as tenderly solicitous of Pamela and her affairs as he was heretofore brutally desirous. Pamela is presented to his friends and, although she is surveyed by them at first with all the curiosity directed toward a prize mare, is accepted by most of them. Mr. B—'s sister, Lady Davers, who has all this while highly disapproved of her brother's conduct, is not, however, to be so easily reconciled to her brother's marriage to a servant girl. Yet even Lady Davers is, let it be said, finally won to reconciliation. Pamela, now Mrs. B—, is somewhat alarmed by the intelligence that Mr. B— has had a previous intrigue with one Miss Sally Godfrey, but her fears of any continuance of that affair are allayed, and when she meets it by chance she is graciously kind to the child that the two have had. Pamela has by this time so definitely intrenched herself in her husband's affections that he receives both her mother and father into his Bedfordshire mansion "with great goodness and complaisance."

At this point in the story, the second part of *Pamela* is begun, and this again turns the course of the narrative from its form as a journal to that of letters. In 103 letters, almost totally devoid of any action whatsoever, the rise of Pamela into complete power as the wife of Mr. B— is presented, along with Pamela's thoughts on the ethical problems that face her during this rise, her considerations of the social world, her attitude concerning the rearing of children after the birth of her first son, and so on. The letters here, unlike those which begin the story of Pamela and which are exchanged largely between Pamela and her parents, are exchanged between several correspondents and there are present a few letters which, although they concern Pamela, are neither from or to her. This, of course, indicates the expansion of the epistolary method which Richardson indulged in when he became more thoroughly acquainted with its possibilities as a narrative medium.

To us today it seems peculiar that a novel put in letter form, as is *Pamela*, should have been once so tremendously popular, and when we further realize that this novel is a series of letters, the purpose of which is to teach propriety and morals, its attraction is still further to be wondered at. It is true that English fiction from Richardson to Galsworthy has had, for the most part, to do with a purpose, but either the thesis has been so carefully woven into the plot as not to obtrude itself, or it has had something to do with a question with which the reader is interested for its own sake. Sentimentality, however, could be purveyed to the public in letter form as well as it could in any other form, and here we find the quality in *Pamela* which caught the interest of so vast a majority of its readers. Into the microcosmic circle of Richardson, where he was a little god, came Pamela, and Pamela fitted into her surroundings and into the events of which she was a victim just as the well-brought-up young lady of the

1740's should have done. In addition, Mr. B—, Lady Davers, Mrs. Jewkes, are likewise realistic creations and are consistent in what they do in their own little worlds. Pamela herself may assume, when we think of her in retrospect, more and more the role of an ideal of virtue, as that quality was then advocated in women.

There is a distinct modernity in *Pamela* and much of this is to be found in the character of the heroine herself. There is no better instance of this modernity, however, than is to be found in the fact that the girl falls in love with her would-be seducer. Perhaps there are some who might feel that this is too close to the questionable technique of our modern "movies" to ring true, and that Pamela's seeming *volte face* bespeaks inconsistency in character delineation. It is more truthfully to be said that this very *volte face* is an indication of the fact that the author was drawing consistently the picture of a girl who, although she may not have had full control over the emotion of love (and there seems to be no patent reason why a servant girl of Pamela's type would not have fallen in love with the dashing Mr. B—) is determined, none the less, to preserve her virtue no matter what the cost, thereby showing herself as wise as she is virtuous. But, again, we do not receive any sensation of the wrenching of circumstances, nor is there really anything basically melodramatic in the fact that Pamela falls in love with Mr. B—.

Pamela is one of those—one is almost tempted to say unfortunate—books of which the heroine was so popular that the author had to accede to popular demand and write a sequel. While Pamela's reactions to high life, devoid as they are of almost any conflict whatsoever, may not be of as much interest as are her early struggles with their carefully handled element of suspense, the tremendous popularity of the work is hereby unmistakably proven in the very existence of a sequel.

Clarissa, the tremendous and tragic novel that followed *Pamela,* tells the story of an innocent and virtuous, but obstinate, young girl, Clarissa Harlowe, the beautiful daughter of a family of some social degree, and the persecution of that girl by family and lover. The Harlowe family is motivated, with the sole exception of Clarissa, by avarice and, although Clarissa has turned over her fortune to her father and brother for management, the father, the brother James, the sister Arabella, and even the mother of the girl desire her marriage with one Mr. Solmes, an alliance that is distinctly to the advantage of the entire family but repugnant to the girl herself. Arabella has a suitor who is called Robert Lovelace, a handsome and debonair and dissipated young man of exceedingly doubtful morals; but this suitor finds himself more interested in Clarissa than in her sister. The Harlowe family is disturbed by Clarissa's aversion to Solmes and as a result treats her with the utmost cruelty. In the meantime, Lovelace has transferred his suit to Clarissa, a fact which further enrages her sister against the girl. Lovelace himself has likewise been offended at the hands of the Harlowe family and is tempted by a desire to humiliate these people. He has a secret agent in the family in the person of one of their servants and is thereby able to carry on his work, though absent, even in their very midst. He surprises Clarissa in a woodhouse and, after her fright has worn off, succeeds in gaining her confidence to a considerable degree, and some of her confidence as suitor which he had not heretofore gained. Clarissa now learns that a day has been arranged for her marriage to Mr. Solmes, and her brother and sister declare that they wish the handling of their sister left to them. Poor Clarissa is attacked on all sides by aunts, uncles, cousins, and even more distant relations; while she stands in a state of vacillation between a desire to look upon Lovelace with the utmost favor and a feeling of uncertainty concerning his intentions. For a considerable period the unkindnesses of her family continue, along with the persistences of Mr. Solmes and Clarissa's own firm resistance to him. She meets Lovelace once or twice and her inclinations toward him are again turned by further indication of the looseness of his character. Clarissa begins to formulate a plan whereby she may leave her family. The

mother of Miss Howe, Clarissa's dearest friend, to whom she
writes most of her letters, refuses to take Clarissa into her
own home against the wishes of the Harlowe family and that
avenue of escape is thus closed to the girl. In desperation, she
writes to Lovelace that she will meet him and go with him to
seek, even though she knows nothing of them except from
stray report, the protection of the ladies of his family. Immediately, she repents this step and attempts to retrace it by
writing another letter, this time one of negation, to Lovelace.
The young roué, however, pretends not to have received the
second letter, and Clarissa is forced to meet him outside her
father's gates. During the meeting, Leman (the agent of
Lovelace in the Harlowe household) sets up a cry and Clarissa, thinking herself discovered, rushes off with Lovelace.
The man now no longer holds honorable intentions concerning Clarissa because his vanity and pride have been piqued
by her many refusals of him. Yet he loves the girl. His conduct toward her, however, as soon as he has her with him
alone, changes so that she herself is aware of the change. He
installs her in lodgings in St. Albans and, although she pleads
with him to leave her, he none the less stays by her side so
that she is convinced that she must ultimately marry him.
She refuses his proposal because of the offensive manner in
which it is offered. Clarissa, seeing a greater possibility of escape, proposes that they go to London, and Lovelace pretends
to allow her to choose rooms there, but those she chooses
prove to be kept by a woman who is actually in the employ of
Lovelace. Together, they go up to London, where the story is
continued. The man still continues to delude the girl with
offers of marriage and prospective plans of the house they are
to occupy after their marriage. Clarissa is somewhat alarmed
by the fact that, although Lovelace talks constantly of marriage, he never once sets a possible day for the ceremony. Yet
Clarissa is so innocent that it seems inevitable that she
should ultimately meet disaster. An evening she spends with
her lover's friends disgusts her with them and makes her
even less ready to marry Lovelace than she was before. The

man, however, has certain marriage settlements drawn up in seeming preparation for a wedding. Yet Clarissa will not hasten matters. She begins to devise, with her friend Miss Howe, a means of escape from London, but Lovelace succeeds in preventing this by introducing to Clarissa one Captain Tomlinson, who pretends to be a close friend of Clarissa's Uncle John, from whom he brings news that the girl's family will be reconciled to her if they are certain she has married Lovelace. Clarissa relents of her hardness and shows a distinct favor toward Lovelace; he attempts, however, to take so gross an advantage of this that she turns from him and decides definitely that her only possible course is one of escape. She goes to Hampstead, to which place Lovelace follows her along with the Captain and again offers her marriage. Meanwhile, he has intercepted a letter from Miss Howe to Clarissa and substitutes for it one of his own invention, which so impresses the girl that she again changes her mind and decides to accept him. Lovelace produces a license and urges Clarissa to go with his aunt, Lady Betty, and his cousin, Charlotte Montague, to the house of his uncle where the marriage will take place. Lovelace then procures two women to impersonate his relations and bears the girl off to what she believes is Montague House, but actually carries her back to London. It is here that Lovelace at length succeeds in ruining her against her will, and the horrified and distracted girl lapses into delirium. Lovelace becomes violently conscious of the fact that he really loves Clarissa and, when she has somewhat recovered, again offers her marriage which she rejects with all the unyielding pride of which she is capable. Her body is violated; her will is not. From this point on in the story the heroine remains absolutely adamant and Lovelace, although he retires to the estate of his uncle, from which he bombards the girl with letters begging that she marry him, is absolutely unable to break her unflagging resistance. The girl retires to the house of a mercer in Covent Garden where she succeeds, by means of correspondence with several people, in further unearthing the villainous plans of her lover. Here she is discovered by a woman with whom she once lived, who has her arrested for debt. Lovelace learns of this and appoints his friend, Belford, to save Clarissa. From this point on, Belford becomes the girl's friend and guardian. Clarissa is, in the meantime, growing weaker and weaker from an illness that is induced largely by intense mental disturbances, and the continuance of these renders her condition dangerous. Meantime, her cousin Morden, also her guardian, returns from abroad and hurries to her assistance, but discovers that she has not long to live. Lovelace is informed of what has come about and he is in an agony of despair. Clarissa dies, however, and the horror of Lovelace is equalled only by that of the Harlowe family, which now blames itself for the tragedy. Lovelace retires to the continent, whither Morden follows him. The two eventually meet and engage in a duel in which Lovelace is mortally wounded and dies with the words, "Let this expiate," on his lips.

Clarissa is undoubtedly the younger sister and imitator of Pamela, but the tiresome and sometimes forced quality that prevails in Pamela is not to be found in the writings of Clarissa, perhaps because she writes out of the potent anxiety of her distress. The style and sentiments of the writing rise in proportion as the catastrophe approaches. Likewise, since the chief people of this book are almost all persons of some distinction, who may be claimed to have received greater instruction than the innocent country girl of *Pamela*, the author has had an additional opportunity to intersperse, in the course of the work, a greater number of reflections concerning the tendencies of life and human nature, and to express these opinions according to the dicta of polite and cultivated society, so that the opinions may thereby be rendered more elegant and, at the same time, more useful. Instead of a statue of a lover, who never speaks but by the organs of another, we have in *Clarissa* a lover who is himself one of the chief correspondents and who writes a great number of letters marked by a fervor of expression and a careless, humorous gaiety not to be thought fitting to the correspondence of a lady of the period without some suggestion of indecency. Thus, by having Lovelace write himself, much is given the reader that needs must have been omitted for the sake of morality, had Clarissa or others of the ladies done all the letter writing.

There is, likewise, in *Clarissa* more description than is to be found in *Pamela*, and we have an almost uninterrupted series of scenes described with a graphic reality. Our curiosity is thus not only aroused but likewise gratified. All the description contained here, however, whether it is character, scene, or action, is marked by a distinct advance toward the natural, an advance which Richardson made steadily and, in the light of his feelings concerning romance, we may conclude, deliberately. We should remember that in the romances we had nothing but representations of the illustrious actions of illustrious persons. All was as nearly ideal as possible. Above all, the emotion of love is so universally presented as a predominant one as to take precedence over all other emotions. It is especially true of the French writings of the type that the authors appeared to be ignorant of all the virtues except that of loving with ardor and constancy.

Such, however, was not the aim of Richardson here. It has already been intimated that *Clarissa* represents a great step forward from *Pamela* in the technique which it shows. Here, the letters are sent from more than one person or group of persons, and we are inevitably made to feel that hereby more characters sweep into the circle of our vital concern. But, more important than that, there is the increased purpose and more accurate aim of this novel which must be taken into consideration. We cannot help feeling that the moral aim, which was always Richardson's, is here sustained with greater distinction than it is in *Pamela*. As Dr. Phelps has so well said: "Clarissa is certainly 'a pure woman faithfully' presented."[4] (Unlike poor Tess, Clarissa is a gentlewoman, and this is the more remarkable in the face of the fact that we cannot feel that her boorish family is, in any sense of the

---

[4] *The Works of Samuel Richardson.* Introductions by William Lyon Phelps, *Clarissa*, vol. I, p. XXXIII, New York, 1902.

word, a group of gentlefolk.) Plainly indicating his aim here, the author himself says in volume IV of *Clarissa*—" 'Much more lively and affecting must be the style of those who write in the height of a present distress; the mind tortured by the pangs of uncertainty (the events then hidden in the womb of fate) ; than the dry, narrative, unanimated style of a person relating dangers and difficulties surmounted, can be; the re- later perfectly at ease; and if himself unmoved by his own story, not likely greatly to affect the reader.' " How different is this from the doctrine that great art is produced only when the event is concluded and the mind is once more in a state of tranquillity!

It is at an ultimate naturalism that Richardson is most definitely aiming in *Clarissa*. Already this had been at- tempted in France. It was Marivaux that endeavored to bring back his countrymen to nature. His *Marianne* and *Paysan Parvenu* are paintings after life; in these the author speaks less and his characters more; but even Marivaux did not dare to entertain his readers with private and domestic oc- currences. True it is that his Marianne speaks like a girl of wit, who loves a kind of general virtue, which consists in pre- ferring her honor to the gratification of her tenderest wishes. But the particulars which constitute a virtuous life are not exhibited; there is no representation of the minutiae of Vir- tue; no example of *her* conduct to those by whom she is sur- rounded as equals, superiors, or inferiors. *Marianne* is a kind of chronicle in which some memorable adventures are well described. The flow of naturalism was a steadily increasing one, but nowhere in France or England did it reach so domi- nant a peak, not even in *Pamela,* as it does in *Clarissa*. *Cla- rissa* is not a mere chronicle of memorable adventures. It is a history in which the events of the heroine's life follow each other in an uninterrupted succession. Her letters are un- doubtedly full of reflections and remarks which seem to be the result of great knowledge of mankind, yet the whole is within the reach of every capacity and is calculated to make every reader wiser and better. None the less, we do not feel any wrenching of naturalness in the wisdom displayed by this girl, for it is a natural wisdom inspired by her personal virtue combined with her present circumstance, rather than the development of a wide and all-embracing knowledge of mankind. What Marivaux perhaps did not dare to do, Richardson did in *Clarissa*. There are strong intimations of this approaching ideal of naturalness in *Pamela*, and even what there is of high romance in that novel is logically explicable through the medium of the leading character and the situation in which she finds herself. But *Clarissa* is the novel which establishes, once and for all, the necessity of verisimilitude to all great fiction.

Beyond this, it succeeds in printing upon the literature of the day its own leading characters as infallible models. Just as is Clarissa herself the paragon and touchstone of highest virtue tragically assaulted, just so Lovelace is the prototype of the eighteenth-century roué; so much so that Napoleon, when he heard the name of Lovelace attached to an English officer, remarked that that was the name of the man in *Clarissa*;[5] so are Miss Howe and Mr. Belford the models upon which the confidante and the confidant of every heroine and hero are made. Beyond these four, it may be said that there is not a single character in the novel, the characteristics of whom are not impressed upon all his letters as the bust of a king is upon the coin of his country. The style of every letter is admirably adapted to the character of the writer. Here, again, is the triumph of verisimilitude.

The two Richardson novels, now considered, are essentially the stories of women. The third novel, *Sir Charles Grandison,* has as its chief protagonist a man, the most perfect prototype of society's gentleman in all English fiction, with the possible exception of George Meredith's Sir Willoughby Patterne. The story is as follows: Miss Harriet Byron, who has been for many years an orphan, is reared by her grandparents, who have conducted her in the paths

[5] *The Collected Essays and Addresses of Augustine Birrell*, New York, 1923, I, p. 219.

of virtue. Her grandfather is now dead and she is living with her uncle, Mr. Selby. Although she is the possessor of but a small fortune, Miss Byron is the recipient of the attentions of many of the young men who live in her vicinage. The girl goes up to London, however, and there continues to attract the attention of young men. Chief among these are young Mr. Fowler, nephew of a Welsh baronet, and Sir Hargrave Pollexfen, a handsome and wealthy roué, distinctly reminiscent of Lovelace. Harriet will, however, have nothing to do with either of them, despite the fact that Sir Hargrave is both confident and persistent and Mr. Fowler persistent but pathetic through the medium of his uncle. Sir Hargrave resorts to foul means to capture the favor of the girl and, by means of engaging one of his henchmen in her service (a device already used in *Clarissa*) has her carried off from a masquerade ball to a house in Paddington. She struggles to escape and, in so doing, receives a slight injury which frightens her abductor so that he decides to remove her to his country house. On the road they are met by an unknown gentleman in a coach. Harriet manages to scream for help, and she is rescued from Sir Hargrave by the gentleman who takes her to the home of his sisters. The gentleman, of course, proves to be Sir Charles Grandison, who is thereby given a late and dramatic entrance into the story. Richardson is extremely fond of these late entrances, as may be noted also from the fact that Colonel Morden enters the story of *Clarissa* almost at the very conclusion to act as a sudden and dramatic instrument of retribution. The rescue of Harriet has two results: Sir Charles is called upon to fight a duel, although he himself is opposed to duelling; and Harriet finds herself falling in love with him. Sir Charles avoids fighting the duel by disarming his adversary and then by delivering him a homily on the evils of duelling, which completely convinces Sir Hargrave of his wrong. The grace with which Sir Charles handles this situation is characteristic of his procedure through the entire story. Sir Charles is impressed by Harriet's charms, but he will not commit himself on the subject. In the meantime, the Countess of D— presents her son, the Earl of D—, as a possible husband for Harriet. The girl has no desire for his attentions. Her letters to her grandmother, Mrs. Selby, reveal to her clearly that Harriet is in love with Charles. In order to expedite the romance between them Mrs. Selby indicates Harriet's true interest to the Countess, hoping that the word will eventually travel back to the Grandisons. The heroine now pays another visit to the Grandison sisters. Sir Charles chooses to be absent on business and Harriet suspects it is because of her presence that he has done this. A close friendship grows up, however, between Harriet and the hero's two sisters. Sir Charles returns and, although he conducts himself with the utmost kindness toward Harriet, makes no advances. Finally, he takes her into his confidence. Some years before, when first abroad in Italy, he became deeply attached to the della Poretta family because of his rescue of the son, Jeronymo, from a band of assassins. He was received into their house and allowed to teach English to their only daughter, Clementina. The two fell in love with each other and the family, when it discovered the mutual attachment, proposed terms upon which the two might marry. Sir Charles rejected the terms because of their impossible one-sidedness and returned to England. Meanwhile, Clementina fell into a sort of madness upon losing him and the family has now written him asking him to come to Italy to discuss new terms. At the close of his narrative Sir Charles leaves Harriet, himself in an uncertain state of emotion. Harriet is, of course, much distressed by this. She begins to realize that Sir Charles' problem is the conflict between his affection for her and his duty to Clementina. The young man departs for Italy, leaving Harriet in a very desperate but none the less self-controlled state. When he arrives in Italy, Sir Charles has several interviews with the della Poretta family, all of which prove ultimately satisfactory, and matters begin to look exceedingly hopeless for the English girl. At the last moment, however, Clementina herself suddenly suffers a change of heart and decides that, though her love is.

great, it would be impossible for her to marry a heretic, and advises Sir Charles that he return to England and marry an Englishwoman. Although he indicates profound regret, the young man relinquishes his rights to Clementina and returns to England in haste, where he begins to pay court to Harriet. He is forced to meet one of Harriet's suitors, Greville, on the "field of honor," but disarms him as dexterously as he formerly did Sir Hargrave. Harriet and Sir Charles are happily and formally engaged and married. At the last moment Clementina appears in England, having run from the attentions of an unwelcome suitor to seek the protection of her former lover. She is generously received by Sir Charles and Lady Grandison and taken under their protection. The della Poretta family follows and is likewise graciously received. Sir Charles, with his usual finesse, gains Clementina's consent that she will accept the suit of the heretofore unwelcome Count of Belvedere and the story closes on the departure of the Italian guests for Italy, the complete happiness of all concerned, and the joy of the heroine in the possession of the matchless Sir Charles.

Thus Richardson excuses the length of *Sir Charles Grandison*, the longest novel he has given us:

The nature of familiar letters, written, as it were, to the *moment*, while the heart is agitated by hopes and fears, on events undecided, must plead an excuse for the bulk of a collection of this kind. Mere facts and characters might be comprised in a much smaller compass: but, would they be equally interesting? It happens fortunately, that an account of the juvenile years of the principal person is narratively given in some of the letters. As many, however, as could be spared have been omitted. There is not one episode in the whole nor, after *Sir Charles Grandison* is introduced, one letter inserted but what tends to illustrate the principal design. Those which precede his introduction will not, it is hoped, be judged unnecessary on the whole, as they tend to make the reader acquainted with persons, the history of most of whom is closely interwoven with that of Sir Charles.[6]

⁶ *Sir Charles Grandison*, Preface, p. xxxix.

And although there are moments when we may feel the inclination to quarrel with the author's obvious intimation that verbosity is a virtue, with his sincerity we can ever quarrel. The sort of all-consuming passion that virtue becomes in the hands of Richardson renders Sir Charles an endurable creation, if not quite human and alive.

In *Sir Charles Grandison* are displayed that profound knowledge of men and things, that masterly skill in narrative and description for which Richardson is so justly admired. The characters of Miss Byron, of Sir Hargrave Pollexfen, of Charlotte Grandison show us human nature in its true dignity, its devious villainy, and its tantalizing sprightliness, respectively; all three are characterizations of the utmost fidelity. A somewhat too perfect conception detracts from the fidelity of Sir Charles himself; but he is, despite this, one of the two most notable and memorable figures Richardson has given us. In *Sir Charles Grandison* the narrative is judiciously conducted; if the events and adventures are fewer than in other works of this nature, the interesting scenes and affecting and moving situations centered about these fewer events are much more numerous, the heart is more frequently and more deeply touched (although it is never wrung by the pathos that affects it in the reading of *Clarissa*), the curiosity of the reader is continually engaged and, equally, continually gratified. Those who desire only a story and are delighted only by a multiplicity of ingenious events may find that there are too many places in which this novel pauses for too long a time and that it suffers from too many interruptions and from the reproduction of unnecessary descriptions and tedious conversations. But these descriptions and conversations, and not the story itself, are the most valuable, instructive, and distinctive part of the work. The minute and exact descriptions of the air, the attitude, the manner, the every motion of every person on every occasion animates and enlives the work, and sets the persons concerned unmistakably before our eyes. We faithfully believe that we see them and imagine ourselves to be of their company. Besides, there is here such an energy of expression, such a complete delicacy of sentiment, such justness of observation of human conduct, such animated quickness of repartee, such sudden turns and strokes of wit, all properly divided and appropriated according to the divergent characters of the persons involved, as to diversify charmingly these conversations and events narrated in letters and render them both entertaining and useful. Horace's rule of *utile dulci* was never more happily followed than in *Sir Charles Grandison*.

In this book, the author has completed his plan, of which *Pamela* and *Clarissa* are parts. In *Pamela* he intended to show the beauty and superiority of virtue in an unpolished mind, with the temporal rewards which it frequently obtains, and to render the character of the libertine contemptible. His chief design in *Clarissa* was to show the excellence of virtue in a delicate and finely sensitive being, though it was not to be rewarded in this life, and to represent the life of a libertine with every adventitious advantage, as an object not only of contempt but even of horror. In *Sir Charles Grandison* he proposed to present yet another aspect of the superiority of virtue, and by exhibiting the character and actions of a man of true honor, to show that every natural and accidental advantage is improved by virtue and piety, that these polish elegance, heighten dignity, and produce universal love, esteem, and veneration. The three novels present a trilogy of virtue; beyond that they present a trilogy of virtue triumphant, but not that alone—these are the panorama of virtue triumphant through infinite struggle.

It is of imperative necessity, in approaching Richardson's use of the epistolary mode, to consider what else goes into the making of his novels, from what exactly he has gathered his material, and to what compositional forms certain phases of his novels might be paralleled. It has already been stated, of course, that the atmosphere of the closet drama and that of Richardson's novels is strikingly similar.[7] Certainly it is true that his novels grew out of a small circle, mostly ladies,

---

[7] Brian W. Downs, *Richardson*, Chapter IV, Section 3.

of which Richardson was himself the guiding spirit and mentor. As a result, a sort of sentimental idealism was bound to arise. This is undoubtedly suggestive of the closet drama. But those who delve beneath the first lines and outward aspects of his work will find no lack of realistic treatment in Richardson. This, essentially, is not of the closet drama but of a more realistic variety of writing.

The essay of the day, too, had its influence on the novel, and it is too well known a fact to need pointing out here that the narrative element in Richardson's and Fielding's first novels very closely resembles that of the essay. But the essay happens to be even closer to Richardson at one point than is allowed by any mere question of abstract influence. In *Sir Charles Grandison*, Grandma Shirley says: "The present age is greatly obligated to the authors of the *Spectator*." Beyond this, however, it has been argued that the very story of Pamela herself recurred to Richardson's mind from the *Spectator* when the *Familiar Letters* were to be begun. Mr. C. H. Huffman in his dissertation, *The 18th Century Novel in Theory and Practise*,[8] indicates that Richardson got his first clue from the essay-narrative which appeared in the *Spectator* for Saturday, May 10, 1712. It tells a story of "intended seduction ending in a marriage." A servant girl, Amanda, is desired by the lord of the manor because of her great beauty. He makes immoral advances to her which she rejects. Letters pass between her and her parents in which the parents are informed of the girl's distress. The lord of the manor intercepts one of these letters and is so impressed by the virtue of these good people that he changes his intentions, offers marriage to the girl and protection to her parents. Virtue is rewarded and all ends happily. This story was then a part of Richardson's material for many years, and he told Aaron Hill that he had recommended it to many of his friends but that none of them would hear of it. Three of the *Familiar Letters* further reminded Richardson of a true story.[9] Since the author's only

---

[8] Dayton, Virginia, pp. 13-15.

[9] Clara L. Thomson, *Samuel Richardson—A Critical Study*, London, 1900, pp. 153-55.

literary essay since boyhood, even in that period when he used to write love letters secretly for a circle of girls, had been the letter, it is not to be wondered at, that he employed the letter form to present the stories he told in his novels, and that he should have gone to his own letter collection, if this story in the *Spectator* is not the suggestive source of *Pamela*, for the basis of his own first novel.

It has, of course, already been established that letter writing was at this time an art, and that its peripatetic pilgrimage enabled it to stand with reference to the age much as the newspaper stands with reference to our own. To Richardson, then, and to those imbued with the Richardsonian spirit, one's basic qualities were to be measured largely by the finesse with which one could write a letter, and a young lady able to write letters with the magnificent indifference to time and space that was possessed by a Pamela, a Clarissa Harlowe, or a Harriet Byron, was a creature far beyond the uninspiring average. Thus, the long practice and proficiency in letter writing which Richardson himself had, led him not only to the composition of letter-novels, but also to the creation of characters who were themselves endowed with a major ability to write letters. And it must be stated that not only the heroines of the three novels are proficient epistolarians, but many of their supporting characters are also. Thus, Mr. Andrews, Miss Howe, Lovelace, Belford, Miss Selby, Sir Charles Grandison, Charlotte Grandison, and half a dozen others of Richardson's characters are copious and accomplished writers of letters.

The "character" has long been a part of English literature, and we are able to find strong indications of it in the epistles of the eighteenth century. The letters served in lieu of long descriptions of a subjective sort that often prove extraneous, and by means of the letters the reader was able to define the personality of the writer for himself and to compare that with similar pictures of such a person which he might have gleaned from his own experience. All of this quality of the "character" in the letter Richardson carefully adopted and adapted to his own novelistic purposes. In his postscript to *Clarissa*, Richardson writes: "The letters and conversation, when the story makes the slowest progress, are presumed to be characteristic." Thus, introspectively, the character sketches are rendered individual at the same time they are made to become part of the whole, and the mere fact that we are able, as readers, to wander at will among the characters, even when important decisions are being made, and are able to watch the processes of determination at moments of crisis adds to the poignancy and verisimilitude of the work. The thought caught on the wing, one of the basic principles of Richardson's writing, is thus presented to us with greater clarity and immediacy than would be otherwise possible. The necessity for the author's stepping down from his platform is thus obviated to a large degree.

No form of composition, in poetry or prose, admits of greater variety than the epistolary, since there are few subjects that may not be discussed through the medium of the letter. But the epistolary form has advantages peculiar to itself. It places the reader in the position of a confidential friend, thus creating a connecting contact between writer and reader, a contact Richardson always strove to preserve without resorting to direct address. The animated and dramatic nature of the letter likewise enables it to make a more forcible and lasting impression upon the mind of the reader, than could be expected from a composition purely narrative or didactic. Of these advantages, no writer of the epistolary novel has made greater or more effective use than has Richardson, and he has lost no opportunity of appealing, when it could be judiciously done, to the feelings and sentiments of those to whom he is supposed to be immediately addressing himself. Richardson seemed to find in the letter of his day all these things, the great range of subjects, intimate discussions, and ease of presentation, to a greater extent than was to be found in any other form of writing. Of manners and of subjects personal, domestic, social, religious, and political, the novel was already full. It was in the form of the letter, however, that the moral aspect, so all-important to the conception of Richardson, was most unconsciously and naturally set forth, because moral implications and discussions were natural to the letter as a distinct eighteenth-century mode. Thus, it was already a literary device for one intimate friend or relative to write to another, who was usually in some sort of ethical difficulty, in order to give moral instructions or advice. When we remember, then, that the drama was a decaying art, but that it had been vastly popular, it seems most just that its place should be taken by the letter, which was in itself a highly dramatic device, the soliloquy, written out rather than spoken. If we are to grant that an actor has many advantages in his favor, such as gesture, vocal inflection, emphasis, and facial expression, we must also grant that the greater art is that of the letter, since it presents all that is to be found in the soliloquy through the medium of the intimations of the written word alone. All that Richardson found awaiting him, in the form of the letter, he seemed then to find admirably fitted to the telling of stories as he himself felt they should be told, and of novels as he believed they should be presented.

Perhaps most important to remember of Samuel Richardson's epistolary novel is, that since he has been in the habit of writing love letters for young ladies of his acquaintance since his early youth, that since he was himself an inveterate letter writer, it was the most natural thing in the world for him to write letters, and thus we find his novels not so much novels put into the form of letters for the sake of convenience as letters expanded naturally to the length of novels. The naturalness of the form of the letter to Richardson's genius has already been several times indicated, but it cannot be too often stressed. To some other authors who used this form in imitation of Richardson, the shape of a correspondence proved but an awkward expedient; but Richardson, unlike these, for the most part, later and imitative writers, worked up to his conception of the novel from a basic conception of it as a collection of letters. His method, therefore, came spontaneously to him. He started, then, from the plan of writing letters to illustrate a given point of morality and, in order to make the letters more attractive and more convincing, fell upon the device of attributing them to a fictitious character. The result was, in the first instance, the huge tract called *Pamela*, in most respects the least good of his works, the most distinctive feature of which is that it shows an amazing fertility in an especially feminine art. There are few of us who have not, at one time or another, suffered from the lengthy outpourings that only a feminine correspondent may send us; it is seldom attractive to us now when we have so little time to devote to the mere perusal of letters; but it must be remembered that since the days of Richardson that which was an art, the art of letter writing, has paled to a secondary means of communication and has, to a certain extent, remained in that place. But the art of the eighteenth-century letter was a serious business. In medieval days, the chatelaine sat, surrounded by her handmaidens, making gorgeous tapestries. This was the pride of her life. In the eighteenth century the letter, to a great extent, took the place of the tapestry. That there is, then, no greater collection of epistolary tapestries than the three novels of Richardson is beyond the shadow of a doubt. It is out of this very overflow of letter writing that comes the charge that Richardson's characters could not have had time to pass through any incident or even episode because all their time was spent in writing letters. That this is a charge not patently true, although it may be supported by some consideration of the overwhelming fertility of Miss Byron, the heroine of *Sir Charles Grandison*, lies in the obvious fact that no fictitious personage is ever bound by the actual limits of a narrow human capacity. The great novelist does not want us to believe, even if the subtitle of his story may state it so, that his novel is a genuine narrative; nor does he want us to mistake it for one. Since any apparent lack of reality is compensated for by the fact that we are let into the finite thoughts and secrets of the characters, an advantage it is almost impossible to obtain in real life, we cannot blame Richardson because his characters indicate a power of writing which no mortal could ever attain to. After all, fiction usually proves to be a higher reality.

It must be remembered, however, that the epistolary form as we find it at the close is a far more fully developed impulse than it is in Richardson's earliest work, no matter how rapid that development may be and how elaborate the previous apprenticeship at letter writing. Richardson is the great exemplar, the figure that looms large on the horizon of the epistolarians. But he, too, had a period of beginning. Thus in *Pamela* we may say that the author was still feeling his way about, not necessarily in the same stumbling fashion in which the young novice feels for a method, but rather as the very careful, conscientiously painstaking and experienced man cautiously sets about doing a thing. Thus, we have in this novel a combination of letters and journal, to be given reformulation in the later novels, which consequently took a form entirely epistolary. Again, even though we might wish for a greater variety in the authorship of the letters here and even though we might feel that Pamela herself is too persistently at the helm of her own ship, yet the diary-journal effect of this undoubtedly lends the autobiographic tone to the narrative which has so often been achieved later by the use of the first person. Dr. Ernest A. Baker says of Richardson that he is the novelist of personality.[10] This is true, and in no author do we get to know the processes of thought of the characters better than we do in these novels of Richardson. The fact that Pamela writes out her own part brings her even closer to us. It is a most intimate sort of autobiography. Yet it was toward epistolary biography, not toward journal biography, that the novelist was always striving.

As for the letters themselves in *Pamela*, they are for the most part natural, absorbing, and admirably fitted to the parts of the story they tell. The fact that Pamela is away from home in order that she may write home the story of her dis-

[10] *History of the English Novel*, IV, p. 71.

tresses is all a part of epistolary inevitability. We, who must always make allowances for reality in any work, can surely make that small grant here when the result achieved is viewed and enjoyed. If any fault is to be found with them, it is that Richardson has not yet learned to wield the novel in letters with all the flexibility that he later acquired.

Richardson's great care in the writing of his letters, and his great knowledge of the fact that letters are the best medium for the revelation of the soul, is nowhere better shown than in *Clarissa*, his second novel, which consists of letters written not only from the heroine, as is almost exclusively the case in *Pamela*, but likewise from the other characters. No novel in the English language presents a more penetrating study of the secret places of the soul and the deep anguish of that soul when it is violated than does this. Here, the epistolary mastery of Richardson is seen rising to the peak which it maintains throughout the entirety of *Sir Charles Grandison*. One of the greatest steps forward in these last two novels is the fact that we are allowed to learn all that everyone concerned with the central story of the two chief characters has to say, in the form of letters, about the matter. Clarissa, Lovelace, Belford, and Anna Howe are almost all epistolary novelists in their own rights. So are Sir Charles Grandison, Harriet Byron, Miss Selby, and Charlotte Grandison. And the distinct style of each correspondent is faithfully reproduced with a singular vivacity. There is something of a fault in this very perfection, since the author himself never appears and is thus obliged to trust his characters with the trumpeting of their own good qualities. Yet, in the final analysis, this criticism need not be directed more wholly at the epistolary method than at the narrative in the first person.

Before we proceed to an estimation of the work of Samuel Richardson in its entirety, however cautiously made, it is not only well, but eminently fitting that we indicate some record of the estimation put upon that work by the contemporaries of the author, who, in some respects, are the most able judges. The historical estimate and valuation of the work of any given author sometimes has a degree of finality about it that a contemporary estimate cannot attain to. Lord Byron is not a greater poet because of the burning enthusiasm of most of his contemporaries for his work, but rather a less because of the colder estimate set upon it by later great critics who have judged it historically. On the other hand, if the work of Shakespeare had been looked upon for several centuries since his death with indifferent eye, we could not well afford to discard the facts of the unprecedented acceptance which it received at the hands of its contemporaries. Therefore, in our attempted judgment of Richardson, colored as it is by the realization that there have been sound critics who have belittled him, we must likewise take into consideration the emotions with which his contemporaries received his work and the opinions they expressed concerning these three great novels. One enthusiastic admirer of the period said that, if all books were to be burned, at least *Pamela* and the Bible must be saved.[11] There is likewise preserved the story of Sir John Herschel, who tells of the blacksmith who was accustomed to collect his neighbors around his anvil and there read them the story of *Pamela*. So tense was their interest and so great their concern that, when Mr. B— married Pamela, these people succeeded in procuring the keys to the village church and joyfully rang its bells.[12] Dr. Johnson says that there was more real knowledge of humanity in one letter of Richardson[13] than in all of *Tom Jones*. Edward Young, author of *Night Thoughts*, considered Richardson "an instrument of Providence."[14] Even Lady Mary Wortley Montagu, in a letter to her daughter, admits reluctant admiration, always a flattering tribute to worth:

This Richardson is a strange fellow. I heartily despise him, and eagerly read him, nay, sob over his works in a most scandalous manner. The two first tomes of Clarissa touched me, as being

---

[11] William Forsyth, *The Novels and Novelists of the Eighteenth Century*, VII, p. 214.
[12] *Ibid.*, p. 215.
[13] *Ibid.*, p. 219.
[14] Leslie Stephen, *Hours in a Library*, "Richardson's Novels," I, p. 54.

very resembling to my maiden days; and I find in the pictures of Sir Thomas Grandison and his lady, what I have heard of my mother, and seen of my father.[15]

But perhaps the tenderest letter is that from the wife of the German poet, Klopstock, in which she writes:

Having finished your Clarissa (oh, the heavenly book!) I would prayed you to write the history of the manly Clarissa, but I had not courage enough at that time. I should have it no more to-day, as this is only my first English letter; but I am now Klopstock's wife, and then I was only the single young girl. You have since written the manly Clarissa without my prayer. Oh, you have done it to the great joy and thanks of all your happy readers! Now you can write no more. You must write the history of an Angel.[16]

All of these are but pale indications of the overwhelming enthusiasm with which the novels themselves were received at the time of their writing or, at least, a few decades after their dissemination.

There were, of course, adverse contemporary criticisms. Mrs. Montagu declared that "*Sir Charles Grandison* was lacking in two of the prime merits of narrative, brevity and elegance."[17] Fielding, likewise, contended that the epistolary style was not a fitting one for the novelist and that the best novelists had not, to date, made use of it.[18]

In the light of what has been said of Richardson by his contemporaries, of what has been deeply felt by simpler hearts than those of critics for the novels of this man, of what tributes have been laid at his feet by later ages, we can but be impressed by the intrinsic greatness of the man as a writer of novels and a wielder of human emotions.

We must remember that today one is hardly expected, unless he is a student of Richardson, to read any one of this

[15] *Works of the Right Honourable Lady Mary Wortley Montagu Including Her Correspondence, Poems, and Essays*, IV, p. 268, Letter to the Countess of Bute, September 22, 1755. London, 1803.
[16] *The Collected Essays and Addresses of Augustine Birrell*, New York, 1923, pp. 216-217.
[17] Downs, *op. cit.*, Chapter IV.
[18] *Ibid.*, Chapter IV, Section 2, p. 93.

author's novels word for word and page by page. He simply has not the time. The epistolary method is, of necessity, slow moving. Richardson, however, had no intention of writing for the amusement of the railway traveler who found himself in the deplorable state of having half an hour to kill by reading. An eminent musician has recently said that the automobile has spoiled our love for music because speed is in itself a sort of intoxication and takes us away from the several hours of comfortable enjoyment which music might bring us. And in literature the same is true. Richardson wrote for an age that had the leisure to read long novels. We are, on the other hand, no longer willing to bear with Harriet, Sir Charles, Clarissa, and Pamela in their long effusions. Only the old may read them. The tabloid monster must be glutted. When he said that there is more knowledge of the heart in one letter of Richardson than in all of *Tom Jones* and when Erskine remarked to him, "Surely, Sir, Richardson is very tedious," Dr. Johnson answered, "Why, Sir, if you were to read Richardson for the story your patience would be so much fretted that you would hang yourself; but you must read him for the sentiment and consider the story as only giving occasion to the sentiment."[19]

To those of us who stop to pause, however, to make some attempt at appraisement of an author we have just read, the size of the family of immortals he has created is of considerable moment. Shakespeare could stand by the immortality of his character creations alone. Richardson, like Cervantes, has given us two "figures against the sky," two characters that have become household words, bound as they are by the weaknesses inseparable from their age and the country of their origin, inferior as they are to the highest ideals of the greatest poets, distorted by the conventional standards in which their creator moved—in Clarissa and Sir Charles.

Richardson is always the shepherd watching the path his characters are about to take and guiding the development of his plot. As Sir Leslie Stephen has said:

[19] Forsyth, *op. cit.*, p. 219.

. . . for one ought not to conclude an article upon Richardson without a moral. It is that a purpose may be a very dangerous thing for a novelist in so far as it leads him to try means of persuasion not appropriate to his art; but when, as with Richardson, it implies a keen interest in an imaginary world, a desire to set forth in the most forcible way what are the great springs of action of human beings by showing them under appropriate situations, then it may be a source of such power of fascination as is exercised by the greatest writers alone.[20]

It is, of course, Richardson's later method, that of having the characters act as minor novelists, that has had the greatest vogue in imitation. Advantages the method surely has, for no matter how much we may be interested in any one single character, the addition of two or three or more other characters and their interests rarely proves fatal to the original one, but rather augments it with the power of variation. No one may say that Harriet or Clarissa is of less interest to us because our attention is directly diverted from them on occasion to other people in their stories.

We must remember that the old doctrine that literature must instruct as well as delight is part of the blood and bone of Richardson's creation. Romance, which only amused and entertained, was definitely frowned upon by the author. Richardson wished "to propose the brightest and most perfect examples to our imitation," and Sir Charles Grandison, for instance, is undoubtedly proposed as an example for his principles and conduct. That Richardson had the courage to sustain this proposal is indicated by the fact that he dared to refuse to let Sir Charles fight duels. If we accept the statement that the first great novelists, and this is especially true of Richardson, used the story as a vehicle for instruction, then must we be ready to overlook a slight lack of inevitability in the epistolary form as practised by Richardson for that purpose and to conclude that this inevitability, already mentioned, is largely due to the insistence of the author upon a purpose for his work. Today we are definitely accus-

[20] *Hours in a Library,* p. 93.

tomed to the omniscient point of view assumed by authors;
the epistolary style is merely this omniscient point of view
used subjectively. We are beside the character who is doing
the writing, not only observing the results but also helping
to guide the pen, to give direction to the flow of his ideas,
and in the end we feel that we have a part in the play and
that its conclusion is therefore logical and inevitable because
we have played that play through along with the characters
and have brought about the proper ending and one that is
indubitably stamped with the high coinage of moral instruction.

Richardson's three novels might well be compared to Wagner's "Ring." Both works have a *leit-motif*. In Richardson
it is the triumph of good; in Wagner it is Fate, the master
of us all. Of course, it may be argued that Wagner's figures
are more firmly knitted into a unity than are Richardson's,
but simply a change of name or situation does not signify a
basic change in fundamental character (as may be seen from
a perusal of the plots of the three novels), so that while Richardson has changed his people to fit his various plots, they
surely remain unmistakably stamped with the similarity
which exists in all of Richardson's brain-children and act as
much in accordance with his tenets as do Wagner's creations.
But most important is the fact that each man, great in his own
way, felt the urge to give to the world his reiterated feeling.

In summary conclusion, it might be pointed out that Richardson is great in so many aspects of literary composition
that the true significance of this combinate greatness may be
received only by a review of all the many things he has given
us. Few great novelists have given us so many memorable, if
not supreme, characters as has Richardson. He has drawn for
us, as has already been stated, two of the first water. The first
is Clarissa. She is not the "dainty rogue in porcelain"; she
is a figurine in spun glass. Clarissa is a study in the utmost
delicacy of feminine nature. She is virtuous; she is lovely; she
is proud; she is motivated by a wholeness of self which extends beyond the merely physical into the psychic. The de-

struction of Clarissa lies not only in her physical violation, but likewise in the violation of her finely balanced soul, her exquisitely isolated spirit. Yet Clarissa is not entirely without faults. She shares with her impossible family a definite degree of stubbornness which sometimes leads her to distress, but where there is so much perfection, it is affectation to make a point of looking for faults. The second unmatchable character in Richardson is Sir Charles Grandison. At the outset it is best to admit that Sir Charles is a consummate prig; but we are rather thankful for his priggishness in what might otherwise prove a too unhumanly perfect individual. Sir Charles is a representative of that type which so many novelists and dramatists have attempted to create and which so few have succeeded in doing: the perfect gentleman. This virtuous, gracious, kindly (and, it must necessarily be added) personally handsome young man is undoubtedly a paragon, but he is likewise distinctly an individual. Among a society of careless sportsmen and duellists, Sir Charles has the admirable courage to stand against the practice of fighting. He has the strength to disarm his enemies at will; therefore there can be no suspicion levelled against him that he is a coward. On the other hand, Sir Charles goes his way conscious of the fact that he need not care for the opinions of others; he is above suspicion; but it is not this so much as the extreme courage of his convictions that forces him to oppose duels and, in the same spirit, to refuse to bob the tails of his horses, a really humanitarian tendency! The characterization to be found in these two figures does not begin or end the powers of character drawing which is to be found in Richardson. But little behind these two major figures are those of Lovelace, the libertine, torn as surely in struggle as is Clarissa herself and seeking the destruction of the purity of the thing he really loves, a man not all bad, but humanly confused; the tenacious Pamela whose virtue is not lighted by a spiritual inspiration as is that of Clarissa, and a girl who is determined to get the best out of present life that is possible for her; the delightful Miss Byron, paragon of sentimental heroines; and the sprightly Charlotte Grandison whose cavalier treatment of her husband is full indication that she was in the very vanguard of militant women. In addition to these characters Richardson has given us a whole series of prolonged sketches. The beastly Sir Hargrave; the female ogre, Mrs. Jewkes; the persistent Mr. B—; the elusive and graceful Clementina, certainly a character "etched in moonlight"; and the wise Miss Howe, are some of those who remain to us as distinguishable and distinct individuals.

Along with the power of characterization, Richardson displays an equally admirable power of dramatic writing. The three novels are filled with long passages of drama which, although they are very likely to seem concentrated with relation to the entire length of the novels in which they occur, are themselves examples of an amazing ability to sustain dramatic effort at a high pitch for a considerable length of time and to retain the original impulse over the space of many written pages. Thus, we remember that frantic scene from *Pamela*, so breathlessly portrayed, in which the heroine, terrified beyond endurance, flies to the pond with suicidal intentions and then, overcoming temptation, and emotionally exhausted, dragging herself to the wood-house, falls there in a bedraggled heap. *Clarissa* gives us that great and fearful scene of Clarissa's first recovery after her violation, punctuated as it is with passages of inarticulate suffering and bursting into wild and fully expressed accusation; but there is likewise to be held in memory as a dramatic moment of tightest fibre the scene of Clarissa's flight with Lovelace and, as a recollection of the pathetic at its most moving best, the scene of Clarissa's death. There is, to be sure, less of the truly dramatic in *Sir Charles Grandison*, but Miss Byron's lengthy adventure with Sir Hargrave is well sustained drama and rises from climax to climax in slow and careful, but mightily sustained, progression. There is no drama in Richardson, however, more tremendous, more insinuating, more powerful in its effect upon the emotions than that, already mentioned, of Clarissa's recovery. Here are drama and pathos wrought in equal measures.

She would have spoken, but could not, looking down my guilt into confusion. A mouse might have been heard passing over the floor: her own light feet and rustling silks could not have prevented it; for she seemed to tread on air, to be all soul. She passed backwards and forwards, now towards me, now towards the door several times, before speech could get the better of indignation; and at last, "O thou contemptible and abandoned Lovelace, thinkest thou that I see not through this poor villainous plot of thine, and of these thy wicked accomplices?

"Ye vile women, who perhaps have been the ruin, body and soul, of hundreds of innocents (you show me *how*, in full assembly) know that I am not married. Ruined, as I am, by your help, I bless God, I am *not* married to this miscreant; and I have friends that will demand my honour at your hands! And to whose authority I will apply; for none has this man over me. Look to it, then, what further insults you offer me. I am a person, though thus vilely betrayed, of rank and fortune. I never will be his; and, to your utter ruin, will find friends to pursue you; and now I have this full proof of your detestable wickedness, will have no mercy upon you."[21]

Certainly, there is in this passage no dramatic conflict between the characters involved, for Lovelace has attained to a physical triumph. But the conflict lies in the strong expression, perhaps the very peak of expression in the entire novel, of Clarissa's valiant struggle to preserve her personal identity. From this point of view, what has been recorded and what, in the novel itself, follows immediately upon its heels is the great scene of the entire work. If digression from the point might be indulged in here, it might be remarked that Clarissa, long before the time of George Meredith, is one of those heroines described, not as walking, but as swimming, across a room.

There seems scarce need for a discussion here of Richardson's mastery of philosophy in these works; they are all philosophy. But there is need to refute the statement that Rich-

[21] *Clarissa*, Vol. VI, pp. 64-65.

ardson has no humor. Perhaps, in the exaggeration of sentiment in which he sometimes indulges, there is an unconscious
humor which has led critics to state that the man is humorless.
The reader, however, who accepts the quirks of Miss Charlotte
Grandison (a character somewhat more modern to the present generation than she would seem to the several generations
immediately before), her treatment of the male sex, her
pungent wit, her insistence on being both seen and heard,
can but believe in the true humor of this creation. There
is humor in the scene in which Lovelace rehearses his minions
in the actions of gentlefolk; humor in any one of a dozen
other scenes, and it is almost always, appropriately enough,
the humor of circumstance. To those, then, who believe
Richardson lacking in this quality, it may be suggested that
it is they who lack.

The mastery of Richardson over all the forms of expression that go toward the making of a novel is further to be
seen in his power of dialogue, that power through which he
gives body to both character and scene. It has already been
noted how definitely the expression of the many letters suits
the varying characters by whom they are written. The in-
tricacies of dialogue are likewise used to point the mood and
meaning of scene. If we were to progress from Lovelace's re-
hearsing the two women as his cousin and his aunt, to the
death of Clarissa, to the scene in which Harriet Byron rejects
Sir Hargrave, to a snatch of the speech of Charlotte Grandison, we should see at once how varied are the nuances of
Richardson's dialogue, how admirably he knew how to use
not only the long and majestic many-syllabled sentence, but
the brief phrase (as when he writes, "Who ever spoke of her
jewels that beheld her face?") and the single word, as in the
use of the word "disgusts" which Miss Byron and Sir Hargrave fling back and forth at each other.

That Richardson is pioneer and innovator, beyond all
this, in these novels, needs only the pointing of the fact that
he gave to the literature of his day the establishment of a new
form, the novel in letters. Further than this, that Richardson

used the analytical, sentimental novel of his day, then so popular, to express the new form, shows his canniness, and his understanding of his public. But that the work remained enormously popular after his death is to be later shown. That Richardson had the courage not to have the greatest of his novels end happily speaks eloquently of his devotion to art for art's sake and of his realization of the fact that it was not fitting to end a novel happily wherein such an ending would destroy the great meaning of its pages that one soul may not destroy the individuality of another soul without some fearful disaster ensuing.

To find a novelist, finally, in whom there are combined in such happy profusion and such generous amounts, almost all the requisites necessary to the creating of great novels: power of characterization, dramatic impulse, animation of dialogue, pathos, sentiment, humor and, above all, a strongly basic conception of original idea which he, as an author, is able to carry out through three long and undeniably complete novels according to his own convictions and by means of his own courage in the face of his knowledge of society, is to find a novelist to whom none can deny the often applied but less often deserved name of greatness. It was not only in the epistolary sense, be it remembered, that Samuel Richardson was an innovator in his day; he likewise revealed the society of the time to itself, sometimes to its distress. But he did not only do this; he did not only dare to write two huge novels in which he, a mere man, chose to use as the center and focus of his work his deepest knowledge of the inner spirit of woman; he was likewise able to transcend the limitations of the age in which he lived so that his own greatness might live for future ages, that greatness which is so difficult, in the final analysis, to give definition to, but which is unfailingly marked by the unflinching faithfulness in writing to the reiterant impulses of his own spirit and which gives him place beside and kinship with those few novelists who reveal the same sort of greatness, Hardy and Conrad, Balzac and Zola, Tolstoi and Dostoievski.

VI

THE EPISTOLARY NOVEL FROM
RICHARDSON TO 1800

ALTHOUGH there are undoubtedly other factors contributory
to the development of the epistolary novel in the eighteenth
century until almost the beginning of the nineteenth, it must
be stated with unmistakable emphasis that it is largely due
to the tremendous success of Samuel Richardson, a success
paralleled only by that of such overwhelming triumphs as was
Shakespeare's in the Elizabethan theatre and Joseph Conrad's in the contemporary novel, that the novel written in
the form of Richardson's three great novels grew in steady
scope until it reached a peak at the middle of the ninth
decade of the century.

There have been offered various partial calculations of the
number of works of fiction produced in the eighteenth century. For the period up to 1740 one may consult the list prepared by Charlotte Morgan,[1] wherein is attempted as complete a statistical synopsis as is to be found. From 1740 to
1770, the period in which the formulation of the novel most
definitely takes place, I have been able to note 595 titles,
gathered from reviews and publisher's notices. An estimate,
similarly based on reviews and notices of publications, is
that to be found in *Notes and Queries*, wherein, for the period 1770 to 1800, 1341 titles are estimated.[2] Particularly interesting, in its acute relationship to our subject is the fact

[1] *The Rise of the Novel of Manners*, New York, 1911.
[2] *Notes and Queries for Readers and Writers, Collectors and Librarians*,
Volume 148 (1925), p. 386.

that 361 of these works[3] published between 1741 and 1800, are epistolary, a total of almost one-fifth of the entire fictional output of that period.

Although the epistolary trend does not show its extremely popular scope at once, as early as 1744 there is noticeable a rising interest in the use of the form: *The Memoirs of an Unfortunate Young Nobleman* (1743), and *Felicia to Charlotte* (1744), are both novels in letters in print by the end of this year. In 1745 was published *The Fortunate Orphan; or, Memoirs of the Countess of Marlow*. In 1747, the year that saw the beginning of the publication of *Clarissa*, a sequel to Sarah Fielding's *David Simple* was published, *Familiar Letters between the principal characters in David Simple and others*, and several other epistolary works of minor interest belong to this year. In 1753 publication was begun of *Sir Charles Grandison*. Were the yearly chronicle of publications traced between the appearance of *Pamela* and that of *Sir Charles Grandison*, it would be found that one or two or more works of fiction in the epistolary form are present each year (v. Bibliography of Epistolary Fiction, p. 217). By the time we reach the decade 1760-69, we find at least one author, Mrs. Frances Brooke, who, like Richardson, used the letter-form to the practical exclusion of any other in her novels; and of the year's output of fiction for 1763, at least one-quarter is in the epistolary form. So prevalent is the letter novel becoming by this time that often the statement, ". . . in a Series of Letters" is given on the title page so that the reader may know that here is an epistolary novel and so be lured to its pages. Of significance is the fact that, during this and the following decade, translations of a French epistolarian, Mme. de Beaumont, began to appear in English along with the translations of other French epistolary works. It is not, however, until the beginning of the decade, 1770-79, the third decade of the flourishing of the novel, that we are able to find so overwhelming an indication of the popularity

---

[3] This figure is based upon calculation which must, of necessity, be tentative because of the fact that not all of the books, the titles of which have been discovered, have themselves been found or examined.

of the epistolary novel as that which lies in the presence of eighteen epistolary works of fiction among a publication of twenty-six novels for the year 1770. The year 1771 brings us one of the two or three greatest epistolary novels of the eighteenth century after the novels of Richardson, *The Expedition of Humphrey Clinker*, by Tobias Smollett. The very fact that so important an author as Smollett chose the epistolary as the form of this novel is instance that the letter form of narrative was rapidly approaching its height at this time. That the novel in letters should be at its height at a time when the novel of sentiment and sensibility is extremely popular seems sufficient to indicate that the form and the spirit of the Richardsonian novel were taken over into contemporary fiction in combination. Suffice it to say, however, that, were this not true, there would still remain truth in the statement that the letter itself is an admirable and convenient means whereby the deepest sentiments and sensibilities of characters may be presented, and that the letter, at least in the eighteenth century, was likely to be a delving into the most secret soul of the writer.

In 1777 Henry Mackenzie, like Smollett, succumbed to the epistolary craze, and put *Julia de Roubigné* into letters. This, be it noted, represents sentiment at its height, but it likewise, in the luridness of its plot, points forward to the school of terror. It is in the following year, 1778, that another great epistolary novel appeared, *Evelina*, by Miss Frances Burney.

The new decade, 1780-89, marks at first a continuance of the novel in letters, especially the sentimental epistolary, and toward the very end of the decade, something of a decline in its popularity. The year 1785 still presents a prevalence of novels of sentiment and about half of them are in letters, but after 1786 the epistolary mode suddenly goes out of fashion, and is used decreasingly as the years go on. Seventeen hundred eighty-five would seem to be the turning-point in the epistolary tide. It is almost as if, with the now rapidly growing popularity of the motifs of terror, fear, and horror (in which sentiment is not lost but modified), the novel in the form of letters was no longer considered the most fitting mode of presentation of the material the public wanted most to read. Certainly the letter is scarcely the most admirably adapted medium for the telling of a tale that depends for its climaxes on sudden and often irrational events presented in the form of action. Again, when it is said that the epistolary novel passed suddenly out of fashion, it must be remembered that it held sway, from its beginnings to the peak of its popularity, for over forty years, and that a period of so many years is a long one for any single mode to remain prevalent in the field of writing, where the new is ever being sought after, even by the most conservative. Yet the epistolary form was by no means entirely abandoned, for we have, for instance, in 1787, John Heriot's *The Sorrows of the Heart*; in 1790, *The Confidential Letters of Albert,* a contribution to the Werther series; in 1793, *Marcus Flaminius; or, a View of the Military, Political, and Social Life of the Romans, in a Series of Letters,* by Ellis Cornelia Knight; in 1796, the American edition of *D'Arcy,* by Charlotte Smith.

As has already been stated, it was the tremendous power of the example of Richardson that made possible the epistolary outburst to be found in the eighteenth century, that outburst which took almost thirty years after the publication of the first novel by that author (*Pamela*) to reach its height. But, even beyond this, it is the fact that in Richardson was concentrated, along with his greatness as a writer, the passion of the century for letter writing that made the enormous popularity of the epistolary form possible; that it was not Richardson alone, but the greatness of Richardson in his employment of what was already a common desire of the vast majority of the reading public.

We must not forget, on the other hand, the fact that the eighteenth century was a century of contemplation and investigation; that it was a century in which there was time for thought and for writing, and that much of this writing expressed itself in the communication between individuals by means of the letter. Perhaps this was even facilitated by the introduction of the penny post in 1680, a simple fact in itself.

In passing to an individual consideration of the users of the epistolary form and their personal contributions to that form, we must necessarily divide the writers into the two groups into which they seem naturally to fall. They are those who are well known in the literature of the eighteenth century, aside from their use of the epistolary form—the first class: and those who are essentially "epistolarians" and have produced little or nothing that is not in the form of the letter-novel—the second class. To the first group belong such eminent names as those of Henry Fielding, Tobias Smollett, Clara Reeve, Frances Burney, and so on.

Before proceeding to this first group it is necessary, however, to make some mention of those epistolary works which were, in themselves, either travesties or continuations in one sense or another, of Samuel Richardson's first novel, *Pamela*. This small series not only indicates the tremendous hold which the first novel Richardson ever wrote took upon England and the English readers, but also contains a burlesque of *Pamela* written by that great adversary of Richardson, Henry Fielding. In 1741, there were published two Anti-Pamelas. The first, published by Huggonson, is titled simply, *Anti-Pamela* and is of unknown authorship. The second is called, *Anti-Pamela, or Feign'd Innocence Detected: In a Series of Syrena's Adventures,* and attempts, through the medium of its heroine, Syrena, a girl supposed to be much like Pamela, to present a series of adventures much like those in the novel, *Pamela*. The intent of the work is largely satiric. To 1741 likewise belongs *Pamela Censured*, a book of little consequence. By all means the most notable of this series is that work which has been so largely attributed to the wit of Henry Fielding, *An Apology for the Life of Mrs. Shamela Andrews* (1741). The book is a biting satire of the highspots of *Pamela* and presents its heroine, Shamela, as a scheming wench who deliberately traps her master into marrying her by means of a series of fits and deadly faints. The full title of the little volume gives a much better indication of the intent of the work than could any possible commentary. It is:—

An Apology for the Life of Mrs. Shamela Andrews in which the many notorious Falsehoods and misrepresentations of a Book called PAMELA are exposed and refuted; and all the matchless Arts of that young Politician set in a true and just light. Together with a full Account of all that passed between her and Parson Arthur Williams; whose Character is represented in a manner something different from that which he bears in PAMELA. The whole being exact Copies of authentick Papers delivered to the Editor. Necessary to be had in all FAMILIES. By Conny Keyber.

It may easily be seen from this how deliberately iconoclastic the little satire was designed to be and, it must necessarily be added, that the author succeeded admirably in carrying out the slashing intent he had in mind, even to an amusing burlesquing of the very title of *Pamela*.

The name of Conny Keyber, under which the work was originally published, has been determined to be a compound of the two names of Colley Cibber and Conyers Middleton, both of which men Fielding is reported to have despised. On the subject of the authorship of this squib Brian W. Downs has written with particular conviction, both in his work *Richardson* and in the Introduction to his Edition of *Shamela*. In the latter piece of writing he says—

. . . Was Fielding the author also of *Shamela?*

No conclusive answer can be returned to such a question; we can merely balance the probabilities. On the one hand there is the unlikelihood that a man of sense and genius would return to a subject or combination of subjects with which he had dealt so faithfully.[4] Against this there is a great deal more to set:—First, the fact that *Pamela* had *not* been discredited; Fielding's renewed and persistent wrath against Cibber for the attack upon him in the Apology as a "broken wit" who knew "that, as he was in haste to get money, it would take up less time to be intrepidly abusive than decently entertaining; that to draw the mob after

---

[4] In *Joseph Andrews* (1742).

him, he must rake the channel and pelt their superiors, etc. etc."; then, analogies in language, such as, most obviously, the use of "doth" and "hath" and the Quicklyisms of the heroine and her mother in *Shamela*, which are repeated by Mrs. Slipslop in *Joseph Andrews*; the expansion of Richardson's Mr. B— into Mr. Booby in both books; the names of the two corresponding parsons in Shamela, Tickletext (a parallel to the names of Puzzletext in Fielding's *Grub Street Opera* and of Murdertext in that very Author's Farce of Fielding's in which "Keyber" was first invented) and Oliver (who has the name of one of Fielding's own tutors); the detestation of canting and sacerdotalism as against practical piety and honest living which colours all Fielding's mature work and accounts for the prominence given to Williams in *Shamela*; the resemblance between the title page of *Shamela* and the phraseology with which Fielding first advertised *Jonathan Wild*. . . .[5]

Mr. Downs adds to this already convincing argument the external evidence of a letter of Dampier's (v. Cross, W. L., *The History of Henry Fielding, I*—New Haven, 1918—p. 306) in which Fielding is given credit for the authorship of *Shamela*, and so on. We may then rather safely assume the work to be that of Fielding, in which case that great name has its only entry to epistolary fiction. The delightful *Joseph Andrews*, which is again a sort of parody of *Pamela*, is not in the epistolary form.

Shamela is by intention a frankly undignified, boisterous, unkind burlesque of Richardson's *Pamela* and as such stands in a distinctly reprehensible light. But it is necessary to say of the book that it is the only one of the several works (aside from Fielding's own *Joseph Andrews*) that hinges upon the immediate existence of *Pamela* as *Pamela*, rather than as a new experience in literature, and that reveals in itself any basic creative quality of its own. The author has followed the outline of the original story with careful, one might almost say, with brutal fidelity. He has lent the darting gleams of satire to most of the salient points; has twisted the char-

⁶ Introduction, by Brian W. Downs, to *Shamela*, The Minority Press, Cambridge, England, pp. IX, X.

acters and their motives to suit his own destructive purposes, and has made mocks of the basic moral of *Pamela*. What he has succeeded in doing is to create a short comic poem in prose, conceived in so witty, so vigorous, and so speedy a vein that the whole attains to a definite distinction of its own.

In 1741 we find an example of the fact that at least one writer was poaching on the grounds already assumed by Richardson as his own. A man by the name of Kelly was commissioned by the bookseller Chandler to write a sequel to the already existent parts of *Pamela*[6] and the result was *Pamela's Conduct in High Life*. This is largely written in the epistolary mode, although there is much of the journal contained in its pages. The whole book is characterized by a combination of pious and uninspired nonsense.

In 1742 the story of *Pamela* was again misrepresented in *The True Anti-Pamela: or, Memoirs of Mr. James Parry, Late Organist of Ross in Herefordshire. In which are inserted, His Amours with the Celebrated Miss Powell of Monmouthshire.* This is simply another feeble attempt to go Richardson one better and to create a heroine in the situation, or in one somewhat similar, of Pamela, in order to point out that virtue is not to be found as the chief characteristic of such girls and that they are usually chiefly concerned with the matter of personal and worldly gain.

It need scarcely be said that there would be little or no necessity to make mention of these books were it not for the important part *Pamela* itself plays in them, especially in the matter of form, and that it might not even then be necessary to consider them, even briefly, were not one of them suspected to be the work of Richardson's great counterpart and most formidable rival in the literature of the eighteenth century, Henry Fielding.

Passing to those notable figures of the century who wrote at least one work in the form of letters we come first (Fielding's possible contribution having been considered) to Sarah Fielding, a sister to Henry Fielding. Sarah Fielding was a de-

[6] B. W. Downs, *Richardson*, London and New York, 1928, p. 20.

voted follower of the art of Richardson but, unlike so many others of the followers of that author, her major works are expressed only in the spirit of the master. Miss Fielding did not write her more notable novels, of which *The Adventures of David Simple* (1744), a story with a sort of anæmic Sir Charles Grandison for a hero, is the best known, in the epistolary mode. The continuation of this story, published in 1747 under the title of *Letters between the Chief Characters in David Simple*, was written in letters, but scarcely lends any agreeable distinction to the name of the author. Like the second part of *Pamela*, this later work is characterized by a notable lack of action, and does not attain to the spiritual naïveté, nor the pleasing wholesomeness of *David Simple*.

After Henry Fielding there is no more distinguished "occasional epistolarian" than is Tobias Smollett, who belongs here by right of his epistolary novel, *The Expedition of Humphrey Clinker* (1771). There are many things that remain fixed firmly in our memories from a reading of *Humphrey Clinker*, but it is the great comic creations that remain longest (the comedians—and the rogues), of which the most remarkable are Tabitha Bramble, the amazing Winifred Jenkins (whose letters are among the most completely humorous documents in English literature) and Lieutenant Lismahago, himself a sort of rogue. As a matter of fact, there is very little story in this novel; what Smollett seems to have attempted to present, and he has succeeded admirably in this, is a cross-section of the society and manners of the age humorously treated.

Humphrey Clinker must necessarily be considered, as an epistolary effort, one of the greatest, if not the greatest, of the novels in letters. It presents the same story from a variety of angles, just does that so much later work by Robert Browning, *The Ring and the Book*. As a result, the divergent opinions and outlooks of the various narrators lend a sustained vivacity and utter verisimilitude to the whole. There is no doubt that much of the book is an itinerary through England and Scotland rather than a story in itself, just as was Giraldus Cambrensis' earlier work of the twelfth century, an *Itinerary Through Wales*, and the later *Set in Silver* an automobile tour through England. Smollett is thereby given an opportunity to render his own sharp and sometimes bitter comments on the towns which are thus encountered and the petty lives which he seems to have seen in those towns. The device of the letter undoubtedly aids and abets the steady flow to which the entire work attains and permits the author to cover ground several times which he might otherwise be able to pass over only once. There is little doubt that the reason for the high degree of brilliance which this novel reaches is to be found in the fact that Smollett has adapted his form, the letter, to his guiding spirit, the comic, with the utmost finesse. The result may be a heterogeneous one; but one cannot deny the fact that there is a completeness about this novel to which only a few works attain. When we are through with it we know everyone of any importance in the book thoroughly, an accomplishment on the side of accurate verisimilitude, and we receive, in addition, a definite picture of life as the author enables himself to see it through the eyes of his characters.

The strength of the epistolary form as used in *Humphrey Clinker* lies, beyond a doubt, in the fact that there is so little story told in the novel and so much portrayal of character and manners. No mode of writing could possibly be more admirably adapted to the static sort of novel than is the epistolary.

Another author of the period who chose the epistolary form for what proved to be his last work also, was Henry Mackenzie. After two novels, *The Man of Feeling* (1771) and *Man of the World* (1773), Mackenzie published, in 1777, his solitary epistolary novel, *Julia de Roubigné*. The form came from Richardson; the material and the spirit did not. In this novel we find the letter used to admirable advantage, and it is handled with a skill that makes it seem almost fitting to moments of melodrama. The first, the fourth, and the fifth letters are all excellent examples of exposition in the epistolary manner and should be turned to for that

particular reason. As a matter of fact, the author has striven
for verisimilitude at all times in this work, and nowhere may
this be more clearly seen than in the Sterne-like scoring
through of the word "victim" (p. 155). Indeed, the only
letters in the entire novel that are of little assistance in bearing out the insistent feeling of actuality which the author so
consciously strives for, are those of Savillon, which somehow
seem to be out of the picture.

The novel itself is a melodrama of jealousy, which stands
in need of the tragic height of *Othello* to make it really distinguished. None the less, the Desdemona-like heroine, Julia,
rises after the fashion of Marguerite in *Faust*, pure into
heaven. Yet, the book, as a whole, is good. The author has
written in a vein of sentiment sometimes suggestive of
Sterne. The threads of moral intimation which run through
his story seem to come from Rousseau. The narrative is
smooth and, if full of sentiment, not over-sentimental; nor
is inevitability wrenched at any given point of the story. It
is distinctly to the credit of the author that he has been able
to create so convincing a work of violence, suspicion, and passion in the less emotional epistolary form and has, at the
same time, managed to attain to a degree of honest motivation and character analysis not usually to be found in stories
of so much violence.

In turning to *Evelina; or, the History of a Young Lady's
Entrance into the World* (1778), the first novel written by
Frances Burney, later Mme. D'Arblay, we come upon a work
that is an eighteenth-century landmark. *Evelina*, like the
novels of Richardson, seems to turn almost inevitably to the
epistolary form. It is the very natural outpouring of the feelings of a young girl concerning her plight, experiences, hopes,
desires, and fortunes. As is the case with *Pamela*, this novel
is likewise made up mostly of letters of the heroine to other
people. The expression in letters could not possibly be more
natural. The book itself is a revelation of the attitude of the
heroine largely toward that social class of which she is herself
a member. The observation of the writer is recorded in swift,

bright strokes, sometimes a little superficially when she reveals that woman's quality of skimming over the surface in telling what she has seen. Yet, this occasional superficiality is an integral part of the style of the author, which is characterized by ease of flight, by total lack of strain, by a light humor and pleasant appreciation of the foibles of human beings. There is satire in this work, beyond the shadow of a doubt, but there is in it also something that is new and distinctive. *Evelina* reproduced for the first time in a successful novel the manners and conduct of ordinary domestic society and, by doing this, laid the corner stone of the domestic novel of the century. The use of the letter for the purposes of this novel is highly intelligent on the part of the author, since it has already been several times shown that there is no better medium for the recording of the thoughts and reactions of a young girl to all that is taking place about her than the epistolary.

Of distinctive interest is the appearance of *Harcourt; a Sentimental Novel. In a Series of Letters. By the Authoress of Evelina*. This is ascribed to 1780, two years after the publication of *Evelina*, and raises hopes that here is to be found a new Burney item. If this work is Fanny Burney's, however, it is very different from her better novels, particularly *Evelina*. Internal evidence (both textual and stylistic) is, in my opinion, lacking in *Harcourt*. Too many letters are written by the male sex; there is no Burney study of manners in the book; no true wit; no ever-present comic spirit. All this stands against the possibility of its being the work of Miss Burney. In the face of this, the external evidence of the title-page does not seem sufficient proof to render positive Miss Burney's authorship of this book. More plausible is the explanation that here is an exploitation of a notable name ("by the Authoress of Evelina") similar to that of the name of Richardson in *The History of Sir William Harrington*.

Of peculiar interest is the fact that one of the earliest of historical novels, *The Recess* (1785), by Sophia Lee, is a sort of epistolary novel, although it is not epistolary in spirit. The entire novel is composed of a single letter sent from Matilda to Adelaide Marie de Montmorenci. That it does not preserve the illusion of a letter need scarcely be said.

Among the many novels which Clara Reeve wrote, there are at least two of some importance which are couched in the form of letters. These are *The Two Mentors* (1783) and *The Exiles* (1788). *The Two Mentors*, which is advertised as "a modern story," is a rather successful epistolary effort. There is in it something of the suggestion of the chapter rather than the individual letter, especially when the first letter invokes a joyous mood; the second, as deliberately, one of melancholy. There is, furthermore, no definite verisimilitude as to just when the letters are supposed to have been written, nor does this lack seem to bother the author particularly. Likewise, it must be said that there is no "taking the pen in hand" to be found, although Saville speaks of writing "journal-wise" (p. 132). The book itself is full of the spirit, the society, the beliefs, and the criticisms of the age to which it belongs and, on those grounds, maintains a lively interest in its own "modernity." There is considerable sentiment in it and the work closes with the moral, "Virtue is the only thing certain upon earth" (p. 316), which indicates how strongly the Richardsonian doctrine of virtue triumphant was holding in the fiction of the period. Certainly the narrative here is good, and there are but few exaggerated effects. When Clara Reeve wrote a Gothic story in *The Old English Baron* (1775) she, in my opinion, outshone Walpole. In the epistolary medium she has proved herself almost as apt, and anyone who likes a book full of good sense, learning and, above all, reason and reasonableness should turn to Clara Reeve for it. Furthermore, there is present in this particular novel a distinct artistic quality in the fact that there is little in it that would stamp it as indelibly feminine, although the male sex is once or twice attacked with truly feminine vigor. Her later *The School for Widows* (1791), is also epistolary.

The Exiles; or, Memoirs of the Count de Cronstadt is not, by any means, entirely an epistolary novel, but rather a personal history told in the first person. There are letters from more than one writer, it is true, but there are also memoirs, patches of narrative, letters within letters and, in the very first volume (p. 47) there is presented "A dialogue between an Uncle, an old Batchelor of sixty-three, and his Nephew, a Student of Seventeen." The result is, then, something of a hodge-podge in its general effect, although the work itself is one of the better novels of the ultra-sentimental school. As it progresses, the book becomes less and less epistolary and more strictly narrative, but there is no point at which the use of the letter disappears for an over-prolonged space. The novel itself is moral, didactic, and sentimental and, after its recording of an unhappy ending, proceeds slightly into the second generation, on speculations of the possible lot of which it closes. The use of the many letters in the course of the narrative in this book is plain indication of the fact that the letter had come into its own as a literary device, even in the "straight" novel, and that the epistolary fashion was a waning one.

The romantic and prolific Mrs. Charlotte Smith has like-wise contributed three novels to the epistolary catalogue in *Desmond* (1792); *D'Arcy* (1796); and *The Solitary Wanderer* (1801). The last novel belongs to that period after the beginning of the nineteenth century in which the epistolary form was distinctly on the decline. The first novel, *Desmond,* has an interesting preface in which Mrs. Smith doubts her ability (as McFee excuses his choice later) to make a novel go as well in letters as in the narrative which was her accustomed medium in her earlier work. When one has read the book, however, any thought of her possible failure is dispersed. The book opens in June, and the letter first disclosed to us somewhat suggests the dramatist's lifting of the curtain at a certain point in a speech. Here we enter Lionel Desmond's life, through this letter to his friend Erasmus Bethel, at a moment when much has already happened which we are made to feel from the very opening sentence might have been of immediate interest to us. Although the first few letters al-

ternate as letter and answer, soon all the letters are from
Desmond to Bethel and are addressed from various parts of
France, where Desmond is traveling with Waverly. Volume II
introduces us, at a somewhat late date, to the two main female
protagonists, Fanny Waverly and Geraldine Verney, who
likewise write much. When Desmond lies ill, as a result of
a duel, his doctor, William Carmichael, carries on his correspondence for him. We are thus given the chief correspondents of this novel and among them they carry on, in lively
fashion, a sentimental and somewhat Werther-like tale. Of
particular interest to the student of this period should be
that letter from Geraldine Verney in which she discusses the
books of the period, in survey, and renders criticisms of
them.[7] *D'Arcy* is a brief novel in letters and, indeed, seems to
depend on its brevity for its success. Even at the very outset,
the exposition is briefly but well put, and the flow of the
narrative is admirably smooth throughout the work. Altogether, the story has an exciting first few pages and gives additional proof that the letter may be used with complete conviction to tell of quickly moving events when given to the
proper character to use. In this novel there is no mass of
details to flounder through and the return to reason (even
though there is present considerable evidence of sensibility),
a movement in which Charlotte Smith was one of the pio-
neers, is here again made clear, and all in all the result is a
rattling good story. The letters themselves are not absurdly
long and, taken as a whole, they result in picturing for us a
closely knit and entertaining story. Along with her exercise
of reason, we are able to see the humanitarianism of the author plainly depicted in this novel, and certainly this adds
to the story a sympathetic quality which is particularly
pleasing.

In turning to that large group of what might be called
"minor epistolarians," that is, authors of somewhat less than
first rank who have written entirely in the epistolary mode,
it must be especially noted that this term, as applied to them,

[7] Letter XII, vol. II, pp. 164-175.

although it may mean that they did not stand in the very front rank of authorship during the period, is not meant to indicate that they were without importance in themselves.

As early as 1755 we have *The Card* (an amazingly simple title for a fictional work of the eighteenth century) by one John Kidgell. As frontispiece to the volume there appears the picture of a card and under it the statement: "The grand figure represents a human Creature. The Dart in his right Hand intimates Cruelty: the black spot on the left denotes Artifice and Disguise; the yellow in his Raiment is a Sign of Jealousy, and the red of Anger; the Flower at his feet betokens Vivacity of Genius and the Feather in his Cap bespeaks Promotion." John Kidgell was a clergyman; and it is no new thing to see the clergyman turn satirist.

The Card, although it may not be strictly called a novel, is of the novel kind. It is chiefly a satire of human foibles and as such is full of a trenchant comic spirit. It satirizes, in its form, the letters of Richardson, and the society of the day is cunningly taken off in such passages as that of the literary ball, the grand tour, and so on. Sentiment is laughed at very freely and that particular form of it, sentimentality, which held in its grip so many contemporary writers, is made the subject of high ridicule. The book does not contain a great variety of events; nor are those which it does contain such as to elevate or surprise the reader to any considerable extent. The work is principally a literary correspondence which exhibits justly many of the humors of life, so as to inculcate some precept, which is not the less important because its object is a trifle, since upon trifles many of the comforts and felicities of life are known to depend. Here, then, we see not only the Richardsonian form in the letters, but likewise the Richardsonian spirit in the morals attached to the incidents presented.

Of the authors here considered as essential epistolarians, there is no more constant a writer than Mrs. Frances Brooke. She has given us, in *The History of Lady Julia Mandeville* (1763) and *The History of Emily Montague* (1769), two works which are, despite their many defects, sufficient to establish her as an author of considerable competence. In 1770 she likewise made a translation, in letter form, of the *Memoirs of the Marquis de St. Forlaix*, to be considered later. There is a certain weakness undoubtedly revealed in the lack of variety of Mrs. Brooke's epistolary style, and we find in both of these novels that men and women alike write in the same feminine vein. Especially is this true of Henry Mandeville in *Lady Julia Mandeville* who, although he is not an effeminate man, betrays an attention to details in his letters which is more characteristic of the feminine than of the masculine mind. If we are to consider these novels in themselves, aside from their epistolary quality, we are inclined to feel that there is in them a great deal of ado about very little incident. The plots are somewhat too thinly sustained and the psychological inward struggles are so completely externalized that often all subtlety is lost. Here we miss that element so strong in the great novel of inner conflict and so pertinent to the epistolary novel, individual analysis, and can only hope that it does exist even if we cannot see it. None the less, both of these novels are distinctly alive, if not vibrant, and entirely sincere, if not quite true. Mrs. Brooke has somewhat more sentimentality in her novels than sentiment, but she succeeds in presenting it with a drooping grace that is not ineffectual. Both of her heroines are at times "reserved, silent, absent" creatures,[8] their "charming eyes" filled with "a melancholy languor." It is for this reason, chiefly, that the heroines' confidantes, more sprightly in nature, are more attractive characterizations here than the heroines themselves.

Something of a departure is to be found in *Emily Montague* in the local color to be found in the scenes that take place in Canada, but there is no real innovation to be found in either of these epistolary novels aside from this. Both are written under the influence of the Richardsonian form and

---

[8] Mrs. Frances Brooke, *The History of Lady Julia Mandeville*, London, 1763, I, p. 49.

spirit, and the sentiment which Richardson himself has pro-
jected finds exaggeration here because Mrs. Brooke lacked
the penetrating knowledge of the human soul necessary to
explain sentiment convincingly.

Mrs. Brooke has given us, however, two other works in
which letters play a large part. In 1760 she published her
first work, not strictly a novel but rather a collection of
sentiments linked by character, *Letters from Juliet, Lady
Catesby, to her Friend, Lady Henrietta Campley.* This is a
translation. The other novel of this sort which has come from
the ingenious Mrs. Brooke is *The History of Charles Mandeville* (1790), a sequel to *Lady Julia Mandeville,* written some
twenty-seven years after that novel was published. It is the
traditional sequel in that it is distinctly inferior to the work
it attempts to follow.

Mrs. Griffith's *The Delicate Distress* (1769), is a work
much like that of Mrs. Brooke in that it is chiefly sentimental;
indeed, almost the closing lines are:

Captain Beaumont presented me with his and his father's pictures; he had before given me Charlotte's portrait.—Alas! it was
a useless gift, as her dear image is too sadly graved on my sad
heart![9]

The entire novel may be guessed at from these few lines.
The letters themselves are in Mrs. Brooke's manner; they
suffer from the monotony of the author's injecting herself into all of them rather than permitting each individual
letter to express the personality of its writer. Again, the
letters indicate that omniscient quality which detracts from
the verisimilitude of such novels; even those which are lost
and never reach their destination are shown to the reader so
that he must assume the ability to read over the writer's
shoulder rather than over the receiver's.

Perhaps the two most notable things about Mrs. Brooke's
the *History of Charles Mandeville* have but little bearing on
the epistolary style. The first is that the little girl in the story

[9] P. 158.

is allowed to talk baby talk, although it was not until later, in the nineteenth century, that children in books were given to talk and act like children and not like miniature adults. The second is that the dialogue in this work is put in quotations, which tends to destroy the illusion of the letter and give the entire book something of the semblance of narrative. Indeed, the whole work is more nearly a series of animated essays on life and customs in India than a novel. Of the books of which we have just spoken and of the epistolary composition that need be mentioned only in passing—*The Excursion; a Novel* (1777)—it should be said that, though we may disagree with the mode of her writings and even with their *ton*, we must admire the sincerity, plodding and forthright, and the pluckiness of this woman, in writing so many volumes so competently.

An author who belongs in this category because of the importance of a single epistolary composition, a distinguished one, although her Oriental tale, *The History of Nourjahad* (1767), is of considerable importance in the development of that type, is Mrs. Frances Sheridan, important not only because she was the mother of Richard Brinsley Sheridan, but likewise because of her own significance as a novelist and a playwright. Her epistolary work is the *Memoirs of Miss Sidney Bidulph. Extracted from her own Journal, and Now First Published,* in three volumes, and its continuation in two volumes, *The Conclusion of the Memoirs of Miss Sidney Bidulph, as prepared for the Press by the Late Editor of the Former Part* (1761-67). The work itself is an epistolary novel of sentiment, written much in the Richardsonian tradition. The story is an involved one and the manner in which the author, by means of letters, proceeds through the mazes of her plot is highly skillful. Although there are moments of melodrama in the book and moments in which the imagination of the reader is called upon to bear a somewhat heavier load than is desirable, there is a distinct conviction in the presentation here of lives which seem to be ruled by Robert Burns' dictum of the "best-laid schemes o' mice an' men." The characters are well drawn, especially in the cases of the hero and the Galahadian Miss Sidney herself; the letters are exceedingly well composed and are full of a lively verisimilitude; the plan of the whole story is executed with forethought and care. Undoubtedly, this is one of the best of the lesser novels of the day.

Mrs. Sarah Scott has contributed at least two epistolary attempts to the literature of the period. The first is, *A Description of Millenium Hall, and the Country Adjacent: Together with the Characters of the Inhabitants, and such historical Anecdotes and Reflections, as may excite in the Reader proper Sentiments of Humanity, and lead to the Love of Virtue* (1762); the second is *The Test of Filial Duty. In a Series of Letters between Miss Emilia Leonard, and Miss Charlotte Arlington. A Novel* (1772). *Millenium Hall* is not a novel and it is not, strictly speaking, epistolary. It is, rather, a description and a series of histories presented in such form that they seem to be told in the course of a long letter addressed to "Dear Sir" (p. 1), and concluded, "I am, Sir" (p. 262). The device is an obvious one and we may as well read for "dear sir" the words "dear reader." The effect is scarcely that of a letter.

The Test of Filial Duty presents one of the few novels among these many the fictional time of which is dated. Here the time of the book is January 5, 1769 to November 14, 1769, a device which must have added considerably to the immediacy of the story. Certainly, however, it is scarcely a fictional necessity in the epistolary story. The early letters in this work are very serious and sober and, one feels, are almost in the mood of moralizing sermons. Like *Millenium Hall*, they are meant perhaps to evoke the proper human sentiments in the hearts of the readers. Again, in this work, we have a novel in which nothing happens, and any news we get comes to us third hand. The letters themselves are rather stilted in composition, but once we become accustomed to the style we find that the substance is far superior to that of the many lesser novels in letters, just as is the element of common

sense more distinctly noticeable once we become accustomed
to the over-moralizing in which the author indulges. Mrs.
Scott is here revealed as an author of little power, but of
much homely sense and considerable ability to express herself within the limits of the letter without once exhausting
the infinite possibilities of the letter form.

Because of their relationship, it is well to consider the epistolary works of the Minifies and the Gunnings within close
range of each other. Miss Susanna Minifie (later Mrs. Gunning) wrote many novels, both by herself and with her sister,
and she is of considerable individual importance as the possible nominal head of this writing tribe. The epistolary works
of the Miss Minifies are, chiefly, the *Histories of Lady Frances
A— and Lady Caroline S—* (1763); *The Picture, a Novel*
(1766); *Barford Abbey: A Novel in a Series of Letters*
(1768); *The Cottage, a Novel: in a Series of Letters* (1769);
The Count de Poland (1780); and *Coombe Wood* (1783).
Of all of these, the third, fourth, fifth, and sixth may be attributed to Miss Minifie alone. *Coombe Wood* may be considered as representative of these novels by the Miss Minifies.
Here the author follows the frequent custom of the day in
wanting to be known as the editor of the letters, instead of as
their author, thereby lending the air of verisimilitude which
was so anxiously sought after in most of the literature of the
midcentury. According to the epistolary method there is no
other way of obtaining this conviction of reality than by the
editor having under his thumb all of the letters at the time
of his writing or arranging the series; thereby he is given
knowledge of all that has occurred. He is not making use of
the omniscient point of view, but he is essentially an intimate
and confidant of the characters involved.

Coombe Wood is somewhat too consistently written in the
"all-will-soon-be-over" style of sensibility. Much of the novel
is over-hectic and too consciously sentimental, and the style
of the whole is peculiarly stilted and artificial. The novels
of the Miss Minifies are generally built on the very thinnest
sorts of plot and material; the stories are told in an involved

manner, and the chronological order is not followed with the strictest accuracy; indeed, the time element rarely enters as such into these novels which seem to be cast in a perpetual eternity of night and day, though certainly some wrenching of the element of time is always allowable in the epistolary work. As epistolary efforts in the purely mechanical sense, these novels mark no advance, but rather a step backwards from the work of Richardson for, although they present the letters of several groups, there is seldom offered a letter in return to any already written.

When we turn to the *Memoirs of Mary*, a later novel (1793), by the now Mrs. Gunning, we find that the author has developed a further knowledge of the epistolary style in which she worked so much to enable her to present occasional replies. Thus, Letter V is sent in answer to Letter III, even though Letter IV is permitted to intervene for no obvious reason. There is a distinct improvement in style, likewise, over the earlier novels and, although events happen with an amazing slowness, the work is done in a smooth manner and the descriptions of people therein are especially clear and convincing. Working with a story that is so definitely autobiographical as is this, Mrs. Gunning could not have chosen a more satisfactory medium than the epistolary. The novel itself is distinctly one in "letters and narrative," a form that grew somewhat popular as the century advanced to its close as a sort of last flourish of the epistolary style. The portion of the novel that is written as a journal is of good length, as is the case later in Sir Walter Scott's *Redgauntlet* (1824), but it is not written in the style of a journal or diary at all, and seems to be an exact complement and supplement to the letters that the heroine earlier wrote her grandmother, and is therefore only a pseudo-journal. It is interesting to note, however, one or two innovations in this book. Joseph Conrad's technique of introducing characters at a point midway through certain events in the story in which they appear seems to be somewhat anticipated by Mrs. Gunning here in her method of giving a block of antecedent events, returning to and proceeding with the story and then giving some more antecedent events. Again, Mrs. Gunning makes use of the very unusual device of giving only extracts from a letter instead of an entire letter, as in Letter XXXIII (volume III). In short, the author has learned well the epistolary mode.

The Gipsy Countess (1799), the work of Miss Gunning, is a work in letters in which the letters themselves do not seem to be such, but are journalistic in tone. Miss Gunning undoubtedly wins for herself in this novel the distinction of being the most long-winded writer in the eighteenth century after Richardson himself. Moreover, as one proceeds through the story there appears to him to be less and less excuse for letters as the medium in which to present this novel. Lady Julia tells her history in short snatches, each snatch constituting a letter written to her brother in India, when all could have been as well accomplished in one large, single packet. The narrative itself is a peculiar, somewhat Conradian mixture of writing in the present of the present and the present retrospectively considered, and the result is the creation of a highly artificial impression. At one point, indeed (Letter XLII), the intermingling of the story of the present with the story of the past becomes so confused that the reader is at a loss to make out just what it is that is taking place. Altogether, *The Gipsy Countess* represents a very inadequate attempt of an author to write a story in letters for its own sake and with no thought to the inevitability of the form itself. This is, of course, but a single indication of the fact that the true epistolary form was losing its pristine grip as a literary medium of dominant use.

An author of French blood who wrote his novels in English is M. Pierre Henri Treyssac de Vergy. His first epistolary novel appeared in 1770, *Henrietta, Countess Osenvor. A Sentimental Novel in a Series of Letters,* and the caption on the title page, "Love and virtue held the pen," goes far to tell us of what de Vergy chiefly wrote. Other epistolary novels of this author are: *Mistakes of the Heart; or, the Memoirs of Lady Caroline Pelham and Lady Victoria Nevil* (1769-72) ; *Palin-*

ode; or, the Triumphs of Virtue Over Love (1771); and *The Lovers; or, the Memoirs of Lady Mary Sc— and the Hon. Miss Amelia B—* (1772). *Henrietta* is a novel of extreme sentimentality in which nothing happens; the heroine does not even die lest the sensibilities of the reader be too deeply shocked. The whole is a sort of analytical spiritual argument with the faintest suggestion of plot occasionally inserted. Again, the letters are such in little more than mere designation. The *Mistakes of the Heart* is somewhat more sprightly, but does not bear any overweight of animation. Most of these novels are alike in being static and artificial but, despite the fact that de Vergy was anathema to the reviewers of his day, they are scarcely more mediocre than many of the lesser works here considered.

Helen-Maria Williams has contributed *Anecdotes of a Convent* (1771); *Letters between an English Lady and her Friend at Paris* (1770); and *Letters Written in France in the Summer of 1790. To a Friend in England; containing various Anecdotes relative to the French Revolution, and the Memoirs of Mons. and Madame De F—* (1790, vol. II, 1792). The nearest approach to a novel among these three is the *Anecdotes of a Convent*, but all three are rather works of an experimental nature, more nearly allied to the epistolary outposts preceding Richardson than to works of a fictional nature.

William Renwick is the author of *Genuine Distresses of Damon and Celia. In a Series of Letters, between the late General Crawford, Sir John Huffey Delaval, Bart., Sir Francis Blake Delaval, K.B., and two Unfortunate Lovers* (1772); and *The Solicitudes of Absence* (1788). Both are novels of sentiment. The latter, however, departs from the purposes of the novel in letters to a considerable extent. It opens as an autobiography and continues as a straight narrative (despite the fact that it is in letters!). The insertion of so many verses, likewise, tends to make the whole rather gauche as a narrative. The letters, and there are many of them, seem to be written at random, serving no particular point and achieving no particular end. The narrative, at the beginning of each chapter, sets the letter that is to follow and tries to give it its raison d'être. The procedure seems original to a certain extent, but the lack of result does not warrant such originality, which only serves to ruin any apparent verisimilitude.

A minor epistolarian of considerable éclat is S. J. Pratt (Courtney Melmoth), the author of *The Pupil of Pleasure* (1777); *The Tutor of Truth* (1779); and *Emma Corbett; or, the Miseries of Civil War* (1780), all in letters. All three of these novels are of considerable interest but the last, and perhaps the best, is of particular note because it concerns itself with the American Revolution. Pratt himself seems to have been a man of considerable wisdom and, as a result of this, we are able to find some good things in his novels. In *Emma Corbett* the narrative is good, simple (in the sense that there is little encumbrance of plot), and the letters themselves are excellently fitted to the roles and the styles of the several personages. Perhaps the language is a trifle too literary and thus detracts from the liveliness of the work, but this is relieved by frequent gleams of humor, rather more humor indeed than is usually to be found in novels of so definitely sentimental a turn as are these of Pratt.

This author has made excellent use of the epistolary form, and in Letter LVIII, he achieves real dramatic fervor by means of his skill in the use of the letter. It makes the reader see clearly the advantages of the epistolary style and its ability to lend verisimilitude to the description of an event progressively as if it were just happening. Nor do we feel any wrench in believing in the very presence of such an event.

Aside from the epistolary significance of *Emma Corbett*, it is of individual interest. The different sides which Emma and her father take pattern the novel much after the Civil War literature in America, in which the Southern girl's lover is almost always in the Union army. Indeed, the favorite theme of the novel of sentiment is love barred with obstacles, the father of the girl being the usual obstacle; and here we have an excellent example of the formula. The novel itself is pseudo-historical, and it presents one of the earliest appearances of General Washington in fiction. Certainly the melodramatic tone is fully present in this work; the sudden meetings, greetings, and deaths are remarkable, and the piling of one incident upon another is exhausting. Although the sentiment of the story may point to Richardson, the general method employed here by Pratt would seem to be that of Defoe, in the use of one detail of narrative after another. Indeed, this is true of almost all of the writings of Pratt in the field of fiction. On the other hand, the epic sweep of Fielding and the minute dissection of Richardson are alike lacking in this particular author.

Another quite prolific epistolary novelist is Mrs. Cartwright, who has contributed: *The Generous Sister. In a Series of Letters* (1779); *Letters Moral and Entertaining* (1781); *The Duped Guardian; or, the Amant Malade. In a Series of Letters* (1786); *The Platonic Marriage. In a Series of Letters* (1786); *Retaliation; or, the History of Sir Edward Oswald, and Lady Frances Seymour* (1787). Of these, the *Letters Moral and Entertaining* scarcely belongs in this category, since it is not primarily a work of continuous fiction, but rather belongs to the ilk of the pre-Richardsonian collection of letters. The most notable work by Mrs. Cartwright is *Retaliation*, a novel of much sentiment, many flaws, and endless letters. One may judge the length of these letters by picking at random. Letter XXVI (volume III), extends from page sixty-two to page 158; Letter XXXI (volume IV) extends from page fifty-four to page 147, presented with several "in continuations," a device which was anticipated in *Evelina* and, to a slight extent, in Richardson likewise. There are also in *Retaliation* shorter letters of some ten or twelve pages. One may thereby judge of the degree of verisimilitude this novel attains. Mrs. Cartwright is scarcely of more than passing interest in the field of epistolary fiction, despite the fluency with which she has written.

Of similar degree is William Coombe, more important for his writing of *Dr. Syntax* than for his epistolary novels, which are: *Letters Supposed to have been Written by Yorick and Eliza* (1779) ; *Letters between Two Lovers and their Friends* (1781) ; and *Original Love Letters, between a Lady of Quality, and a Person of Inferior Station* (1784) , the last of which embodies something of a "new" theme. The novels themselves have no particular distinction.

Of infinitely greater importance in the pageant of the letter-novel in the eighteenth century is Robert Bage, at least four of whose works: *Mount Henneth* (1782) ; *Barham Downs* (1784) ; *The Fair Syrian* (1787) ; and *James Wallace* (1788) , are in epistolary form. The novels of this author are scarcely novels of sentiment. Bage has attempted to use the novel as a social force and has succeeded well. It is interesting to observe that, despite the fact that these novels of Bage are written in letters, the epistolary novels wane with the vogue for works of just the social type Bage tried to write. The basic motivation of his work seems to lie in the two words "amuse" and "instruct" and, even though he is perhaps better known for his *Man As He Is* (1792) , and *Hermsprong; or, Man As He Is Not* (1796) , his epistolary efforts hold their own with all but his best novel, *Hermsprong*. Bage is definitely a student of society and, as such, his novels take on something of the tone of propaganda. In addition to this tendency, there is humor in almost all of these writings, a quality that certainly is not the dominant force in the epistolary novel, especially when it is too closely allied (as it is so often) with the lack-humor of too much sentiment. In his letters Bage always tries for verisimilitude and, when he has a Frenchman writing letters, as is the case in *The Fair Syrian*, he inserts much French. In this particular case the result is not exactly what might be desired. The conventions of fiction require not too many excursions into foreign languages. In another respect, the author adheres to these conventions by "omitting to publish" certain letters that would be repetitious and by hastening the narrative occasionally by means of a passage of straight narrative prose. He does not indulge in replies to letters to any great extent, but he makes a definite effort to establish the personality of the individual writer in the letter he or she writes and, in *The Fair Syrian* especially, the characterization he thus obtains is splendid.

Whatever may be the faults of Bage, his crisp, often epigrammatic style is sufficiently alive to hold our interest to a degree that other, even better, epistolarians, do not attain to so easily in their works.

Four other names that require individual mention here are those of William Robinson, John Potter, Mrs. Charlotte Lennox, an author of considerable worth who did not do her best work in the epistolary field, and Mrs. Mary Robinson, she who was the celebrated "Perdita" Robinson. William Robinson wrote two epistolary works: *Love Fragments. A Series of Letters* (1782) and *Sydney St. Aubyn. In a Series of Letters* (1794). John Potter wrote *The Virtuous Villagers. In a Series of Letters* (1784) and *The Favourites of Felicity. In a Series of Letters* (1785). Charlotte Lennox wrote *Euphemia* (1790). Mary Robinson wrote *The Shrine of Bertha. In a Series of Letters* (1794); *The Widow; or, A Picture of Modern Times. A Novel. In a series of Letters* (1794); and *The False Friend; a Domestic Story* (1799). Among these several works there is little of real epistolary interest. *The Favourites of Felicity* is a light, sentimental novel in three volumes distinguished by occasional glimpses of humor. It concerns itself, from time to time, with a timid sort of social criticism and bears heavily upon France and things French for its material. The letters are unbelievably long and extend over many pages of unanimated description. Any verisimilitude which the novel might possess is thereby pitifully swamped if not entirely annihilated. Even *Euphemia*, by the author of *The Adventures of Arabella; or, The Female Quixote* (1752), a work which was a distinct innovation in its day, is an epistolary novel no better than passing fair. In Mrs. Robinson's *The False Friend*, there is to be seen an interesting attempt to use letters for the purely domestic novel, a form introduced by the vogue of the matchless *Evelina*. Yet

none of these serves to advance or distinguish the epistolary
mode as do many of their predecessors.

Aside from these, two works, both dated 1790, have been
assigned to Mrs. Radcliffe, and deserve passing mention. They
are: *The Fate of Velina De Guidova;* and *Radzivil.*

There are, beyond the writers already presented, a number
of authors, mostly minor, all of whom have contributed but
a single work (or, at the most, two) to the epistolary catalogue. There are over forty names to be considered here.

It is not to be thought that all of these writers are one-
book writers; they are, upon the whole, merely the writers
of but one epistolary work to be recorded here. The first of
them is, by reason of the date of his work, John Cleland, the
author of the *Memoirs of Fanny Hill* (1749). Mrs. Seymour
wrote, in 1753, *The Conduct of a Married Life. In a Series
of Letters,* and James Seguin published, in 1755, *Letters of
Princess Zilia to Prince Aza of Peru.*

John Langhorne's *The Correspondence of Theodosius and
Constantia* (1765), is a limpid and graceful work in many
respects, but seems to be old-fashioned even by comparison
with other works of its own period. *The History of Alicia
Montagu,* in 1767, comes from Mrs. Jane Marishall, a novel
very much of its time, in which the author makes use of the
already famous name of Montagu, and creates a work that
may be related to Mrs. Bennett's *Agnes de Courci* so far as
ardent sentimentality is concerned.

Richard Griffith is represented by *The Gordian Knot* in
1769; Mrs. Skinn by *The Old Maid; or, The History of Miss
Ravensworth. In a Series of Letters,* in 1770; and Thomas
Hull by *The History of Sir William Harrington,* in 1771.
Sir William Harrington is a sentimental novel of practically
no merit, but considerable audacity. On the title-page the
author has presented this full caption: *The History of Sir
William Harrington. Written Some Years Since, and revised
and corrected by the late Mr. Richardson, Author of Sir
Charles Grandison, Clarissa, etc.* We may thereby see that,
even in the eighteenth century, there were those who were

not above trading on famous names and, since Richardson
was at this time not alive to defend his reputation, the audacity of the author, Hull, is both patent and reprehensible.
He was, however, sufficiently dealt with by the reviewers of
his day.[10]

M. de Guys is here represented by *A Sentimental Journey
Through Greece*, in 1772, patterned after the famous work
of Sterne of similar caption; Mrs. Fogerty by *Memoirs of
Colonel Digby and Miss Stanley. In a Series of Letters,* in
1773; Charles Johnstone by *The Pilgrim*, in 1775, an epistolary work in the mode of the time which happens, in this
case, to be rather a collection of memoirs, opinions, and adventures than a novel; and R. Roberts by *The Peruvian Letters,* in 1775. In 1776 came Mrs. Griffith's *The Story of Lady
Juliana Harley. A Novel, in Letters;* John Seally's *Loves of
Calisto and Emira; or, The Fatal Legacy;* and Menella Bute
Smedley's *The Maiden Aunt.* The year was a rather slim
one, perhaps because of the American Revolution, and Miss
Smedley's novel is only another piece of sentiment and intrigue. Mrs. Griffith's work is of considerably greater merit.

The History of Miss Temple, by Miss Rogers, came in
1777, and *Memoirs of the Marchioness de Louvoi,* by Lady
Mary Walker, belongs to the same year.

Of particular interest is that curious volume, *John Buncle,
Jr.,* by Thomas Cogan, published in 1778. The story, what
there is of it, starts, oddly enough, with the ninth letter. Indeed, this book is not a novel in our customary use of the
word, but rather are the separate parts novelle, each day
having a story to be told and some new philosophical point to
be discussed. This little book of pocket philosophy was put
into the form of letters only that it might be in the vogue,
for it is safe to say that any writing, in order to "go over" at
this time, needed only to be put in letters; hence the raison
d'être for the form of *John Buncle, Jr.* The Sterne influence
may be seen in this volume in the manner in which the
Preface and Errata are put last; the ninth letter is first, and

---

[10] *Monthly Review,* Monthly Catalogue, London, Vol. XLIV (March 1771),
Article 31, pp. 262, 263.

there is given an air of general inconsequence, of much material merely hanging together. The book is, like most parodies and satires, chiefly interesting for the ludicrous lights it throws on the too popular and too widely accepted ideas of the day. Thus, the fictional rank of the book seems inferior, upon the whole, to its satirical rank.

The year 1779 brings a sentimental novel by Miss Nugent and Miss Taylor of Twickenham, *The Indiscreet Marriage; or, Henry and Sophia Sommerville. In a Series of Letters.*

The letters that appear in Sir Herbert Croft's *Love and Madness* (1780), are of special interest for one reason. When the lovers write to each other, they actually tell each other the news and gossip of the day, things which they know will be of interest, and thus their letters attain to a high degree of verisimilitude. Usually, when two people write to each other, their letters do contain such material, even though they are lovers. It is this which so many of the other epistolarians of this group seem to forget. In this single respect, then, the letters in *Love and Madness* are among the best.

We again turn to a novel of almost Richardsonian length in Miss Palmer's *Female Stability; or, The History of Miss Belville,* published in 1780, the form of which is letters and replies to them. Miss Palmer employs a method of alternation, especially between the letters of Adeline and Sir James Thomson, so that the reader may not find time to become too tired of an excess of sensibility before he is "humorously engaged." This author is likewise adroit in the handling of her plots, and there are here four in all, perhaps five, which she weaves in and out with skill and aplomb. In this novel, almost every last detail is given in every last letter yet, at the same time, although we are hereby given an enormous amount of detail, especially concerning the people who figure in the story, we really see little of them. The milieu is vague and, upon the whole, the essential element of two souls struggling in conflict, described by letter and at some distance, must necessarily result in a greatly lowered tension. Another weakness of the epistolary form as here employed is to be found

in the fact that Miss Belville stands always in the necessity
of describing how desperate half a dozen men or so are for
love of her. This weakness, which results in an enforced ego-
tism, is, of course, analogous to the same fault in narrative
in the first person, or the autobiographical form.

Dr. Dodd is here represented by *The Magdalen*, 1784; and
Mrs. Hampden Pye by *Theodosius and Arabella. A Novel
in a Series of Letters*, 1786. The latter novel is done with considerable asperity and, although it is almost totally lacking
in both depth and action, none the less must have proved
most entertaining and amusing to the readers of its day because of its tart and pointed discussions of many things timely
in the course of its pages. John Dent's *The Force of Love.
In a Series of Letters*, and Miss Lucy Peacock's *The Rambles
of Fancy; or, Moral and Interesting Tales*, were likewise published in the same year as *Theodosius and Arabella*.

Another representative author of this group is Mrs. James
Keir with her epistolary novel, *The History of Miss Greville*,
published in 1787. This story was written to combat "a
prejudice very frequently entertained in early life—that none
but a first attachment can be a happy one." Julia Greville is
the heroine; her confidante-correspondent is Miss Lucy Herbert. Mrs. Keir was a Scotch woman and succeeded in incor-
porating in her novel some of her Scotch wit and canniness.
A delightful point is made in the next to the last letter of this
novel where Lucy Herbert, now married, signs herself—
"Lucy Her—no-no—Stanley." The book is well written
and a thoroughgoing example of the epistolary novel of
sensibility.

We must turn to John Heriot's *The Sorrows of the Heart*
(1787), to find a real man of feeling, a hero who bursts into
tears on not too much provocation, but rather because of
an unconscious relationship to Werther or Harley in Mackenzie's book. He is a hero the very tone of whom lends the
novel the probable distinction of being the most sentimental
of all the type. The exaggeration here is one of sentiment,
not of caricature. Again, the plot is so thin and so little hap-

pens that the book seems to have moved forward, as it is read, only in dates. Unhappily, these over-sentimental and over-sensible people do not suffer from *mal du siècle*. That comes later.

Agnes de Courci (1789), by Mrs. Bennett, is distinguished by the fact that it is a domestic tale. This does not, however, rob its letters of the privilege of being full of sentiment from time to time. The whole work, indeed, is weakened by too many tears and too much melodrama. For those who think of domestic fiction as represented by the trials of Fielding's Amelia, or the sprightly adventures in society of Miss Burney's Evelina, this book of Mrs. Bennett's is not such. In the same year, Mrs. Gomersall gave to the world *Eleonora. In a Series of Letters written by a Female Inhabitant of Leeds in Yorkshire*. A book of that year which seems to have been written by one who knew upper society is *The History of Lady Caroline Rivers*, by Mrs. Elizabeth Todd. The fact that almost all of the letters are written by two people (although volume II opens with a letter from Lord Rake to James Rattle, Esq., the first to be written by anyone other than Caroline or her friend Louisa) does not help to make for variety. The story itself is not at all unusual, but it is told in lively style, and Lady Caroline might have come out of the pages of Frances Burney.

Richard Cumberland was an author of considerable popularity in the eighteenth century and, although a minor novelist, was of excellent tissue. He is represented in the epistolary category by but a single work, *Arundel* (1789). This is notable, aside from its intrinsic merit, for the fact that the "editor" has added to his work a happy ending, told in a closing letter from "editor" to "reader" very much in the tone of the closing chapters so usual in the Victorian novel, especially in those of Dickens and Thackeray. What is admirable in this work is the fact that, with a set of thoroughly stereotyped characters: the hard, obstinate father; the faithful mother; the rich, swaggering villain; the usual vivacious confidante, and the usual hero and heroine—with these people

and with story material that is not full of suspense, the author
has succeeded in concocting a thoroughly absorbing and
even-paced work. There is here the same good humor and the
same largeness of spirits that we find in Fielding, while the
occasional mawkishness of Richardson and that author's
over-attentiveness to unimportant details are entirely lacking. The clever arrangement of the letters, that is, the accuracy of letter and answer and the juxtaposition of varying
points of view by means of the letter, here succeed in showing
the epistolary mode at its best.

Miss Parsons published *The History of Miss Meredith* and
the Reverend James Thomson published *The Denial; or, the
Happy Retreat* in 1790. *The History of Miss Meredith* is
merely another of those novels of sentiment in letters in which
tears, violence, and too much sensibility are unwisely inter-
mingled.

Illicit Love, by Mrs. Morris (1791), is an exceedingly sentimental and artificial novel in letters written upon the subject of man's unfaithfulness. It attempts to rise to tragic dignity, but its stylistic excesses succeed in making it merely
maudlin. Mrs. Rowson, an Englishwoman who published
much in America, published in England, in 1791, *Mentoria;
or, the Young Lady's Friend,* an essay-like work in letters
which opens, interestingly enough, with *Verses Addressed to
a Young Lady, on Her Leaving School* and a brief *History of
Mentoria,* before it proceeds to the letters themselves. The
entire work is extraordinarily static.

Anna St. Ives, A Novel, by Thomas Holcroft, appeared in
1792. While this three-volume epistolary novel is full of sentiment and melodrama as excessive as that combination in
most of its companion novels, it is written with a firmness of
expression that places it somewhat higher than many of the
minor epistolary works. Its chief distinction lies in its composition rather than in its story or its spirit. E. Cornelia
Knight is represented by *Marcus Flaminius* in 1792, and
William Hutchinson by *The Doubtful Marriage,* in 1793.
The first is a mere catalogue of opinions and adventures—not

a novel. The second is an ultra-sentimental novel with an amazing lot of dialogue in it.

In *Juliana Ormeston* (1793), subtitled *The Fraternal Victim*, Mrs. Harley has provided herself with a large canvas, teeming with characters and a number of plots all being run conjointly. The author uses all the machinery of the novel of the seventies: there are letters, villains who steal letters and pictures, duped old parents, dainty maidens married to incorrigible rogues, and so on. Yet the style is excellent, and the narrative runs along without any noticeable interruption in any place. There is much in the tone of these letters that comes out of Richardson. The style of letter that Anna Harcourt writes comes out of Richardson's Miss Howe, for instance, and the prototypes of almost all the types of letters here are to be found somewhere in Richardson's three novels.

The Conflict, A Sentimental Tale, in a Series of Letters (1793), places the name of Mr. Heron on the list and, despite the fact that she belongs chiefly to the nineteenth century and is not largely an epistolarian, the name of Maria Edgeworth appears in 1795 with *The Letters of Julia and Caroline*. The same year brings *A Tour to Milford Haven in the Year 1791*, by Mrs. Morgan, a sort of travel story in letters. J. J. Cambar's *Clementina Bedford. In Letters and Narrative*, notable because there is indicated in the subtitle the mixture of letters and narrative, belongs to 1796, and Mrs. Harriet Lee's *Clara Lennox; or, The Distressed Widow. A Novel. Founded on Facts. Interspersed with an Historical Description of The Isle of Man*, to 1797. *Clara Lennox* is distinguished by its large amount of graceful and pleasing description, much of which is far more satisfactory than the story in which it is contained. The novel itself is a sentimental one, and the letters are mediocre and rather given to frequent "laying down of pens" and "taking up of pens." The story works to a rather pathetic conclusion, well sustained and made memorable by the fact that, upon the death of the man she loves, Clara does not faint.

When his death, which took place soon after her quitting the room, was announced to her, she received it without any of those noisy and exclamatory emotions which generally characterize our sex; her bosom heaved with suppressed sighs, and her whole frame was agitated and convulsed; a settled gloom is displayed on her countenance, and her whole deportment too plainly announces the poignant grief which preys on her spirits.[11]

It may be noticed, of course, from what has been said concerning the sentimental novels in letters of this and the preceding groups, that the sentimental novelists of the eighteenth century found two fields of endeavor very fruitful. Either they chose the amours and courtship of young unmarried couples which usually ended happily; or the post-marital affairs of a couple into which jealousy entered. The plight of the "distressed widow" is a rare one among these works. The unmarried state seems to be preferred since it is easier to write a plot in which two young lovers are kept apart, easier to invent ways and means of keeping them apart, and easier to inculcate action into such a plot. Of course, an immediate separation after marriage is sometimes used to great advantage, as is a secret marriage afterwards denied as a marriage at all by the man. Out of all this comes what is perhaps the chief criticism of many of these sentimental novels. These types, as stories, were in themselves very repetitious, and they were, beyond that, overmuch used.

Should there be any doubt by this time of the overwhelming popularity of the epistolary novel of this period, it might be dispelled by a presentation of the fact that the original English novels in letters were not sufficient to glut the desire for such. There were, in addition, translations of a number of novels in letters from the French. Only the more important of these need be considered. Mention has already been made of the translation by Mrs. Frances Brooke, published in 1760, of the *Letters from Juliet, Lady Catesby, to her Friend, Lady Henrietta Campley.* The book itself is extraordinarily dull and, since the giving of histories was at this

[11] *Clara Lennox,* II, p. 205.

time very popular, the author indulged in the practice to a considerable extent. The book itself reverts to *Pamela* for its prototype in the journal quality it employs, which is notably inferior to that of the earlier work. On the other hand, the work is not totally lacking in good qualities, and the author reveals a mastery of the ability to do excellent characterizations in vignettes of single sentences, although this may be the power of the translator. Again, there is a lack of reality in the fact that Lady Catesby, in her passion for writing letters, writes even while her visitors are talking. Nothing happens in this book, and the plot that holds it together is extremely thin and the narrative uninteresting and, indeed, a bit egotistically biased, since there must necessarily be few who can care for every thought that Lady Catesby has, and she seems to record every thought without due regard to its importance. There is, in this work, some analysis of emotions and reasons for actions, and a slight indication of psychological study, but that conflict, so essential to drama, even in a novel, is utterly lacking, even within the soul of Lady Catesby herself. Mrs. Brooke likewise translated another work from the French in *Memoirs of the Marquis de St. Forlaix. Translated from the French of Mons. Framery,* a highly pitched novel of sentiment that moves with considerable speed and is couched in letters, the occasional haste of which, the broken endings, the expression of mental anguish, and the feeling of immediacy, lend the entire novel considerable verisimilitude.

There was translated into English in 1765 *The History of the Marquis de Roselle,* the work of a rather prolific French writer, Mme. Elie de Beaumont (not to be confused with Mme. le Prince de Beaumont, author of *La Nouvelle Clarisse,* 1767). Two other epistolary works translated into English from the French of Mme. de Beaumont are *Letters from Emerance to Lucy,* and *The History of a Young Lady of Distinction.* This Frenchwoman, the translations of whose works seemed to enjoy a considerable popularity in England, wrote chiefly novels of sensibility and used the epistolary form with considerable constancy. The letters attain to a certain degree of reality by their constantly varying length, and those which comprise *The History of the Marquis de Roselle* are not only dated, but likewise note the place from which they were written, as well. This is a pleasant epistolarian, but scarcely a significant one in the panorama of English letter-novelists.

Letters from Elizabeth Sophia de Valière, by Madam Riccoboni, was translated by Mr. Maceuen in 1772. This book is again a sort of combination novel and memoirs, in which there is considerable sentimentality and emotion, but there is also present more than an occasional touch of the French finesse. The letters, too, are relieved of over-monotony by their comparative brevity in most cases. Another rather important translation from the French is that of *The Fatal Effects of Inconstancy; or, Letters of the Marchioness de Syrcé, the Count de Mirbelle, and others* (1772). This is a sort of combination scandal romance and sentimental novel, and it indulges in an unconscionable amount of self-analysis, most of which is of the self-pitying type, before it finally works to its sad and melancholic conclusion. The effect is that of a series of memoirs much more than of a series of letters.

Perhaps the most important of these translations is *Dangerous Connections* (1784), from the French *Liaisons Dangereuses*, by Choderlos de Laclos. This gives us a distinct contrast in many respects to the English novel of sentiment written in letters. It contains less actual sentiment, less true sensibility and more sex, more finesse in the handling of affairs of sex than is to be found in any of the English novels of the 1780's. The proverbial French talent for the handling of *affaires de coeur* exquisitely, is well illustrated by past masters and past mistresses playing, in this book, at their *jeux d'esprits et de coeur*. The English novels of the period are as awkwardly and painfully sentimental in the pursuit of such games as are the German. On the other hand, there is no real characterization in this novel; there is a flood of endless repetition to be found in it; the carrying on of a correspondence between people in the very same castle deprives the book of verisimilitude, and practically nothing at all happens with an almost romantic monotony.

Of peculiar interest is the translation, in 1792, of *The Female Werter*, from the French of M. Perrin. This work, in two volumes, follows closely the story of the German *Werther*, making a woman, instead of a man, the chief figure in the tale. There is here endless sentimentality, a plethora of description, and a ceaseless iteration of the fatal effects of unrequited love. Indeed it would be difficult to find a more completely sentimental representative of the *Werter* series of imitations.

In turning to that large number of epistolary fictional works of the eighteenth century to which there have been assigned the names of no authors, a problem in arrangement is again faced. Because, however, these works indicate clearly the rise and fall of the epistolary novel in the century, it has been thought best to have them divided into the products of separate decades.

The first ten years of the beginnings of the rise of the epistolary novel, 1740-49, the decade in which Richardson first appeared as a novelist, have little to offer us of an anonymous nature. There are some six titles in all: *Sephallisa to Sylvius. A Letter from a Lady in the Country to her Lover in Town* (1743); *Felicia to Charlotte; or, Letters from a Young Lady in the Country, to a Friend in Town* (1744); *The Letters from a Young Painter Abroad to his Friends in England* (1747); *Letters Wrote by a Peruvian Lady* (1748); *The Letters between Sylvia and Philander* (1749); and *The Petticoat-Pensioners* (1749). These volumes are, taken as a whole, not a part of the Richardsonian tradition of the novel or story in letters at all, but remnants of the epistolary impulse to be found among the precursors of Richardson, especially of the travels in letters.

The next decade, 1750-59, shows something of an increase in the epistolary form; it yields about twelve titles in all.

As yet there is no great indication, however, of the epistolary flowering to come, and with the possible exception of *The Memoirs of an Unfortunate Young Nobleman* (1757), all of the works of this decade look back beyond Richardson. There is to be noticed here, on the other hand, the same prevalence of the statement "letters of" in the titles, that was to be seen in the epistolary works of the preceding ten years. There is likewise to be found in these works some attempt at pseudo-reality. *Memoirs of an Unfortunate Young Nobleman* pretends to tell the actual adventures of a young man who has been sent in slavery to the colonies, a fiction founded on fact.

It is not until we reach the decade 1760-69, that we are able to observe a tremendous increase in the epistolary output, during a period almost twenty years after the publication of *Pamela*. Here there may be estimated to be at least thirty-two epistolary titles. Representative[12] of these books may be considered: *Sophronia* (1761); *Letters between Emilia and Harriet* (1762); *The History of Miss Lucinda Courtney* (1764); *The Faithful Fugitive* (1766); *The History of Miss Emilia Belville* (1767); *The History of Miss Pittborough* (1767); *The Distressed Lovers; or, the History of Edward and Eliza. In a Series of Letters* (1768); *The Unexpected Wedding. In a Series of Letters* (1768); *The Exemplary Mother* (1769); *The Fruitless Repentance; or, the History of Miss Kitty Le Fever* (1769); and the *History of Eliza Musgrove* (1769). *Sophronia; or, Letters to the Ladies* is a series of letters from a woman of society in which she narrates a slender story interspersed with the events of the day. The first twelve letters are all from Sophronia and are long and monotonous, nor does this monotony change when the letters begin to alternate between Sophronia and Amoret. This is one of the dullest works of its kind, and there is really no effort made to incorporate into it anything of an exciting nature. The result may easily be guessed at. *The Letters between Emilia and Harriet* is another example of epistles on

---

[12] It is to be noted that the books here presented as representative of the epistolary works by unknown authors, are limited and defined to a large extent by the ability of the author of this work to procure them.

and for important occasions, in which there is but the most slender thread of continuity, here obtained by means of the two writers, and an even slighter thread of fictitious intimation. *The History of Miss Lucinda Courtney* is a good example of the epistolary "history" of the day and is a pleasant concoction of sensibility, mild villainy, and female distress, the high spots of which are a combination of the misfortunes of Clarissa and Miss Harriet Byron. At the conclusion of this novel, however, the heroine, like Miss Byron, is "the happiest woman in England" in the possession of a perfect lover. The letters in which this novel are written are as much like those of Richardson as the author could possibly make them, to the extent, indeed, of an occasional symptom of copy creeping in.

The typical sentimental novel of the age is to be found in *The Distressed Lovers*, full of woes and tears, and ending in the death of the hero. It closes with the significant words: "To the *feeling* reader, few words are forcible; on the *unfeeling* one, the strongest will have no effect."[13] One may judge herefrom what sort of reader certain eighteenth-century novelists asked and expected. *The Exemplary Mother* is likewise a novel of sentiment, but proceeds with considerable force and employs the device of melodrama, which was beginning to be introduced during this decade. *The History of Eliza Musgrove* is much more quiet in its emotions than the usual sentimental novel of its day and succeeds in portraying more sentiment than sentimentality. It likewise rises to a sudden tragic climax of death that is very moving. There is in it something of the domestic novel, and it ends on a note that is distinctly quiet, rather than on one of deep mourning or hysteria, as do so many of its sister novels.

The Faithful Fugitive; *The History of Miss Belville*; *The Unexpected Wedding*; *The History of Miss Pittborough*; *The History of Miss Sommerville*; and *The Fruitless Repentance* are all routine novels of sentiment done in letters, and one is as much an example of the mediocre epistolary novel of the

[13] *The Distressed Lovers*, p. 131.

period as is another. *The History of Miss Pittborough* and *The History of Miss Sommerville* are distinguished by a degree of animation which sometimes passes for humor. They are all, however, excessive in their sentiment and suffer, on the whole, from the fact that their letters are too long for the material they contain. On the other hand, they all represent the spectacle of the epistolary novel as it was gaining hold of the popular mind.

Again we see, in this department of anonymous novels, the notable forward leap of the epistolary novel characteristic of the 70's and 80's almost as soon as we enter those years. For the decade 1770-79 there are some sixty-eight epistolary novels of unknown authorship among the publications of the period. A mere perusal of the titles of this group is sufficient to indicate certain facts. It will be seen that the "histories," "letters," and "memoirs" are still popular, and when not prefixed to the titles often occur in the subtitles. We see how popular was the use of the subtitle itself, and especially the use of the particular subtitle, "history of." The use of the caption, "in a series of letters," is frequent and may be found to be more so if one is to look through the novels with their accompanying full titles (v. Bibliography). Again, many of these works are listed as "novels," the word becoming an indicative part of their heading. It is impossible, likewise, not to notice the extremely sentimental tone of most of these titles, the prevalence amongst them of "distressed," "unhappy," "unfortunate," "self-deceived," "suspicious," and words of similar import, certainly a clear expression of the tendency of this and the early part of the following decade which had been steadily growing for some years since the time of Samuel Richardson.

A consideration of the books themselves involves such divergent and representative works as: *Constantia; or, The Distressed Friend* (1770); *The Maid of Quality* (1770); *The Letters from Clara; or, The Effusions of the Heart* (1771); *The Cautious Lover; or, the History of Lord Woburn* (1772); *Female Frailty; or, the History of Miss Wroughton*

(1772); *The Double Disappointment; or, The History of Charles Marlow* (1774); *The Correspondents* (1775); *The History of Eliza Warwick* (1777); *The Mutability of Human Life; or, the Memoirs of Adelaide, Marchioness of Melville* (1777); *The History of Melinda Harley* (1778); *The Unfortunate Union; or, the Test of Virtue* (1778); *The Letters from Henrietta to Morvina* (1778); *Coxheath Camp. A Novel, in a Series of Letters* (1779); *The Relapse* (1779); and *The Wedding Ring; or, The History of Miss Sidney* (1779).

We may assume the author of the over-tearful *Constantia* to be a woman. This is quite one of the most sentimental works of its kind and indicates that such sentimentality may exist in a book that is, aside from that, very well conceived and written. In contrast to it stands such a book as *The Maid of Quality; or, the History of Lady Lucy Layton* which is a most self-contained and smooth-flowing work and belongs to that group of novels in which the happy ending is allowed the reader after an enforced period of distress. *The Cautious Lover* is a sentimental novel in letters in which there is some animation arising from the presence of something like a convincing brevity in the letters themselves. This is, like *The Maid of Quality*, a novel with a happy ending, the ending being a little eulogy of praise of woman and wife; and, as a whole, the work does not descend to the sentimental depths that are plumbed by some of these novels. We may assume the author to be a man. Even more surprising than the *Cautious Lover* in the brisk and animated fashion of its style is *Female Frailty*, adorned by a most diverting characterization in the figure of the heroine, one of those attractive and self-willed girls so admirably fitted, in novels, to bring down tragedy upon their own heads. This book, written with a certain degree of reality, much emotion of a sincere sort, sympathetic in its general tone, and moving with a remarkable speed to its unhappy close, is by all means to be named one of the very best of this group. Quite in contrast to it is *The Double Disappointment*, one of those epistolary novels that is a miracle of repetition—such repetition as should be spared most readers. There is really nothing at all to distinguish this book except its poorness. It is humdrum, hackneyed in theme, and lacking in strength of diction, characterization, and thematic treatment. Indeed, this is as poor a book as has ever been written (or, worse, published), and the whole of it, presented in 450 pages, could have been done in three. Another one of the less satisfying of these novels in *The Mutability of Human Life*, in which the title is used as a lever to effect ups and downs of the most extravagant sort. The book is further weakened by a pseudo-religious spirit pervading parts of the narrative, which makes the whole rather cheaper than it would otherwise have been. The letters, too, may be said to be not especially well written and inevitability is so violently wrenched in them that even the happy ending seems forced, though it was surely to be expected.

There is considerably more action, more social satire, and more characterization in *Coxheath Camp* than there is in most of these novels, and if the letters are filled with dialogue we are able to forgive this on the grounds of their animation. Although this work is anonymous, the solid competence of it, the admirable characterization, the occasional pseudo-humor, and the fact that it is so intimately concerned with war, seem to ally it to the similar work of Samuel Jackson Pratt. *The Relapse* is distinguished by the fact that certain characters in it, like Mr. Sedley and his wife, are reminiscent of Fielding characters, without the rich humanness of the latter's characterizations. We find a heroine amongst them who would have, in the 50's and 60's, written her "history," but in this decade she presents her story as a "novel" instead. The letters are by no means the least good features of this work. They are, at times, very convincing, as, for instance, the first letter in the series to use exposition. Its sets forth the situation of Miss Hastings succinctly and in an interesting fashion, without waxing too expository. *The Wedding Ring; or, the History of Miss Sidney* is a narrative of considerable liveliness; especially good are the letters from Captain

M'Daniel and Patrick O'Neale (Sir Harry Beaumont). The slightly picaresque tone they lend to this novel is a welcome relief from the excessive sentiment of most of the novels of its decade. There is a quality of "thinking aloud" in the letters here presented, and this is precisely what the epistolary novel should consist of and, incidentally, why the letter resembles, or should resemble, a natural soliloquy. In a letter from Miss Sidney to Miss Woodley (p. 88—the letters in this volume are not numbered) the question is again brought to mind of the device of telling the reader, by some reference, that such and such a letter is missing, and does not appear. This is supposed to lend verisimilitude; but how can we find convincing the absence of this letter or that, when all the others appear, unless we are specifically told, as we are occasionally (as in *Dangerous Connections*, for instance) that the letter has been mislaid or destroyed? All told, this is an excellent novel, somewhat anticipatory of Maria Edgeworth, and continues excellent to the very end. The conclusion has somewhat too much of "and they lived happily ever after" in the mode so popular later in the conclusory chapters of the Victorian novel. Furthermore, the author steps down from his platform, after the fashion of Fielding and Thackeray, only less effectively so; letters are forgotten; and the result is a weakened ending to an otherwise good work.

Just as these three books, along with *Female Frailty*, are representative of the best of this group, so are such works as *The Letters from Clara*; *The Correspondents*; *The History of Melinda Harley*; and *The Unfortunate Union* representative of the most ordinary epistolary publications of the day. *The Letters from Clara* is the usual novel of sentiment of the period here overarticulated in the form of heavily woeful epistles. *The Correspondents* is a monotonous book, too delicately composed, but somewhat surprises its reader by the variety of its letters, short ones and long ones being placed side by side with something of an agreeable effect. A sentimental bit couched in the usual epistolary form is *The History of Melinda Harley*. The only two notable features of this work are that it has humor and that it closes with straight, non-epistolary narrative in which the threads of the story are tied together for the reader. *The Unfortunate Union* is the Richardsonian impulse run riot in the hands of one who does not know how to handle it. As a result, such phrases as "the pearly drop stood in her eye" (p. 319), appear too frequently to ensure any real sort of felicity of expression.

At least two real curiosities are to be found among these books in *The Letters from Henrietta to Morvina* and *The History of Eliza Warwick*. The former is a very late example of the pre-Richardsonian series of travel letters, this time being of "anecdotes historical and amusing of the different courts and countries through which" Henrietta has journeyed and the letters occasioned by what she has observed. *The History of Eliza Warwick* is an even more curious sort of epistolary work. After two or three introductory letters in which Eliza is besought to write her "history" in a letter to her love, the epistolary intent disappears and we have an autobiographical story, or one of memoir type, appearing in its stead. This form grew very popular during the 60's and 70's when the "history" was still a preferred title and the epistolary form was undoubtedly rising to its height. Thus we have here a sort of fusion of two things, but not the satisfactory fusion that we get from the reality of an interchange of letters between two or more people. We are reminded, however, of the fact that this "history" is contained in a letter, by the frequent insertion of "my Lord," and occasionally the style and the tense of a verb may remind us of this otherwise almost forgotten fact.

The next decade, 1780-89, as has already been noted, contains the epistolary peak somewhere around the date 1785. During this period there were published at least seventy-five epistolary novels of anonymous authorship, among which may be seen a distinct decline in the use of "histories," "letters," and "memoirs" in favor of more individual and characteristic titles, and these three words, once so prevalent as leading titles, are now relegated entirely to subtitles or dropped altogether. Likewise the use of the subtitle still remains popular and the predominance of the caption, "in a series of letters," in the title has indisputably increased, especially up to the date 1785.

Typical of this group are such novels as: *Masquerades* (1780); *Colonel Ormsby; or, The Genuine History of an Irish Nobleman in the French Service* (1782); *The Ring, In a Series of Letters* (1783); *The History of Lord Belford and Miss Sylvia Woodley* (1784); *The Confessions of a Coquet* (1785); *The Disinterested Nabob* (1785); *The Nabob* (1785); *The Rencontre; or, the Transition of a Moment. In a Series of Letters* (1785); *Juliana* (1786); *The Letters of Charlotte during her connection with Werter* (1786); *Orlando and Seraphina* (1787); *Death's a Friend* (1788); *Eliza Cleland* (1788); *The Life of Miss Catlane; or, The Ill Effects of a Hasty Marriage* (1788); *The School for Fathers; or, The Victim of a Curse* (1788); *St. Julian's Abbey. In a Series of Letters* (1788); *Argus; The House-Dog at Eadlip* (1789); and *The Predestined Wife. In a Series of Letters* (1789).

Not only has the author of *Argus; The House-Dog at Eadlip* (1789) succeeded in hitting upon a quaint and unusual title but he has created, as well, a rather sprightly novel in letters in three long but interesting volumes. The letters are convincing and true to character and (a rare quality) those written from woman to woman are more sentimental than those from man to man (a proper thing). The story is long, but well sustained; the style varies between the didactic and the philosophic.

There is something of the picaresque romance in *Colonel Ormsby; or, the Genuine History of an Irish Nobleman in the French Service,* which distinguishes it from most of these novels, despite its hysteria and welter of sentimental love and tears. The sense of adventure in its pages succeeds in lifting it above the more mediocre tone to which it might otherwise be limited. *The Nabob* has a preface of considerable interest in which the noses of the critical brethren are pulled with a

lively will. As in so many sentimental novels, so here are the
letters the hero and heroine write as sober in tone as those
written by their parents. Yet this is a well written novel and,
by comparison with many another of this group, is fast moving. In addition to this, it has real wittiness and there is little
excess of sentimentality. The letters themselves are definitely
in keeping with the nature of the characters writing them,
and this is as important to the novel in letters as is the keeping in character of dialogue to a play. When we come to *Eliza
Cleland* we find a book of greater significance than any of
the preceding. The novel opens on a pleasant note of con-
templative quiet and, at the same time, starts to point its
moral almost at once. The introduction of remarks by the
editor is an unusual occurrence. It is a practice distinctly
away from the epistolary form and smacks of the influence
of Fielding. In themselves the remarks are too obvious to
have much interest. Yet this is a well written novel, and its
greatest defect is, perhaps, the so little mingling of the separate plots; each is permitted to wander through its own blithe
course with astonishingly little reference to any of the others,
until they have reached a point at which they fuse only long
after they should have done so. This novel, too, indulges in
an excess of sentiment, despite the fact that it is one of the
better products. Evidently the English had not yet learned
that marvelous self-control which they later acquired. Full
of sentiment and moralizing, some of which it must be said
is extraordinarily good, is *The Predestined Wife*, by the author of *Eliza Cleland*. This novel is every bit as well written
as the latter, and goes far to convince us that the author of
both must have been a woman, perhaps most because both
books are subtly permeated by a feeling that the author is
always on the woman's side of the dispute whenever one
arises, but not so violently on the woman's side as to be
stamped a man. The letters here are too effusive, on the
whole, and suffer from too much "in continuation"; but they
are usually "in the story" and are written with skill and sincerity. *The Life of Miss Catlane* is again a superior book.

The manner in which it opens by having the heroine write to three different people about the same thing seems both ingenious and natural, and to this is added the fact that she has the same thing to tell in a way that is suitable to each and the individual temperament of each. Whoever was the author of this book possessed a rational mind, considerable humor, and a sense of the fitness of things. The first fifty pages of *St. Julian's Abbey* prove that the author has experience and that he knows how to write a novel of sentiment with some sensibility, without becoming too exaggeratedly effusive. The title itself is an excellent Gothic one, but this is not a Gothic novel. (The only known Gothic novel in letters is *The Subterranean Cavern; or, Memoirs of Antoinette de Monflorance*, 1798). *St. Julian's Abbey* ends abruptly, and we cannot help feeling that the author has looked at his *Othello* and his *Julia de Roubigné*; but the story is interesting withal, even though the characters are all patterns. The letters themselves are well done in the letter-and-reply mode and this is, for the epistolary novel, the best possible form.

There seems to be a notable excess of sentimentality among these novels, and *Masquerades; or, What You Will* is an extremely sentimental telling of the dictum that "all the world's a stage, and all the men and women merely players." Its chief distinction lies in the fact that its subtitle and that of Shakespeare's *Twelfth Night* are the same. *The Rencontre* presents a gradual rise from excessive misery to unspeakable happiness through an endless maze of sorrows and difficulties, while *Orlando and Seraphina: A Turkish Story* revels in suffering, the entire effect of which is scarcely edifying. *Death's a Friend* is of the same ilk and is filled with gusts of agony and passion, with the heavy sighs of betrayed innocence and with a conclusory convulsion of sorrow. *The School for Fathers*, which is one of those hybrid works that is partly epistolary and partly in memoirs, is weakened by excess sentimentality and melodrama. Incidentally, the title "school" seems to have been a popular epistolary one in the eighteenth century. In 1763 was published *The School for Wives*; in

1776 was published *The School for Husbands*, a highly sentimental and involved tract against the keeping of mistresses;
and in 1788 came not only *The School for Fathers* but likewise *The School for Tutors*. Finally in 1791 came Clara
Reeve's *The School for Widows*.

Circumlocution is, in addition, one of the outstanding
faults of several of these novels, but in none does it find so
deep a well and fountainhead as in *Juliana*. In reading this
work, one is not impressed by any excessive length of the letters themselves, because of the length of the sentences of
which they are composed. The book contains a great deal of
moralizing; much recitation of "histories," and a considerable amount of character analysis, but there is little plot and
no real characterization. It concludes, however, with the
triumph of virtue and thereby assumes a sort of sanctity.

Representative of the worst of these works is *The Ring*.
This novel requires considerable indulgence, and when we
reach a midway point, at which a conversation heard some
time before is set down with unflinching accuracy after it is
over, that indulgence is likely to break down. Here is a book
in which, although there are elopements, escapes and so on,
very little happens. The characters are negligible chiefly because types are presented as characters. Although not repetitious, the narrative is long, and one must feel that what is
told here could easily have been presented in a much shorter
compass. The art of condensation was not at this time, however, one particularly sought after.

Among these works, *The Disinterested Nabob* is interesting chiefly because it purports to portray actual local color,
in this case the color of India, while *The Letters of Charlotte*
is important because it is one of that number of imitative
novels which were inspired by Goethe's epistolary work, *Die
Leiden des Jungen Werthers* (1774). This English imitation represents the very height of sentiment and suffers not
only from that but also from the fact that only the letters of
Charlotte may be given the reader, the story being thus rendered peculiarly one-sided. It is superior, however, to *The*

Confidential Letters of Albert, from his First Attachment to Charlotte to her Death: from the Sorrows of Werter, another link in the growing Werter series which came in 1790 and *Stellins; or, the New Werter* (1793) which is a slavish imitation of Goethe, full of *mal du siècle,* devoid of anything that might prove of potent interest to the reader, and scarcely worth the paper it was printed on.

The History of Lord Belford and Miss Sylvia Woodley is representative of a hang-over of the "history" literature in letters, written by an author of obviously little talent in a mode for which he had no real gift. *The Confessions of a Coquet* is likewise in this tradition, but there is to be found in this book greater variety because of the occasional appearance of brief letters.

By the time that we come to the last ten years of the eighteenth century we find fewer books of this group than for a period of twenty-five years or so before; the publication of anonymous epistolary works approximates but twenty-seven. Among these we notice a tendency slowly rising of the title to stand alone without any subtitle, or of the caption following the title to be simply "a novel."

We may present here, as representative works, *Hermione; or the Orphan Sisters* (1791); *Memoirs of a Scots Heiress* (1791); *Monimia. A Novel* (1791); *The Vale of Felicity; or, Sylvan Happiness* (1791); *The Fair Imposter* (1792); *Belleville Lodge. A Novel* (1793); *Original Letters of Sir John Falstaff* (1796); *Derwent Priory; or, the Memoirs of an Orphan, in a Series of Letters* (1798); and *Geraldina. A Novel, founded on a Recent Event* (1798).

Among the best of these is *The Vale of Felicity* which, although it is much too saccharine, is smooth and graceful in its writing, pleasant and not too affected. *Belleville Lodge* is likewise a thoroughly good epistolary novel in which the author seems to know his way about in the medium he is using. The letter-and-answer method is employed here, especially in the first part of the book, with considerable success. A good deal of the tone of actuality is incorporated in the letters of *Derwent Priory; or, the Memoirs of an Orphan*, and the epistles which pass between Miss Lumly and Lady Laura are alive and sprightly with the common interests of two women commonly shared. The author of this book is either a woman or is a man endowed with considerable power in drawing imaginary women from his own store of experience of the sex. There is a great deal more in the trifles of this book, the frills and fancies of life, than there is in the love story it presents which characterizes the usual sentimental romance. The technique of breaking off a correspondence at an interesting point, to turn to another one, is used in *Geraldina*. Suspense is thus created in a rather elementary but effective fashion and our interest held to the story. Again, in this novel, we see the convention of the epistolary mode whereby even foreigners must write their letters in English. There is in this book, however, a distinct departure from the convention of the novel of sentiment, in the elopement of Geraldina with a former lover, a matter which bespeaks the growing freedom of women and which would have been almost impossible in a novel of this sort ten years earlier. That Geraldina is execrated for the act does not alter the fact that she did it. The novel is, for 1798, slightly old-fashioned in form, since, as has been shown, the epistolary novel had now passed its day; yet this one is admirably done. *Geraldina* distinctly belongs to the fast fading novel of sentiment rather than to the school of theory or to the school of the Gothic tale, both of which were, at the time of the writing of this novel, growing into great prominence.

Representative of the less satisfactory works are such novels as *Hermione, Monimia,* and *The Fair Imposter. Hermione* has a bit of the "mysterious" in it in the finding of the manuscript in a drawer, a device already employed by Sarah Fielding and Johnstone. The story itself, much of which is told in journal form instead of letters, is a most retarded one, and there is in it a plethora of mere talk. Of course, in such an epistolary novel as this, where a more or less day-by-day chronicle method is employed, we cannot expect crystallization of character, action, or even thought. The copy of *Mo-nimia* which I possess is unopened, certainly an eloquent and just commentary on its popularity. The name Monimia is that of the heroine of Smollett's work, *Ferdinand, Count Fathom* (1753), and also of the heroine of *The Orphan* by Thomas Otway (1680), but any possible reference to the genius of either of these two men stops here. As in *Geraldina*, we see here an example of the epistolary novel after the form had passed its height. *The Fair Imposter* makes use of two of the stock names of the eighteenth century, Mowbray and Beaumont, and the name of the heroine is Clara Howard, the same as that of the heroine of Charles Brockden Brown's epistolary novel bearing that name. The plot of this novel, like that of so many plays, has little to recommend it except an ingenious mixing up of right and wrong. There is no great conflict; no great issue at stake to grip us. Nor are the figures of sufficient stature to impress us with their importance, and thus our interest is scarcely maintained in them to a degree that makes us care. The letters themselves suffer from the same lack of individuality as do the characters.

Even at this late date there is to be found a series of memoirs, and among the books of this decade there was published *The Memoirs of a Scots Heiress* which is not, strictly speaking, epistolary. It is a direct narrative interspersed with a considerable number of letters in the course of the story, given in their proper places. We may see from this that by the time this novel was published and the epistolary novel was on the wane, it was none the less leaving its trace upon the "straight" novel in the form of occasional letters used to add verisimilitude to the story that was being told. Another literary curiosity of this group that is of greater interest than the preceding is that quaint little work *Original Letters of Sir John Falstaff and His Friends; now first made public by a Gentleman, a Descendant of Dame Quickly*. In this thin volume is presented a series of letters to and from most of the characters that appear in the *King Henry IV* plays and *The Merry Wives of Windsor*, by which these figures are reconstructed with loving hands and a knowing mentality. The letters are all written with a subtle appreciation of their supposed writers and a striving to present each after the fashion in which each might have written. Thus, in the letters of Sir Hugh Evans, the same sort of broken English is made use of that appears in the original Shakespeare plays. The result is a little packet of absorbing and lively letters in which a group of figures, to which many of us are devoted, reappears with a striking resemblance to their originals.

This résumé of the history of the epistolary novel in the eighteenth century serves to show, then, its rise on the tidal wave of Richardsonianism; its enormous and rapid popularity moving to a peak at the middle of the ninth decade of the century, and its sudden decline, chiefly because it was overworked, not to extinction but into sudden abeyance, from which it was to leave behind the letter as an almost indispensable literary device and the novel in letters as a literary form to continue from time to time down through English literature to this very present.

As a literary type, the epistolary novel may be compared to the Italian *Commedia dell' Arte* in that in both the actors are supposed to write out their own parts as they go along. Just as a play has the parts and lines ready made for the actor, so has the novel of the "omniscient" point of view. But the epistolary novel may easily give the simulatory effect of developing as it goes along, as needs be, and as occasions arise. Thus, it is akin to the *Commedia dell' Arte*. On the other hand, the epistolary novel must be looked upon as an artificial form, a sort of combination of principal elements, and it is, for that reason, an acquired taste.

It may be gathered from all that has preceded that there are certain conventions in the epistolary novel, just as there are conventions of lights, make-up, an unseen wall and so on in the theatre. In the epistolary novels of the eighteenth century, the history of a certain person is rarely given in his own letters, as is the case in the novels of Richardson. It is usually recited to one of the letter writers, who, in turn, communicates it further. Again, when the letters in the novel reach such a length that we are made to feel that the character must sit up "after hours" to do them, this, too, we must accept. Thirdly, in the epistolary novel the characters write out their own fates, just as they work out their own fates in comedy. Thus, this sort of novel is more strictly allied, in the broader sense of the word, to comedy than to tragedy. Most of the epistolary novels have been seen to deal with the events in the lives of the heroes and heroines that lead up to marriage. Some of them continue after the marriage; some few start with marriage. But for the purposes of sentiment and sensibility, the unmarried state is best adaptable. Further than this, in the best examples of the type, much of the character development or revelation is made clear to us by means of the type of letter the person writes. Of course, those persons in the story who do not write have to be given to us second or third hand, and they are always presented to us colored, one way or another, by the particular view the writer of the letter in which these persons appear takes of them. What character development there is in the majority of these novels, all except the greatest, is to be found in the stern father, the villain, or the reprobatish male or female. The hero and heroine remain virtually unchanged as a rule, and indeed often seem to be so definitely untouched and untainted by all that has happened to them that we are led to wonder if they may not be fools of nature. This is especially true of the heroines.

In most of these novels the characters belong to the upper class of society, though the poor and unsung peasant or peasant girl occasionally appears as background and, in one epistolary novel, *Peggy and Patty; or, the Sisters of Ashdale* (1783) is celebrated as the heroine.

Some word must be said on the side of the verisimilitude captured by those authors who give only the letters and not the replies to them, assuming that they cannot take the personal and omniscient points of view at one and the same time; but the relief afforded to monotony, and the variety and smoothness which the presentation of replies gives to an epistolary work, more than makes up for any seeming lack of reality. Again, the introduction of dialogue into letters in more than snatches is extremely artificial, since the idea of the thought caught on the wing thereby fairly evanesces. We do not feel that we are present at the most intimate moments, as we are when the secret thoughts of the writer are being communicated to paper. In other words, despite the fact that it may break the monotony of continuous letters, dialogue brings us too close to the novel not in letters, and the differences between the two tend to merge.

As may have already been gathered, the type of narrative which is employed in the epistolary novel is usually a very simple one, as is the plot. The story is usually told in a straightforward manner and, though it proceeds with complications, moves to an appointed end with few real complexities. And, indeed, this sort of story is best when it is told that way, for a basically simple thing made needlessly complex is apt to become obviously artificial.

When we grant that the writing of letters to our friends is a natural impulse; when we grant that therein we tell things, we narrate events, gossip, anecdotes; give advice; describe people and places and so on, are we not also granting that the putting together of all these stories might not possibly make a single story? The artificial, or synthetic, quality of it all lies in the bringing together of letters from a varied group of people who have not really logical connection, but seem to be banded together by fate just to suit the purposes of the novelist for the story he happens to have in hand. Herein lies the chief artificiality of the epistolary novel; but it is no greater artificiality, basically, than the omniscience of the author of a novel not in letters, or the knowledge of the playwright behind the scenes in the lives he is about to portray.

Finally, we may arrive at some idea of the tremendous popularity of the epistolary novel when we recall that some "straight" novels (as, for instance, *Henrietta, Countess Osen-*

vor) were divided into letters instead of into chapters. But the popularity of the epistolary novel cannot be better illustrated than by the fact that every author of importance in the eighteenth century used this mode at one time or another, as has already been shown.

VII

THE EPISTOLARY NOVEL IN
ENGLAND SINCE 1800

IN THE course of the preceding chapter it has been stated that the epistolary novel reached its height in England about 1785, after which the fashion for writing novels in the form of letters and correspondences having waned, the graph of the novel in letters may be seen to enter upon a sharp and distinct decline. It has likewise been stated that the epistolary novel left its imprint upon the literature of the day, not only in that it gave the letter to the novel as part of its natural impedimenta, but also in that it made possible the writing, from time to time, of the novel in that particular form. Thus we are able to find, if we investigate the spread of English literature from 1800 to the present day, that there exists, sporadically scattered throughout its vastness, a considerable number of novels and stories in letters. At no period, as will be ultimately seen, may there be said to be a revivification of the epistolary impulse to the extent that it results in a large and concentrated epistolary literature such as has already been found in the eighteenth century. There will, on the other hand, be found several decades in which scarcely an example of the epistolary style is to be recorded. There exists sufficient proof, however, to make with certainty the statement that, even after the period in which the novel in letters ceased to blossom to its fullest extent, it did not die, but has taken its place for almost a century and a half now as a normal form of literature, to be resorted to by the occasional author, from time to time.

To the very opening year of the century belong two epistolary works of fiction, *A Picture of the Age. A Novel* and
*Mordaunt. Sketches of Life, Characters, and Manners, in
Various Countries; including the Memoirs of a French Lady
of Quality. By the Author of Zeluco and Edward* (Dr. John
Moore). Moore had already written letters of a non-fictional
nature for the *Edinburgh Review* before he wrote *Mordaunt*,
which is a curious combination of travel letters, personal history, and foreign scandal. In Volume II (for 144 pages) is presented the "history" (here called the "story") of Madame la
Marquise de—, as narrated by herself to Miss Clifford. The
method used here is that of letter and answer, and indeed
through the entire three volumes the letters are chiefly terse,
natural, and unsentimental. The book is additionally filled
with a large fictional and poetical learning common to its
day. By the time we reach 1804 we have an epistolary novel
which, in the fullness of its bulk, looks back to the novels in
similar form Richardson has given us. This is *The Life of a
Lover. In a Series of Letters* by Sophia Lee, sister to Harriet.
Not only does the title carry us back to the sentimental novel
in letters of the 1770-80's but so, likewise, do the contents of
the six volumes it takes to unfold the story. The first letter
of Volume I opens with the sentence: "The heart of your
Amelia flies, my dear, to embrace and bid you welcome to
your native land! . . ." and this may be said to set the precise
tone of the entire novel. Indeed the author herself, in the
preface to the work, admits that this manuscript, now first
published, which has long lain in her desk, belongs in mood
to another period and has lived on paper through a complete
change in the spirit of literature, a change brought about by
what she calls the "revolutionary system." Although there
is excess of sentiment in the novel itself, it is well written,
the letters achieve some feeling of reality and, when they
diverge into occasional description, it proves to be of a rather
high quality. The reader feels, of course, that Miss Lee was
conscious of almost all the faults of her story, but published
it in spite of them. In *St. Clair; or,The Heiress of Desmond*

(1804), Miss Owenson has given us a lesser epistolary work. This is a sentimental and adventurous novel of some slight skill in presentation and derivative interest in context. The letters themselves, however, give an unfavorable impression of casualness because they are sometimes dated, sometimes addressed, sometimes signed, but most often date, address and signature are all left to the imagination. There was likewise published in 1804 *The India Voyage*, by Mrs. H. Lefanu. This violent novel contains letters that are practically devoid of versimilitude because of their extreme length, their many "in continuations", their failure obviously to address themselves to anyone or be signed by any writer.

Not until the year 1871 was published a work conjectured to have been written in the year 1805. Its title is *Lady Susan*; its author, Jane Austen. Of its original date we must remain uncertain. In the preface to the reprint edition we are told, "The manuscript . . . is not a draft but a fair copy. . . . The watermarks are for the most part of the ornamental kind; but several leaves bear the maker's name, Sharp, and two bear the date, 1805."[1] Of the work itself it may be rightly said that the book is one of Jane Austen's lesser creations, not only in point of size but in point of workmanship as well, when it is compared with the same author's great books. That she early fancied the epistolary mode, which was, by the time of her writing of this, long on the wane, is further indicated by the fact that much of her early work or juvenilia is in letter form. That she is successfully able to carry a story through its entire course in this form is no mean feather in the cap of one for whom the crystal clear stream of lucid narrative ran so supremely well and smoothly. Perhaps the epistolary mode was experimental on the part of the author. Perhaps the fact that Fielding, Fanny Burney, and lesser lights as well, had done their early work in letters while they were feeling about for a method with which to stabilize their talents, may have had some influence here. Whatever else may be said, the experi-

[1] Oxford, 1925.

ment is serious in all respects, and the tongue of the author was not in her cheek as it was when she wrote, *Love and Freindship, Lady Susan,* and so on.

The letters, as they appear here, are not overstrained or overwritten; they are always in character, and they do not show any glaring inconsistencies. Lady Susan herself, though less sharply drawn, reminds one in her resourcefulness and eloquence of Thackeray's Becky Sharpe. Here, again, the terrific sentimentality possible in such a story was avoided.

Love and Freindship, not published until 1922, is, like E. S. Barrett's *The Heroine* (1813), a satire on the sentimental novel. One must read this little work of Jane Austen to appreciate it fully, since it is brimming with humor of the true Austen tang. As a burlesque of the novel of sentiment, *Love and Freindship* is far more hoydenish and in the Fielding tradition than is the more vaunted *Northanger Abbey* with its take-off of Gothic moods and scenes. The very dialogue here, ridiculous in character and in itself, catches the movement, the conscious hysteria, and the well-poised suffering found in the dialogue of the sentimental novel at its height, the period at which, in all probability, Miss Austen began to read. The form, genre, and spirit of the sentimental novel are all delightfully and accurately satirized; even the use of the letter itself is satiric and the result almost masterful. As such a satire, it must take its rightful place with *Shamela, The Female Quixote,* and *The Heroine.*

Jane Austen's unfinished novel in letters, *Lesley Castle,* is, as far as it goes, not nearly so interesting or amusing as *Love and Freindship,* nor does it retain its pace, first set, of high wit and not-too-gentle satire. It is unfair, however, to render any sort of fixed judgment of a fragment. In *Lesley Castle* we have the method of letter and reply used by the author; in *Love and Freindship,* Laura writes all of the letters with the exception of the first. *Lesley Castle* gives the same events from different points of view and is thus in the manner of the best epistolary novels. To cap the climax, as it were, Jane Austen has given us her parody of the Richardsonian letter-writer in *A Collection of Letters,* in which a gently satiric method is employed with considerable effect, and the heavily didactic tone of most letter-writers is thereby admirably burlesqued. Among Jane Austen's scraps is to be found another fictional letter, *The Female Philosopher,* along with two epistolary bits, "A Letter From a Young Lady, whose feelings being too strong for her Judgment led her into the Commission of Errors which her Heart Disapproved," and "A Tour Through Wales—in a Letter from a Young Lady," a burlesque of the travel letter. It may be claimed, then, beyond the shadow of a doubt, that in the earliest work of Jane Austen the epistolary mode predominated.

There was published as early as 1805 an English translation of that important French novel in letters, Madame de Staël's *Delphine.* A year later came Maria Edgeworth's contribution to the epistolary works of the nineteenth century, *Leonora.* This is a sentimental novel and does not rank, by any means, with her Irish stories. In it Miss Edgeworth has none the less employed restraint with the result that her most emotional moments are more moving than they might otherwise be. The letters themselves possess a considerable degree of animation and betray the author of real ability at every turn.

The celebrated "Monk" Lewis, Matthew Gregory, has given us an epistolary novel that is likewise a Gothic romance, but it is not original with him. *Feudal Tyrants; or, The Counts of Carlsheim and Sargans. A Romance* (1806), is a tale of the Gothic school adapted from the German and published in four volumes. It is filled with the trappings of the school and is but condescendingly epistolary. To the same year belongs *The Wild Irish Girl, a National Tale,* by Miss Owenson. This is a highly sentimental and energetic work and depends upon its descriptive beauties for its chief claims to distinction. It has, however, a distinct "national" color which renders it partially noteworthy. *Helen; or, Domestic Occurrences,* by Augusta Ann Hirst, likewise belongs to 1807. The work itself is a pedestrian creation in two volumes and most of the letters in which it is written are as lengthy as the list of subscribers with which the novel is prefixed.

Three epistolary novels, *Christina*; *Leontina*; and *The Spirit of "The Book,"* are brought to light in 1809. *Christina; Princess of Wolfenbuttel: by the author of Caroline of Lichtfield* (Thomas Holcroft), is a translation, or adaptation, from the German. It opens with numerous fragments of a long journal (*Memoirs of a German Princess*), becomes epistolary about midway through the first volume, returns to the journal, and then becomes epistolary for the entirety of its second volume. There is but little real distinction here between journal and letter, and indeed the letters sound peculiarly like a mere addressed journal. *Leontina* is another epistolary translation, this time from the German of Augustus von Kotzebue, the novelist and playwright who has been so popular in adaptation upon the American stage, even so late as the early twentieth century. *Leontina* is a sentimental novel in letters of no particular distinction. *The Spirit of "The Book"; or, Memoirs of Caroline Princess of Hapsburg, a Political and Amatory Romance. Edited by Thomas Ashe, Esq.* is another of the same ilk. It need scarcely be said that this "amatory romance" is of an excessively sentimental sort.

To the year 1810 belongs the *Letters from Mrs. Palmerstone to Her Daughter; Inculcating Morality by Entertaining Narratives,* by Mrs. Hunter of Norwich. This work, which is a sort of glorified letter-writer, full of didacticism and warning, is rather rare in the period of its publication and is, indeed, a definite flash-back to the beginning of the eighteenth century. It is such matters as these that prove revolution in literature to be more a question of progression than of destruction, and we are able to find pre-revolutionary types appearing long after they have been considered dead. Another early eighteenth-century title is to be found in *Memoirs of a Princess; or, First Love. An Historical Romance,* by Olivia W. S. (1812). The historical novel in letters is rather rare in England, and herein lies the chief distinction of this work, which is, however, more sentimental than historical. The close of the story, with its solitary figure awaiting doom on a lonely rock, surrounded by storm and night, is very much in the tradition of the Gothic school of writing.

Entirely different from many of these epistolary productions is that which belongs to the year 1813, *The Heroine,* by Eaton Stannard Barrett. The full title of this book is *The Heroine; or, Adventures of Cherubina,* and the motto is, interestingly if not truly, *L'Histoire d'une femme est toujours un Roman.* This book belongs to the group that includes *The Female Quixote* and *Love and Freindship* in that it satirizes romance and sentiment. It is, in genre, the same sort of satire as *The Female Quixote,* although Mrs. Lennox seems to have written a satire that is truer and less amateurishly insistent because here the heroine is made to mock at herself, and that is hardly conducive to thinking her a sincere "heroine," while the heroine of Mrs. Lennox' satire is entirely serious in her folly. *The Heroine* is rather doggedly cast into the form of letters and even the memoirs are sent by means of letters, just as they are in Mrs. Sarah Scott's *Millenium Hall.* There is an amusing touch of satire employed when Cherry continues to write to Biddy even after she realizes that Biddy has been the instigator of all her troubles. The novel must go on!

After the first few letters, there is nothing really epistolary here save that the chapters are titled "letter." It is all more truly an autobiography. Certainly this novel is sufficient to prove that the autobiographical story is not made more plausible by being cast in letter form so arbitrarily as it is here. There is too much action and too little real stress and, even though the result is supposed to be satire, the result is definitely artificial beyond the demands of the form. This might be called a good epistolary novel only in that the narrative runs so smoothly and so swiftly, but it is in the very fact that the novel moves too swiftly for epistolary narrative that the chief weakness of *The Heroine* lies.

Catherine Hutton has, in *The Welsh Mountaineers* (1817)

and *Oakwood Hall, A Novel; including a description of The Lakes of Cumberland and Westmoreland, and a Part of South Wales* (1819), contributed two epistolary novels to the category. These two novels reveal a minor writer of distinct quality and ability and one who has leaned chiefly toward the epistolary mode in her fictional work. The letters, although they do not particularly smack of inevitability, are lively and readable, especially in *The Welsh Mountaineer*, though the very thing which contributes most to their liveliness, the dialogue, tends to rob them of their reality as letters. In fact, the letters of both novels have rather too much recorded dialogue in them. Although there is something of the fashionable world in both *The Welsh Mountaineer* and *Oakwood Hall*, it is the pictures they present of the countryside, rich with a plausible local color, that are their chief distinction. The local characters are, likewise, particularly convincing and diverting.

In 1818 was published *A Year and a Day*, a novel by Madame Panache. This novel presents a hybrid form of narrative and letters. It is divided into chapters, many of which are entirely in letter, some partly narrative and partly in letter, some entirely narrative. As a result, so definitely narrative in tone are the letters, that the entire novel loses its epistolary semblance and seems to be a "straight" narrative product. This is noticeable of many such novels of the period, and it is especially true of the works of lesser writers.

John Galt, in *The Ayrshire Legatees; or, The Pringle Family* (1821), has handled exactly this situation with considerable aplomb. He has divided his novel into chapters, but each chapter contains a series of letters (all of which possess a continuity of numbering throughout the volume) which do not seem to be a mere continuing of the narrative style but actual letters. John Galt shows himself in this single device, as well as in the writing of the novel itself, one of the better authors represented here and one to be placed beside Maria Edgeworth, whom he resembles in many respects, especially in that of the successful presentation of local color. *The Ayr-*

shire Legatees belongs to what may be considered his West Country series of works, the creations for which he is still memorable. There is humor here and characterization, and a Scotch persistence of philosophy which makes for simple, unadorned reality. The letters themselves are natural and plausible; they fill their rightful place in the novel and seem entirely a part of it rather than something superimposed upon the story for the sake of some nameless effect. Beyond that, they are letters in every sense of the word and in every possible aspect and characteristic. John Galt has given us another epistolary work in *A Rich Man* (1836), a short story in letters. This is an interesting experiment, and the mechanism whereby the author produces all the effect of concentration usually to be found in the short story by means of letters which are, in most works, the indication of diffuseness, bears close examination. The book is a sort of autobiography in letters of the "late Lord Mayor of London," a Scotchman. It is again full of good Scotch sense and biting humor and seems to fall into the form of letters with the utmost and most satisfying ease.

Perhaps the most distinguished name to be found among authors of the nineteenth and twentieth centuries who have done some sort of epistolary work is that of Sir Walter Scott. He has written, in *Redgauntlet* (1824), a novel of an abortive Jacobite rebellion of c. 1765 under the leadership of "Redgauntlet," an irreconcilable partisan of the House of Stuart. As originally published in three volumes, the work comprised three different kinds of novel form. The first volume was in letters; the second was a diary; the third was narrative. In more recent editions, of course, all three volumes are presented as one. None the less, about one third of this speedy and adventurous novel is in the epistolary form. The letters themselves, although somewhat more vigorous than is the case of most of the epistles of eighteenth-century fiction, with the exception of those of such writers as Fielding, Frances Burney, and Smollett, are carefully composed by Scott with an eye to the eighteenth-century tone, and carry off the manners of that period with considerable success. The novel, taken as a whole, is not one of Scott's best; moreover, it suffers something in continuity because of its several changes of form. None the less, it is valiant, if not brilliant; absorbing, if not breath-taking; delightful, if not entirely convincing.

It is interesting to find an author like Bulwer Lytton, romanticist par excellence, using the letter form so long after the greatest vogue of the letter, never particularly well adapted to romance, was past. We find this use in *Falkland* (1827). Unlike Scott, Bulwer carries the epistolary form through to the end in this novel. Like Scott, however, he makes use of three forms: letters, diary, and narrative. The difference between the efforts of the two authors lies in the fact that here the three forms are not separated, but are intertwined.

The first few letters of this novel are all from one person, Erasmus Falkland, to his friend Frederick Monkton, and serve to build up a "history" of Falkland in true eighteenth-century style. At the conclusion of these few, however, the number of correspondents increases. The author introduces stop-gap narrative from time to time, in which events are told the reader which would take many more pages were they in letter form than they do in the form of "straight" narrative. We may conclude from this that condensation of time was perhaps more important in 1827 than it had been in 1777. The mixed style again causes a lessening of inevitability because, while the letters assure us of the reality of the writer and the recipient, the intrusion of the author as narrator makes us feel less certain of the reality of the corresponding characters. The parts of this novel written in letters are much more hectic and inflammatory than the parts of the novel written in narrative. Yet the character analysis that Falkland gives of himself is, despite this, excellent, especially in the early letters. No one of the other characters emerges as more than a type. The whole story has a certain unity, lent it by the love of Falkland for Emily, but it is, in total effect, something of a patchwork quilt: not a true novel in narrative; not a true epistolary novel, either.

Different from *Falkland* in that it is entirely epistolary, but like *Falkland* in that it is romance (indeed, it is more truly romantic in setting than the previous novel) is *Pericles and Aspasia* (1836), by Walter Savage Landor, a novel in letters set in classical splendor. Its very tenderness of beauty renders it a work of but small range and appeal; it seems to be only for those who conceive beauty in their own minds to be something akin to what is presented here. This is a work written with the utmost exquisiteness and delicacy. As an epistolary work, the book is of particular interest because the author shows so plainly in it his knowledge of the letters of the eighteenth century. Landor prefaces the book with an *Advertisement* that begins, "He who opens these Letters for a History of the Times, will be disappointed," and that is strikingly similar in tone to the Richardson prefaces to his great epistolary works. In *Pericles and Aspasia* the letters themselves lack reality; but this is not because of any fault in them, but rather that they partake of the tone of unearthly beauty that pervades the whole of this sensitive creation.

A far less artistically successful effort, and one that is not particularly successful from an epistolary point of view, either, is Anne Brontë's novel, *The Tenant of Wildfell Hall*, published in 1848. Again, this combines the epistolary and the narrative methods, and so undistinguished are the letters as letters that they seem to be but part of the entire narrative, distinct from it in no major respect, and the ultimate effect of the whole is one of narrative in the first person.

One of the most completely delightful of the epistolary works of the nineteenth century is, *The Dodd Family Abroad* (1853-54), by Charles Lever. It is amazing how little this story dates in spite of the obvious factors involved which do date a book, particularly that of the description of contemporary manners. But perhaps the vivacity of style, the true readings of human nature, the vitality of the people who stand forth fully and admirably from their letters—these keep the book young. Moreover, as one reads on in this book, he cannot help being struck by the extraordinary naturalness of it. Each character writes "in character," even to the girl who tries with but half success to assume the worldly air of the Continent. Indeed, from the very first line of the first letter,[2] we are struck by this quality of naturalness that is both undeniable and refreshing, the very quality which makes Richardson's works and *Humphrey Clinker* so good.

The arrangement of the letters, each to a close friend of the writer, may be paralleled with that of the letters in *Humphrey Clinker*. Here, too, even the maid writes. The story is set in the best tradition of the epistolary novel, again as we have it in *Humphrey Clinker*, by having the events discussed from different points of view, in different letters descriptive of the same events. It is just such a case as this, in the final analysis, the history of the adventures of a family abroad reporting to friends, dear friends, at home, in which the epistolary form is most logical. *The Dodd Family* has, as a work in letters, a quality of epistolary inevitability that is not always attained in these novels of later date and, indeed, in some of the less effective works of the epistolary flowering itself. It might well be added that some of the letters in this book have a distinct eighteenth-century flavor, especially such a one as Letter X, from Caroline Dodd to Miss Cox, at Miss Mincing's academy, Black Rock, Ireland, which is a true Richardsonian epistle.

Between the dates of the appearance of the *Dodd Family Abroad* and 1890 there is an amazing lack of epistolary fiction. During these dates the English novel flourished, but the novel in letters seems to have fallen into desuetude. Indeed, there seem to be but two works of any importance composed in the letter form, and both of these were written and one appeared in parts, many years before they were published in book form. These are *The Ramsbottom Letters* (1872), and *Mr. Brown's Letters to a Young Man About Town* (1853).

---

[2] Dear Tom,—Here we are at last—as tired and sea-sick a party as ever landed on the same shore! Letter I, p. 18.

In their 1872 publication *The Ramsbottom Letters,* by Theodore Hook, represent a reprint; they were originally contributed to *John Bull,* somewhere around 1827-29.[3] They are a series of travel letters from one Dorothea Ramsbottom, who is a sort of female Dogberry or nineteenth-century Mrs. Malaprop in her use of the English language, and fills her letters with quaint quips and observations. As a Cambridge undergraduate, Thackeray wrote several essays which he signed Dorothea Ramsbottom, parodies of Hook's work, but these were not in the form of letters.[4] William Makepeace Thackeray's *Mr. Brown's Letters to a Young Man About Town* are, however, supposed to be essays in the form of letters. They do not take the trouble to be addressed or signed; each essay is a separate entity in a separate letter; finally, if we look at such titles to these letters as, "On Tailoring," "On Friendship," "A Word About Balls in Season," "Great and Little Dinners," we may readily see how definitely they are familiar essays with a didactic turn of character and how slightly they are actual letters of any degree of verisimilitude. The dearth of epistolary material during the period previously mentioned is not relieved by the appearance of these two epistolary works.

Of slight epistolary interest is *Mohammed Benani* (1887), an anonymous novel distinguished by the fact that there are, in its context, six lengthy letters, each one making a single chapter of the tale, and written by one of the characters, Frank Weston. The major portion of the story is straight narrative.

With the beginning of the 1890's we find a notable return of the fictional work in letters, the period from 1900 to 1909 being especially full. This may be at least partly attributed to a revival of interest in the eighteenth century under the guiding influence of such lovers of it as Austin Dobson and, perhaps, Edmund Gosse. Perhaps, also, the residuum of sentiment now become self-conscious and developing ironic traits

---

[3] Myron F. Brightfield, *Theodore Hook and His Novels,* Cambridge, 1928, pp. 166, 331.
[4] *Ibid.,* p. 331.

from the mid-century, and the intensive study of literary history combined to show intending writers of a certain kind a mold for expressing thoughts which should have the sort of brittle charm and artistic appropriateness then so delicately cultivated.

The decade opens, from an epistolary point of view, with Charles Francis Keary's *A Mariage de Convenance* (1890), a rather pathetic story of a selfish man and the woman who devotes her life to him with distressing results. But one of the most interesting books to be found here is *Love Letters of a Worldly Woman* (1891), by Mrs. W. K. Clifford, which presents, in three different correspondences, "A Modern Correspondence," "Love Letters of a Worldly Woman," and "On the Wane," the amatory adventures of three women whom the author calls, in the preface to her work, "women who loved the world . . . the round world itself and the people who belong to it." The letters themselves tell their stories with a great deal of literary magnetism. The third correspondence, "On the Wane," which tells of a young man who jilts a girl and then returns to her, only to find she no longer loves him, is particularly fine and is done with a feeling of ironic reality that gives it considerable dramatic power. As epistolary efforts, the correspondences here recorded are of the very best. Distinctly less good is *A Fellowe and His Wife* (1892), by Blanche Willis Howard and William Sharp, although it has some pathos and a little beauty. As a purely epistolary work it is interesting from an experimental viewpoint. The two chief correspondents are the Count Odo von Jaromar and Countess Ilse von Jaromar. The letters of the Count were written by Blanche Willis Howard; the letters of the Countess by William Sharp. It can only be said that the results are not especially distinguished.

From its very subtitle, which is *Being a Series of Sixteen Letters Written by J. Stark Munro, M.B., to his Friend and former Fellow-Student, Herbert Swanborough, of Lowell, Massachusetts, during the Years, 1881-1884,* A. Conan Doyle tries to invest *The Stark Munro Letters* (1894), with a tone of actuality. The story itself, which is a sad one, is effectively told without being the least degree overwrought. The letters as such are somewhat less satisfactory. There are but sixteen of them in a space of over three hundred pages; they are almost all of equal length and are literally packed with dialogue. This, therefore, like so many of the novels which adopted the epistolary method and form by concentrating upon a single correspondent, tends to become almost a narration in the first person.

An epistolary curiosity is to be found in *Wandering Heath* (1895), a series of stories, studies, and sketches by "Q." This is *Letters from Troy, Addressed to Rasselas, Prince of Abyssinia*. There are two of these satirico-literary letters; the first is called "The First Parish Meeting," the second "The Simple Shepherd." They are both of but mild interest and hardly of any significance in a consideration of epistolary fiction. To 1896 belongs *The Saltonstall Gazette*, by Mrs. Ella Fuller Maitland, a series of essays done in the graceful and polished manner of the eighteenth century, and connected by a slight thread of personal reminiscence.

It is of particular interest that that celebrated thriller, *Dracula* (1897), by Bram Stoker, which is so curious a compound of psychology, melodrama, and pseudo-scientific nonsense, should have been written partly in letters and partly in journal. In a sort of foreword at the beginning of the work, the author attempts to add to the actuality of the collection by means of Richardson's device of pretending to be but the arranger of existing material that has somehow fallen into his hands. The correspondents are many and include the unhappy Lucy, Mina Murray, Dr. Seward, and Van Helsing; and almost all of the correspondents, with the notable addition of Jonathan Harker, keep some sort of diary or journal. The most unusual is, of course, Dr. Seward's phonograph diary, spoken by Van Helsing. Unlike the story itself, which is most convincing when read with tongue in cheek, although the author did not write it so, the letters and journal are extraordinarily convincing and seem to be entirely what they are made to represent. In their fullness; their attention to detail; their differences in style with each different correspondent; their record, not only of the main thread of terror in the story but also of the small excursions of human life and thought, they seem to acquire a sort of eighteenth-century completeness. Whatever the tone and substance of the story, the technique is excellent.

Again, in *The Etchingham Letters* (1899), we find a literary correspondence which, like *A Fellowe and His Wife*, is a collaboration. The authors are Sir Frederick Pollock and Ella Fuller Maitland. The two do not seem to have made any obvious division of labor, but to have written together in all the letters regardless of the pretended writer. There is a definite eighteenth-century tone to this book. Of special interest is the fact that it is prefaced with a list of the chief persons of the letters (some fifteen in number) in the true Richardsonian manner. Not all of the characters write letters here. The two chief correspondents are Miss Elizabeth Etchingham and her brother Sir Richard Etchingham. The letters themselves are at all times dignified and befitting writers of the rank and breeding of these characters; sometimes they are both learned and scholarly. In the same year as that in which these letters were published appeared *Like Another Helen*, by "Sydney Carlyn Grier" (Hilda Gregg). This is a story in letters of India in the eighteenth century, concerning itself with the affair of the Black Hole of Calcutta (1755-57), and is the correspondence between two girls. The book is chiefly notable because of the resemblance of one of the girls to Clarissa Harlowe and because the author has succeeded in reproducing the language and atmosphere of the century in which her story is laid with remarkable accuracy and plausibility. Perhaps the influence of such Richardson publications as *The Works of Samuel Richardson*, edited by Leslie Stephen (London, 1883), and *Sir Charles Grandison*, condensed in two volumes by George Saintsbury (London, 1896), is to be found in the Richardsonian tendencies of such works as the immediately preceding.

In the very last year of the nineteenth century was first published *An Englishwoman's Love Letters*, the author of which is Laurence Housman. This may be considered the modern *Love Letters of a Portuguese Nun*. The opening sentence of the first letter, "Beloved,—This is your first letter from me: yet it is not the first letter I have written to you. There are letters to you lying at love's dead-letter office in this same writing . . . ," sets a tone to the book that is strikingly like that of the *Portuguese Letters*. The *Englishwoman's Love Letters* are the longer of the two, the less truly pathetic and the more persistently saccharine. It is the warrior mother alone of the whole story that is memorable. Quaintly enough, the history of the seventeenth-century publication was further paralleled by this at the dawn of the twentieth, for in 1901 came *The Missing Answers*, the full title of which is *An Englishman's Love Letters. Being the Missing Answers to an Englishwoman's Love Letters*. One is reminded of the earlier answers of the "cavalier" to whom the nun's letters were addressed. It is, however, but a fleeting parallel. The later work is anonymous, the device used being the publication, by the friend of the heroine, of the letters from the lover. As used, this device itself is not very convincing and, as for the letters, they form a peak of early twentieth-century sentimentality. The style is flabby, superficial, and even a little childish at times; the whole tone borders upon the ridiculous. But it is interesting to note that there are, at about this time, a rather large number of epistolary novels of sentimental intent, extending throughout the ensuing four or five years. Kin to the two works just mentioned is, *The Letters Which Never Reached Him* (1900), by Elizabeth A. Heyking. They, too, record a hopeless passion ultimately ended by death. Here, however, there is only unforeseen separation, not abandonment. These letters are better done than those of either of the two preceding books and, although extremely sentimental, are relieved by an occasional faint glimmer of humor.

Very much in the manner of the eighteenth-century intimate fictional correspondence is *The Letters of Her Mother to Elizabeth* (1901), by William Rutherford Hayes Trowbridge. They concern themselves with very little indeed, but reveal the soul and wit of a fashionable woman in a thoroughly piquant and lively manner. There is real brilliance to be found here, and the letters may well be claimed as representative of the very best of their kind. *Rosa Amorosa* (1901), by "George Egerton" (Mrs. Golding Bright), is another sentimental record of the letters of a woman in love. Here again is to be found that exaggeration of emotion peculiar to so many of these love correspondences and the ornate nothingnesses which make the reality of feeling over into the birthday-cake artificialities of sentimentality. To this sentimental group likewise belongs the anonymous *Letters of an Actress* (1902).

Another name that belongs with this sentimental group is one of peculiar renown, Elinor Glyn. Three of her works are epistolary: *The Visits of Elizabeth* (1901); *Elizabeth Visits America* (1909); and *Letters to Caroline* (1914), called in America *Your Affectionate Godmother*. All three of these are representative of the distinctly third-rate novels of their time, effusive, sentimental, and unreal. They tell, for the most part, of the adventures of a flighty young girl, the ideal heroine of the day, both abroad and in America, and end with love and kisses. Once the reader is able to accept the heroine as a real creation, he is able to feel that the letters, too, are realities, for they are distinctly "in character" and contain several truly amusing passages. To this group likewise belongs *Matilda's Mabel* (1903), by Neil Lyons, but there is no more distinguished author represented in the sentimental epistolary novel of the earliest years of the twentieth century than is Algernon Charles Swinburne. It is of peculiar significance that one of the greatest of the late Victorian poets should have, in the writing of a novel, made use of the epistolary mode. Although published in 1905, *Love's Cross-Currents* does not really belong, in point of writing, to this period, but rather to the earlier period of Swinburne's youth.

Theodore Watts-Dunton, as the poet tells us in the dedication of this book, resurrected the work when the author had almost forgotten its existence, and Swinburne thereby begs indulgence for the novelistic creation of his earlier days. The subtitle of this work is *A Year's Letters*, and the book is thus given a temporal limit. The novel itself is really excellent, not because of the course of human events that it unfolds particularly, but rather because of the youthful vigor, the feeling for character, the sentimental sympathy, and yet the liveliness with which the story is told. *Love's Cross-Currents* sounds, in its entirety, peculiarly unlike the novel of a poet and strikingly like the novel of a novelist or, perhaps more accurately, the novel of a dramatist. There is much characterization of a penetrating quality in the book and a good deal of carefully handled dramatic conflict. The letters themselves are vivacious and convincing and, at all times, "in character." There are five important correspondents, and all are faithfully indicated by the letters they write. The impetuous lover sounds like an impetuous lover when he writes, and so on; and the letters of Lady Midhurst are a lasting delight. Beyond all this, one is made to feel that the use of the letter form is here the properest medium for the story presented, and that is one of the acid tests of the fitness of the epistolary mode to any given material.

It will be seen, of course, that practically no year of this decade, 1900-1909, fails to produce examples of the epistolary art, and the fact that a work written earlier, as was *Love's Cross-Currents,* should be published at this time, seems to bespeak not only the distinction of Swinburne in 1905, but the favor that was given the novel in letters as well.

The Life, Treason, and Death of James Blount of Breckenhow, Compiled from the Rowlestone Papers, and edited by Beulah Marie Dix (1903), is again a collection of realistic letters telling (with a vigorous attempt at pseudo-actuality on the part of the "editor") the story of a family. The book closes with a personal relation, but the greater part is epis-

tolary. The title and "editing" are both truly in the eighteenth-century manner.

A distinguished name in the world of letters is to be recorded in the next epistolary novel, not a member of the
group of sentimental novels just discussed. The name is that
of George Moore, and the novel is *The Lake* (1905). This
novel is, of course, not entirely epistolary; about one-half of
it is told in "straight" narrative. But the letters, of which
there are many, are a very natural part of the story and, far
from intruding, seem indispensable as a part of the revelation of the soul struggle of Oliver Gogarty. The characters,
certainly the two leading characters of Father Gogarty and
Rose Leicester (Nora Glynne), not only reveal themselves
fully in the letters they write, but are likewise helped to
express themselves fully to the eye of the reader by these letters. Moore makes occasional use of editing the letters presented so that not all of a single letter, in some cases, appears, but rather extracts from that letter are given. The
effect is an entirely satisfactory one, and we feel willing to
rely upon the literary shrewdness of the author to do our
eclecting for us as he writes. The inevitability of the letters
is here made possible by the separation of the two people
between whom they are chiefly exchanged while the bonds
of attachment between them are still at their strongest. Although one feels instinctively that Moore would not have
been successful with the entirely epistolary novel, yet the
use made of letters in *The Lake* is purposeful and complete.

In Vernon Lee's *Hauntings* (1906, 2nd ed.), a collection
of four long tales, two of the pieces are epistolary. These
are: "Dionea, from the Letters of Doctor Alessandro De Rosis
to the Lady Evelyn Savelli, Princess of Sabina," a mysterious
and pseudo-medieval tale, somewhat Hawthorne-like in plot
and construction and full of learned references; and "Oke of
Oakhurst; or, the Phantom Lover" a fantastic, melodramatic
story of a strange woman. The latter is rather absorbingly
written, but neither of the two stories preserves the proper
epistolary illusion.

In 1906, "T.B." (Arthur C. Benson) published *The Upton Letters,* a rather pedestrian correspondence that is full of philosophical comment and literary criticism, rather than of anything of a fictional tendency. In the same year was published, *Listener's Lure* by E. V. Lucas, a well-written book of solid English characteristics. From an epistolary point of view, it is of interest because it makes use of the telegram on several occasions. It makes use, in addition, of brief headings to some of the letters in order to give the reader knowledge of letter omissions, or of failure on the part of the writer to post the letter. This author has given us three other epistolary works in "Life's Little Difficulties" (1907) ; *The Vermilion Box* (1916), and *Verena in the Midst* (1920). "Life's Little Difficulties" is a short piece in *Character and Comedy,* which is a series of short stories. *The Vermilion Box* is a novel of the perplexities of the War in England which is presented in a series of letters that attain to an almost perfect degree of verisimilitude, especially those of "Granny." Likewise a novel is *Verena in the Midst. A Kind of Story.* In this Mr. Richard Haven reappears from *The Vermilion Box,* and there are any number of other well-drawn characters. The book itself is full of a quiet charm. That pleasant author, Mary Annette, Gräfin von Arnim, has written an epistolary novel in *Fräulein Schmidt and Mr. Anstruther* (1907). It is full of the sly, quiet wit, the solid sense and the true feeling for people and life that characterizes most of the work of this author, and the letters themselves, although they have somewhat too much dialogue in them, are intelligent and diverting examples of the fictional epistle used to tell a continuous story.

A particularly enlightening sort of epistolary fiction is *An Ocean Tramp* (1908), by William McFee, in that the only indication of epistolary quality lies in the fact that the author tells us in his preface that the book is in letters. Furthermore, the original title of the volume was *The Letters of an Ocean Tramp.* There is but little indication in the book itself, however, that it is composed of letters; the effect is that of a journal, rather than of a series of epistles. This shrewd and penetrating study of a vagabond is splendidly done, but the author seems to have somewhat mistaken his form in designating it epistolary. In this year was likewise published, *When All the World Is Young,* by Reginald Lucas, in which the course of a young man from Eton to Parliament is traced in letters from a scholarly and wise father.

An eighteenth-century subtitle is to be found in *Uncle's Advice. A Novel in Letters,* by William Hewlett, published in 1909. In the same year was published *Set in Silver,* by C. N. & A. M. Williamson, one of the most delightful of epistolary works, which is chiefly a romance recorded on a motor trip through the British Isles. The letters are very much in the modern medium, impetuous in style and occasionally abbreviated in expression. Most of the letters are from young Audrie Brendon and are accurately young-girlish in tone. But even those that are not written by Audrie are full of wit and flow with a remarkable speed, and they are all encouragingly "in character." If there is any fault to be found with them, it is that there is a "smartness" in all, just as there is in almost all of the speeches of almost all the characters created by Wilde. There is to be found, however, in the very first letter an extremely revelatory remark concerning letter writing, and it is, "Isn't it funny, when you have a lot to tell, it's not half as easy to write a letter as when you've nothing at all to say, and must make up for lack of matter by weaving phrases?" No more accurate criticism of the epistolary mode is to be found anywhere.

To the last year of this decade, 1910, belong two epistolary works. One is *Letters to Sanchia Upon Things as They Are,* by Maurice Hewlett, in which the author presents the supposed correspondence of Mark Senhouse, protagonist of *Halfway House* (1908) ; *Open Country* (1909) ; and *Rest Harrow* (1910), to his ideal Sanchia, to whom he gives advice and with whose absent spirit he communes in sentimental longing. The letters themselves hold very little interest for those who do not already know the characters portrayed in the novels which consider their careers. They are almost essays rather than letters and each is preceded by a long, and often unnecessary, explanatory note.

The second epistolary work of this year is *Gwenda*, by Mabel Barnes-Grundy. The affectation of this book may be leveled at by noting that the name of the heroine is Gwenda, and that she writes most of her letters to her grandmother whom she chooses to call "Granty." There is some humor here, however, and much dignity as the book rises to its melodramatic conclusion. The letters, despite the insistent affectation already mentioned, are letter-like and convincing.

The letters of one Peter Harding to his relatives and friends are given us in *The Corner of Harley Street* in 1911, a book by an anonymous author. The epistles are filled with family affairs, with social criticism, with philosophy, and with a sort of monotony induced by the fact that, no matter who the recipient, the letters are all written in the same tone. There is a total absence of action in the volume. The letters are, however, full of dialogue, and it is safe to say that by this time dialogue has become a recognized, if not an entirely convincing, property of the letter and is used with great frequency and in great profusion. To 1915 belongs an epistolary consideration of some of the aspects of the war in *Aunt Sarah and the War. A Tale of Transformations*, of unknown authorship. Written earlier, but first published, for special reasons, in 1917, is *Christine*, a story in letters by Alice Cholmondeley. The author presents the letters as those of her daughter in Germany to her in England, published after the death of the daughter in a hospital in Stuttgart. In addition they seem to reveal the mental state of Germany and its people before and during the Great War. The revelation of German pride is notable and penetrating without being too condemnatory. The letters themselves are full of hope and despair and ultimate pathos, and are written with much conviction. Another story of a life taken by the war is told in *Jamesie* (1918), by Ethel Sidgwick. The letters in broken English are here especially delightful, and indeed all of the letters are very real and, incidentally, realistically short in many cases. Again, use is made of the occasional telegram with telling effect. The form of the book is very elaborate, with many correspondences handled at once, in addition to the narrative interludes that lie between many of the epistles. None the less, the effect of the whole is that of a singularly complete revelation of human lives without the slightest intimation of prime literary greatness.

Stephen McKenna's *The Confessions of a Well-Meaning Woman* (1922), is an amusing exposé of what might be called the "confessions of an interfering woman." The author has delineated his leading character, Lady Anne Spenworth—a conventional soul with a horror of any sort of class freedom —with considerable accuracy and, although the fact that all the letters are from Lady Anne (essay-like and one-sided) somewhat limits the range of the work, the accuracy of presentation is unimpeachable.

Cosmo Hamilton has published an epistolary novel. This work, *Undelivered Letters from an American Girl to Her English Husband* (1926)—published in America under the title of *Confession*—presents a delightful revelation of the relations between a charming and self-willed girl and the English peer to whom she is engaged. The letters, although too long, are very real, thoroughly up-to-date, and succeed in presenting the modern woman in an admirably sympathetic light. Even the artifice of non-delivery cannot spoil the picture as a whole.

In 1928 was published an intimate record of a husband's love in *The Love Letters of a Husband*. The anonymity of the author has here been carefully preserved. This is the story of a separation between husband and wife because she feels that he has grown tired of her. Ultimately they return to each other at the close of this long correspondence, which is, at times, a very beautiful unfolding of the smouldering flame of love that refuses to die.

To 1929 belongs a collaboration of Hugh Walpole and J. B. Priestley, *Farthing Hall*. The letters present a twentieth-century story done in the eighteenth-century epistolary fashion. There are, as a matter of fact, two stories in this novel: the one a budding romance; the other a broken one. Although the proceedings are all very inconsequential, they are diverting, and it must be said that what is told in the correspondence of two friends might be very dull if presented as "straight" narrative.

Among so many stories of a sentimental bias told in letters from the very beginning of the epistolary impulse to the present, such works as *Humphrey Clinker, Evelina, The Dodd Family Abroad, Dracula,* and so on, stand out, aside from the merits peculiarly their own, because they are epistolary works not in the sentimental mode. Of such a group is *Topsy,* the most recent novel in letters it is possible to record, since it was published in 1931. This is the creation of A. P. Herbert and the letters were written originally for *Punch.* In book form they present the rather diffuse trials and tribulations of a very modern girl, whose combined accidental shrewdness and inherent vacuity are somewhat reminiscent of that notable modern siren, Lorelei Lee. The language of these letters is very much in the jazz idiom and combines what a man thinks is the speech of a flighty modern girl with the speech that might actually be hers. This is not art, but it is all highly diverting and amusing and goes far to indicate that, though but distantly related to the sentimental, psychological novel of the eighteenth century, the enlarged portrait of a girl in all its modern dimensions and contortions may be likewise presented in letters so that it may not only delight but also perhaps instruct.

EPISTOLARY FICTION (PARTICU-
LARLY THE NOVEL) IN FRANCE
AND IN ITALY

THE casting of narrative works of fiction, which we have designated novels, into epistolary form, was a practice by no means limited to the land which gave the greatest examples of the art any more than it was to the century which produced its most distinguished proponents and in which the mode reached its highest peak of development and achievement. Novels were written in this form by French, Italian, American, German, Russian, and other authors. In Brian W. Downs' book on Samuel Richardson, there is included a chapter on "The Consequences of Richardson,"[1] wherein Mr. Downs has included a list of novels in letter form in various other literatures in Europe. He has, however, omitted America from his census, and has treated epistolary fiction in Italy rather slightingly. It may be argued, of course, that the use of this form was not a "consequence" of Richardson, or that Richardson did not introduce into Italy the novel in letters, although admittedly he made it fashionable there. But when one considers the epistolary epidemic, as it may be termed, and sees the germinal *poste restante* marked "England" and knows further than that that Richardson connotes the word "epistolary" in England, one can well feel that he is not jumping to conclusions rashly in ascribing to Richard-

[1] *Richardson*, p. 218.

son the impulse giving strength to the novel in letters and its imitators in England and outside England.

If one were anxious to investigate the subject of the epistolary novel in France completely, the compass of a volume would be necessary. Aside from those works listed by Mr. Downs in his aforementioned chapter, M. Philippe Van Tieghem's edition of *La Nouvelle Héloise; ou Lettres de deux Amants habitans d'une petite Ville au pieds des Alps*, of Rousseau (first exposed for sale in 1761 in Paris), contains the best list collected in one spot convenient to the finger tips.

In 1751, three years after its appearance in England, *Clarissa* appeared in French as *Lettres Angloises ou Histoire de Clarissa Harlove*. In 1755-56 we may note the appearance in French of *Nouvelle Lettres Angloises ou Histoire de Chevalier Grandisson*. These translations are both attributed to Abbé Prévost, the author of *Manon Lescaut*. As early, however, as 1742, there is noted a work which shows that *Pamela* had already made its mark upon the French literary consciousness, for *Antipamela; or Mémoires de M.D.*—appeared at this time, published in London. In 1743, *Anti-Pamela; or, Feign'd Innocence Detected: In a Series of Syrena's Adventures*, possibly by Mrs. Haywood (opines Mr. Downs) was translated into French. The translation of *Pamela* itself appeared in 1742, but this is a book less to the fancy of the French than are Richardson's two later novels. From this date on, through the eighteenth century, as in England, France having looked upon the epistolary mode and having liked it, its popularity was assured. Many imitations of *Pamela*, aside from those already noted, appeared in French. Mme. de Beaumont, who has been previously mentioned for her epistolary fiction, was a Frenchwoman prolific in her imitations of Richardson. Francois-Thomas de Baculard d'Arnaud was another such author. Diderot's *La Réligieuse* is one of the most outstanding instances of Richardson imitation and was published in 1760, almost twenty years after the

appearance of *Pamela*. Laclos' *Liaisons Dangereuses* (translated into English as *Dangerous Connections*) was another.

The true Richardson of France was, however, Jean-Jacques
Rousseau. *La Nouvelle Héloise* (1761), is, like others of his
works, in letters. This work in particular may be compared
with those of Richardson because it, too, had a long train of
imitators. Of great interest, however, is Rousseau's version
of the *Portuguese Letters* in a volume called, *Letters of An
Italian Nun and an English Gentleman* (1781), a series of
sentimental and pathetic letters which are extremely well
written, graceful in phrasing, and of an insistent sadness.
The influence of these on English sentiment was great.

Among the many works which were composed in imitation
of the *Nouvelle Héloise*, M. van Tieghem has listed: *La
Philosophe par Amour; ou, Lettres de deux Amants Pas-
sionnés et vertueux* (1765); *Henriette de Wolmar; ou, la
Mere jalouse de sa Fille, pour servir de suite à la Nouvelle
Héloise* (1768); *Le Nouvel Abailard; ou, Lettres de deux
Amants qui ne se sont jamais vus* (1778), by Réstif de la
Bretonne; *Sophie; ou, Lettres de deux Amies recueillies et
publiées par un citoyen de Genève* (1779); *Lettres de deux
Amants habitants de Lyons, publiées par M. Léonard*
(1783); *La Dernière Héloise; ou, Lettres de Junie Salisbury
recueillies et publiées par M. Dauphin, citoyen de Verdun*
(1784); and *Amours ou Lettres d'Alexis et Justine* (1786).

It is not to be thought, however, that the epistolary impulse in France was entirely dependent upon Richardson. As early as 1607-1619 Honoré d'Urfé's *L'Histoire d'As-
trée*, was a model for epistolary correspondence in France in
the seventeenth century. It was of such tremendous influence
that its use in the eighteenth century as a representative
gem of the epistolary art is not to be wondered at. Then, too,
there were *Lettres Persanes* (1721), by Charles Louis de
Sécondat, Baron de la Brède et de Montesquieu, full of a
graceful humor, a piquancy of phrasing and a perspicacity of
observation that render them particularly lively. If Oliver
Goldsmith could copy this work forty years later in his *Citi-*

zen of the World, surely its widespread use at home need not be thought surprising. The intermixture of the serious with the light vein in these letters keeps them delightful. They are, moreover, valuable as an informative treatment of the manners and customs of Europe as these might be seen through the eyes of two Asiatics. John Davidson, the English poet, made a sympathetic translation of them late in the nineteenth century. Directly in imitation of these are the letters of the French patriot, Jean Paul Marat, *Lettres Polonaises*, written about 1770. In these letters, a young Polish prince traveling through the countries of Europe incognito, writes his extended criticisms of the manners and customs, especially of the social conditions, of the countries through which he has traveled, and sends them chiefly to a friend and to a brother. The letters are, of course, an excuse for Marat to air his opinions of the existing social order.

Not entirely in the same vein, but created by the same impulse as were the *Lettres Persanes* were those two epistolary works which formed a background in France to the development of sentimental fiction in the epistolary form, Alcoforado's *Lettres Portugaises* (1669), and Mme. de Graffigny's *Lettres Peruviennes* (1747), both of great popularity.

When the influence of Richardson on the French epistolary novel is being argued, it must be remembered that there is a high possibility of the existence of an original French epistolary influence on Richardson. Marivaux's two major works of fiction, *La Vie de Marianne* (1731-41), completed after Marivaux's death by Mme. Riccoboni, and *Le Paysan Parvenu* (1735-36), are both in letter form. It was this author, Pierre Carlet de Chamblain de Marivaux, who endeavored to bring back his countrymen to nature, as has already been mentioned (p. 75). In like manner, Samuel Richardson made strong endeavor to turn the tide of fiction into the channels of realism, of everyday occurrences and everyday lives. He succeeded undoubtedly beyond the dreams of Marivaux, and the works of the latter author are, by comparison with those of the English writer, fanciful and light. Yet there are resemblances to be noticed between the attempted realism of Marivaux and the successful realism of Richardson, resemblances that suggest the possibility of Richardson's having somewhat followed the lead of the Frenchman. *Marianne* is, however, episodic. The Richardson book it most suggests, *Clarissa,* is, on the other hand, a history in which the events of the heroine's life follow each other in an uninterrupted succession. Here is one of the chief differences between Richardson and Marivaux. There is no doubt that Richardson had before him the example of Marivaux's novels in the epistolary form. That he was led to couch his own works in that form because of the example of Marivaux is, on the other hand, doubtful, if not entirely incredible.

Even before Marivaux, however, and following in the trail of the *Lettres Portugaises* rather than in that of Marivaux's early work, are such series of love letters as *Lettres de la Marquise de M– au Comte de P–* (1732) and *Lettres Athéniennes* (1732), both the work of Claude Prosper Jolyot de Crébillon (Crébillon *fils*). The latter work may be placed beside Landor's tale of classic love in letters, *Pericles and Aspasia.* In the French work the letters are exchanged between Alcibiades and Aspasia.

To almost the same period of years as the two important epistolary works of Marivaux belong the epistolary works of Madame de Tencin, *Le Comte de Comminge* (1735) and *Malheurs de L'Amour* (1747), two sprightly novels written with a moral purpose but not a great deal of dignity. Already considered in Chapter VI of this work as French epistolary authors whose work was translated into English are Mme. Riccoboni and Mme. Elie de Beaumont. The former is the author of *Lettres de Julie Catesby* (1759), and the latter the author of *Lettres du Marquis de Roselle* (1764), both written in the epistolary form. It might be noted that Mesdames Tencin, Riccoboni, and de Beaumont, along with Mme. de Charrière, author of *Lettres neuchateloises* (1784), and *Caliste; ou Lettres écrites de Lausanne* (1786), and Mme. de Souza, who wrote *Adèle de Senanges* (1794), form a sort of epistolary school of sensibility which extends over a period of some sixty years and is comparable to the similar school of sensibility already considered in the English epistolary novel of the eighteenth century. These French books are, upon the whole, although the works of Mme. Riccoboni and Mme. de Beaumont are thoroughly pleasant, rather pedestrian and uninspired creations, sometimes relieved by a flow of graceful and exquisite writing, but usually overladen with sentiment and sensibility.

Voltaire is the author of an epistolary work in *Les Lettres d'Amabed, traduites par l'Abbé Tamponet,* a piece that may be considered minor in every respect. This was published in 1769. Dependent upon the work of Marivaux for its title and its moral indignation is *Le Paysan Perverti; ou, les Dangers de la ville—histoire récente mise au jour d'après les véritables lettres des personages,* by Réstif de la Bretonne (already mentioned for his imitation of Rousseau), published in 1775.

With the advent of the nineteenth century, the letter novel continued to be written in French from time to time, just as it had in English, and Mme. de Staël used the epistolary form in her sentimental novel *Delphine* (1802). Etienne Pivert de Sénancourt, a later disciple of Rousseau, published *Obermann* in 1804. There is much of Rousseau to be found in this and also much of the fast-growing tendency toward *mal du siècle.* The strongest influence to be seen here is, however, that of a German novel, Johann Wolfgang von Goethe's *Die Leiden des Jungen Werthers* (1774), since nature is sought as a solace for sorrow in the French work just as it is in the original German. The letters are always "in character" and the work is not uninteresting. The form recurs at intervals, and one is apt to find a novel in letters appearing in France at almost any time.

An epistolary novel by Louis Buonaparte, *Marie; ou, les Peines de l'Amour,* was first published in 1812 (translated into English in 1815 as *Maria; or, The Hollanders*). This is a sentimental and involved novel which tells the story of a girl who is thought to be "inaccessible to love." The characters are all rather vague but are, in the typically French manner, all very beautiful. The philosophy of the entire work is summed up in the sentiment (p. 27, vol. I), "The heart which can love twice is unworthy of true happiness!" In the first part of the work most of the letters, sentimental and moralizing in tone, are exchanged between two characters, Julius and Adolphus, but as the story proceeds the correspondence falls into other hands, and the letters grow increasingly longer until Letter LXI assumes the proportions of some eighty-one pages. The chief recommendation of *Marie* is its occasional capturing of the Dutch scene, with which the author was thoroughly familiar.

In 1815 Pigault-Lebrun wrote *Adelaide de Meran* in letters, and Théophile Gautier's most famous (and most notorious) work, *Mlle. de Maupin* (1835), is partly in letters, partly in narrative. Honoré de Balzac, too, tried the epistolary form in *Mémoires de deux Jeunes Mariées* (1842). The contrasts presented between the lives of the two girls who write the letters is the chief point of interest in this novel. In 1869 Daudet's *Lettres de Mon Moulin* appeared. These sketches are altogether delightful and their capturing of background and atmosphere is noteworthy. One of Victor Cherbuliez's most popular novels, *Miss Rovel* (1875), is written in letters. Octave Feuillet published *La Morte* in 1886, translated into English as *Aliette* (1886). Here, the husband, who has just lost his wife, tells the story in letters. The analysis of emotion and of character is interesting throughout. *Mon Oncle Barbassou* (1888), by Mario Uchard, is a sort of modern Arabian Nights story of a young Frenchman who inherits a harem from his Mohammedan uncle, a circumstance which is complicated by the fact that the uncle is not dead. It is composed of letters, almost every one of which is a full, and expansive, chapter in length. There is considerable verbal coloring, some humor, and much adventure in this novel; but the extreme length of the letters, the fact that they lose the tone of letters as the story proceeds and take on the tone of straight narrative, does much to rob the whole of the desired epistolary effect. In 1897 an absorbing work appeared, depicting private life and manners of the late seventeenth century in a thoroughly readable fashion. This is Emmanuel Pierre Rodocanachi's *Tolla la Courtisane; ésquisse de la vie privée à Rome en l'an du Jubilé* 1700. The method of appending notes makes the book seem almost "severely historical," but it is actually epistolary fiction instead. *Le Songe d'une Femme* (Eng. trans. 1927), by Remy de Gourmont, a series of letters concerned almost exclusively with passion, and *Mitsou* (1929), are examples of the present-day use of the form in French.

Thus we see that the use in France of the epistolary form has been a fairly constant one and has persisted through the centuries. It flourished, as in England, mainly in the eighteenth century, and has since been resorted to from time to time for the purpose of fiction.

Turning to epistolary expression in Italy, we find that *Pamela* appeared in translation in 1744-46, and the heroine of the novel had her story made famous in that country by Goldoni's *Pamela Fanciulla* (or *Pamela Nubile*) (1750). Goldoni followed this play with *Pamela Maritata* (1750). *Clarissa* was translated, in novel form, in 1783-86; *Grandison* in 1784-89. Thus we find that the epistolary nóvel reached Italy, from England, save in the case of *Pamela*, rather later than it had France, where Richardson's novels were completely translated by the close of the fifties. In Germany, too, the fifties saw Richardson completely translated. But in Italy the drama was at this time more popular than the novel, and so it was that Pamela became a stage rather than a page heroine. Incidentally, these plays of Goldoni were translated

into English and published in London in 1756. Chiari, in
1759, also published a *Pamela Maritata*, and his novel *Francese in Italia* he based on *Clarissa*.[2] One finds here not so
much the definitely moralistic tone that was so peculiarly
Richardson's; but the impulse of the epistle came from him.
Of course Rousseau was, in France, a nearer neighbor to
Italy, and Goethe's *Werther* was also very popular with the
Italians, but since all go back to Richardson as the fountainhead we may say of Chiari that he, too, does. Mr. Downs
has taken from Arturo Graf the statement that Richardson,
though he did not introduce the epistolary form into Italy,
made it popular there.[3] This is unquestionably a good phrase,
but one that seems upon the whole a trifle vague, for the
translation of *Pamela* dates 1744-46; Chiari's *Francese in
Italia* dates 1762. Richardson was there eighteen years before
Pietro Chiari! And in Chiari's *La Viaggiatrice* there is a very
clear influence of *Pamela*. It is in epistolary form as are three
of his other novels: *La filosofessa italiana*; *La Cantatrice per
disgrazia*; and *La Donna che non si trova* (1762), which is
in imitation of *La Nouvelle Héloise*. As a matter of fact,
Albergati had had it in mind to imitate this Rousseau work
in an epistolary novel but did not do it, and published instead the *Lettere Capricciose piacevoli e varie* in collaboration with Zacchiroli, Compopioni, and Bertalozzi. Thus, if
Richardson did not "introduce" the epistolary form into
Italy, but merely made it "fashionable," then to Chiari must
be given the honor of introducing it. But since Richardson
was most often his model, we may conclude that the introduction was at least under the influence of Richardson if that
author was not himself the immediate impulse. Of course,
Richardson did not introduce epistolary fiction into England, but he made it popular there.

Earlier too, of course, than Chiari are certain other works.
It has been claimed for Italy that the origins of the epistolary
novel are Italian. Europe knew the epistolary novels of

[2] Arturo Graf, *L'Anglo-Mania e L'Influsso Inglese in Italia nel secolo
XVIII*, Torino, 1911.
[3] Graf, *op. cit.*, p. 282; Downs, *op. cit.*, p. 233.

Montesquieu, Richardson, Rousseau, and Goethe. But in 1569 there was already an epistolary novel in Italy, the *Lettere Amorose* of Aloise Pasqualigo, which is the basis for this distinguished claim. In 1684 we have Marana's *L'Esploratore turco e le diliu relazioni segrete alla Porte Ottomana* (Paris). This has been thought to be of French origin, but Natali refutes this conclusively.[4] It is, like Montesquieu's *Lettres Persanes*, a survey of politics and society. It was very popular and appeared in English in the first decade of the eighteenth century. In almost direct imitation of the early work by Marana is *Lo Spione Italiano; ossia corrispondenza segrete e familiare fra il Marchese di Licciocara e il Conte Pifiela, tutti e due viaggiatori incogniti per i diverse corti d'Europa* (1782).

It is, in the final analysis, however, Pietro Chiari who is the leading proponent of the epistolary form in Italy, as has already been intimated. Certainly this is indisputably true of his place in the eighteenth century, if it is not equally true of his place in all Italian literature. It is interesting to note that the general machinery of his epistolary novels is, indeed, very much like that of the sentimental moralistic novel in letters in England. The same extravagances, the same plethora of gallant intrigues, surprises, duels, flights, and of course, tears, are employed in these novels almost as plentifully as they were in England's epistolary works of fiction. I have already indicated that the novel was not the most important form in Italy in the literature of the eighteenth century. It was not, indeed, until the appearance of *Le Ultime Lettere di Jacopo Ortis* in 1799-1802 that the novel became a truly popular form in that country. In other words, Chiari was persistently writing in a form that was not entirely popular during the period in which he wrote. By 1757 he had begun his career as a writer of the picaresque tale with the *Storia di Luigi Manderine*, based on a French original. Thus Concari sums up this really important writer:

> *Non credo che giovi di saperne oltre di codesti romanzi di venture fondati in capricciose combinazioni accozzate senza logica*

[4] *Il Settecento*, 1929.

ne arte; il fin qui detto da un idea dei propisiti dell' autore, che pure scrive per dilettare e istriure, e non ha ne rettitudine ne moralita, se non pervana ostentazione nelle massime e nei discorsi.[5]

Yet this is the man who did so much in Italy to keep the novel alive!

The book which has already been indicated as that which began to popularize the novel in Italy (*Le Ultime Lettere di Jacopo Ortis*) in 1802 did not possess that title when it first appeared in 1799 as *La Vera Storia di due Amanti infelici*. Ugo Foscolo was the author of this celebrated work. It may be said to stand in the same relation to Italian fiction and literary history in general as Goethe's *Werther* does to German, and reflects for Italy the general *mal du siècle* then prominent as a literary fashion on the Continent. In *Obermann* of Sénancour and *Adolphe* of Benjamin Constant we have parallel instances. The importance of *Jacopo Ortis* cannot be overestimated. It was the first work of fiction in Italy to be highly sensitive and to make any attempt at style. As Focolo says in a letter to Goethe in 1802: "I have herein depicted myself, my passions, my time, under the name of a friend in Padua. The work has no intent as an 'invention,' for I have drawn everything from 'truth'. . . ." The tone of the whole is elegiac, an early *In Memoriam*, and one of the few in the epistolary form. The letters themselves are both sensitive and sentimental; yet there is sometimes an almost lyrical quality to the prose that lifts it above the commonplace.

Later in the nineteenth century, along with the influence of Walter Scott on the Italian novel, may be noted several epistolary novels. These are in imitation of, or inspired by, *Jacopo Ortis* and *Werther* largely. In 1817 Giovanni Agrati

[5] "I do not think it is necessary to enquire any further into such romances of adventure revolving about whimsical combination, thrown together without either logic or art. What has been said thus far gives an idea of the purposes of the author who writes to delight and to instruct, and yet does not possess either righteousness or morality, except to display them in his maxims and discourses." T. Concari, *Il Settecento*, p. 398.

published the *Storia di Clarice Visconti duchessa di Milano*. This work was much admired by Manzoni, who wrote in its favor and said that it was such a model of diction that it succeeded in hiding its own paucity of ideas. In 1818 may be noted *Lettere di Giulia Willet*, by the Marchese Orintia Romagnoli Sacrati of Cesena; in 1825 the *Lettere di una Italiana* by the Baroness Carolina Decio Cosenza of Naples. This work is a strange mixture of the pseudo-classical and the heroic-romantic, for we have a Lysander writing to a Cressida and a Count W— to a Clelia. Perhaps such a work may best be called a corruption of the sentimental novel. Cesare Balbo left unfinished an historical romance in epistolary form entitled *Lettere di Alfonso d'Este ed Isabella di Savoia*. It must be remembered that the analysis of passions in a bourgeois society had been made in England, in France, in Germany, even if not in the epistolary novel at least in the expository novel; in other words, contemporary manners had been described in a familiar way. In Italy domestic fiction and the "novel of manners" was not known in 1818 when the *Lettere di Giulia Willet* appeared. Of course there were some people in Italy who considered romance as old-fashioned as did some in England when Mrs. Charlotte Lennox, in 1752, published *The Female Quixote*. In 1819 there appeared in Italy a book which definitely satirized romance, *La Donna delle romanzi*. But it was not until *I promessi sposi* (1830), that the aspect really began to change, and with this change the epistolary novel began to disappear almost completely. About 1825 it died a natural death, after having been in vogue for nearly three-quarters of a century.

Of the work which saw the light in Italy in this form, it may be said that there is only one of lasting importance, and that is Ugo Foscolo's *Lettere Ultime di Jacopo Ortis*. The other novels in epistolary form are more or less transitory in tissue and general worth. But when one remembers that a country which had very little fiction in novel form which was its own before 1830 gave birth to a goodly dozen of epistolary novels, the virulence of this trans-European epidemic can be estimated.

The same general statement may be made of German literature, in which there is to be found, among the several existing epistolary novels, but one that is of true worth and importance. This is, of course, *Die Leiden des Jungen Werthers,* by Johann Wolfgang von Goethe, a novel in letters which first appeared in 1774. Since it was preceded by the epistolary works of Samuel Richardson and Jean-Jacques Rousseau, it is a safe and natural assumption to suppose that Goethe derived at least the suggestion for the form of his work from the novels in letters of Richardson and Rousseau. Goethe followed the path of Rousseau in the spirit that he established in his work and succeeded in setting up a new mode of thought in German social relations and in literature. In that the book encouraged sentimental youths to commit suicide, it achieved a sort of notoriety as well as fame; yet its intrinsic value is a high one. The philosophy, the sentimentality, and the social ethics of the book are derived from Rousseau. On the other hand, the style in which the letters are written; their naturalness; their faithfulness to character (especially in the case of the letters which Werther writes, full as they are of philosophic ramblings and sentimental self-pityings) ; their attempted simple presentation of bourgeois life, are all more closely allied to the work of Richardson than to that of Rousseau.

The book itself is important as a literary work as well as an epistolary one. In this novel, says Wilhelm Scherer, Goethe "protested against a society, which did not understand how to use the brilliant talents of an impetuous young man; he protested against established inequality, against the pride of the nobility . . . ; he protested against prevailing morality, that did not even look upon suicide with compassion; he protested against conventional pedantry of style and against aesthetic rules . . . ; and he protested against the established speech, which the author employed, as a matter of fact, not only with freedom, but even arbitrarily."[6] Whatever else may be said of the book, it must stand undoubtedly as one of the most remarkable and influential of epistolary novels in literature and one as important in its effects as the epistolary novels of Richardson and the *Nouvelle Héloise* of Rousseau.

[6] Wilhelm Scherer, *Geschichte der Deutschen Literatur*, Berlin, 1883, p. 500.

IX

EPISTOLARY FICTION IN AMERICA

THE Epistolary impulse was, of course, not confined to Europe, and there is ample evidence that it early crossed the Atlantic. As early as 1744 *Pamela* was in print in Philadelphia. Benjamin Franklin made an edition of it here, and in the same year there were editions of it in New York and Boston.[1] Richardson's other novels were first issued in this country in abridged form, again in Philadelphia, in 1786. Thus Richardson's work attained popularity in America and seems to have been read to a sufficient degree to warrant printings of them here about the same time that they appeared in Italian translations in Italy, but considerably later than they reached France in French translations. On the other hand, the English editions of these works circulated in America before the dates of their American editions, and it is possible to find these editions in existence here. Beyond this we may feel reasonably sure that even in those far-away days those people who made a point of being strictly in the mode read the "latest" things from London, much as they like to do today.

Undoubtedly the epistles of Benjamin Franklin of a familiar nature, in *Bagatelles*, and the open letters of Francis Hopkinson added something to the literary impulse for letter writing in America, but most significant for us is the fact that what is acknowledged to be the first American novel, *The Power of Sympathy*, was in epistolary form. This is a weak and ineffectually sentimental piece of work of rather hybrid nature once attributed to Sarah Wentworth Morton,

[1] Cambridge History of American Literature, New York, 1917, I, p. 284.

but now doubted to be hers at all. It was published in Boston in 1789. By this time the greatest vogue of the epistolary novel in England was past, but our fiction was sired (some people would prefer grandsired) by a novel in letters, which, although its intrinsic worth may not be very high is, none the less, an epistolary novel. A year later, in 1790, the epistolary strain was carried on with the appearance of *Memoirs of the Bloomsgrove Family. In a Series of Letters to a Respectable citizen of Philadelphia.* The continuation of this title on the title-page of the book itself is interesting because it is in that all-inclusive and didactic tone so common to similar English works some twenty or thirty years previous to this. It is: *Containing Sentiments on a Mode of Domestic Education, suited to the present State of Society, Government and Manners, in the United States of America: and on the Dignity and Importance of the Female Character. With a Variety of Interesting Anecdotes.* The author is Enos Hitchcock, D.D.; the publishers are Thomas and Andrews of Boston; the Dedication is to Mrs. Washington. It is scarcely necessary to point out that this highly instructive work is hardly a novel in the current sense of that term.

In 1792 came Jeremy Belknap's *The Foresters, An American Tale: Being a Sequel to the History of John Bull the Clothier. In a Series of Letters to a Friend.* This is a curiously rambling affair that ought to be read with indicative notes because of its endless topical allusions and political cruxes. It is definitely post-Revolutionary in tone, looking back to the period of accomplishment in the colonies. From that point of view, its present-day interest purely as literature must necessarily prove a very feeble one. In 1793 appeared Gilbert Imlay's *The Emigrants, or the History of An Expatriated Family, being a Delineation of English Character and Manners written in America.* To 1793 also belongs an anonymous work, *The Hapless Orphan; or, Innocent Victims of Revenge. A Novel, founded on Incidents in Real Life. In a Series of Letters from Caroline Francis to Marie B—,* by an American Lady. This was published in Boston by Belknap and Hall. In 1797 a very popular work, *The Coquette; or, Eliza Wharton*, by Hannah Webster Foster, appeared. Mr. Van Doren attests to the great popularity of this work when he states: "*The Coquette* saw thirty editions in forty years."[2] In 1795 came the *Trials of the Human Heart*, by Mrs. Susannah Rowson, printed in Philadelphia. Again, another epistolary novel was published in 1797 under the title of *Infidelity; or, The Victims of Sentiment. A Novel in a Series of Letters*, by Samuel Relf. This was published by W. W. Woodward. That the epistolary novel was popular, is proved by the fact that the title contained in it, in several instances, the information that the work was "in a series of letters." It must be noticed, likewise, how definitely imitative of the titles of English epistolary works many of these American epistolary titles are in their general outlines. The next original work to appear in letter form in America was *The Original Letters of Ferdinand and Isabella*, by John Davis. This belongs to the year 1798. In 1800, at Portsmouth, New Hampshire, there was published[3] anonymously *The Castle of Serrein; or, Abode of Perpetual Pleasures: in a Series of Letters by Seignora R. Interwoven with her own memoirs, etc.*

The next two works to be chronicled are by the most important of the early American novelists, Charles Brockden Brown, the favorite of Shelley, and the American Ann Radcliffe. Just as so many of the greater English authors used the epistolary mode for one or two of their works, so Brown used it in his *Clara Howard; or, The Enthusiasm of Love* (Philadelphia, 1801) and in his *Jane Talbot* (1801). The tenets of the sentimental school seem to be abundantly supported in the former novel by the fact that absolutely nothing happens in the course of the story. To quote Miss Loshe: "The entire book is occupied with the weighing of reasons, the chopping of motives, the analysis of emotions."[4] These generalities may be applied to nine out of ten of the senti-

[2] Carl van Doren, *The American Novel*, New York, 1929, p. 7.
[3] Wegelin, *op. cit.*, p. 6.
[4] Lillie D. Loshe, *The Early American Novel*, New York, 1907 and 1930, pp. 45-48.

mental novels published in England during the latter half of the eighteenth century. Although somewhat more happens in *Jane Talbot* and there is considerable animation in the letters as they proceed, yet there is the same protracted weighing of emotions and analyses of the heart and, at times, the letters sound like any sort of narrative except epistolary. The work is full of sentimental perplexities. It is significant, however, that the man who was the first professional novelist in America should have thought it worth his while to employ the epistolary form twice in his writings.

In 1802 there appeared *The History of Maria Kittle. In a Letter to Miss Ten Eyck,* by Ann Eliza Bleecker. This originally appeared in Vols. I and II of the *New-York Magazine; or, Literary Repository,* 1790-1791.[5] In 1803 came *Emily Hamilton, a Novel founded on incidents in real life,* by a Young Lady of Worcester County (Eliza Vicery). In 1807 *Dangerous Friendship; or, the Letters of Clara D'Albe. Translated from the French by a Lady of Baltimore* was published in Baltimore. In 1808, Miss Hassall published *Secret History; or, the Horrors of St. Domingo, in a Series of Letters by a Lady at Cape Francis to Colonel Burr, late Vice-President of the U. S. Principally during the command of General Rocheambeau.* Two more works of the prolific Mrs. Rowson are in letters and belong here. They are the triply entitled *Sarah; or, The Exemplary Wife; or, Sincerity,* which was published in 1813; and *Rebecca; or, The Fille de Chambre,* the second edition of which is dated 1814. *Sarah,* by the way, had first appeared as a serial in the *Boston Weekly* magazine in 1805. To 1816 belongs *Adelaide. A New and Original Novel,* by a Lady of Philadelphia. In 1823, John Neal published two works, *Seventy-Six* and *Randolph.* Of these two, *Randolph* is done in letters. The chief interest of the work lies in the fact that the narrative is relieved, every now and again, by the criticisms made by Neal of contemporary literature, both English and American. He criticizes some of his own things, but the most delightful remarks are those made

---

⁵ Wegelin, *op. cit.,* p. 11.

on the subjects of Brown and Coleridge. The novel itself is extremely sentimental. In 1824 John Gardiner Calkins Brainard published *Letters found in the Ruins of Fort Braddock, including an interesting American tale, originally published in the Connecticut Mirror.* By 1827 there was a second edition of this work. In 1826 Theodore Sedgwick published *Hints to My Countrymen. By an American.* This work is in letters, interspersed with pieces of verse, anecdotes, and elaborated homilies and is in the good old homespun tradition.

During what is known as the central period of American literature, a Nova Scotian appeared, who may be drafted for American fiction. He is Thomas C. Haliburton, also known by his pen name of "Sam Slick," a Yankee appellation. In 1839 he published *The Letter-Bag of the Great Western; or, Life in a Steamer,* according to a literary device at least as old as Breton's Elizabethan *Packet of Mad Epistles.* The letters tell individual stories and present individual characters, and there is about most of them a distinctly didactic air. Haliburton's work, *Sam Slick's Wise Saws* (1853), although not in letters, is presented to the reader with an introductory letter.

William Ware, another American author belonging to this period, published three historical novels, each of which is in letters. These are: *Letters from Palmyra* (1837), later known as *Zenobia, or The Fall of Palmyra; Probus; or, Rome in the Third Century. In Letters of Lucius M. Piso from Rome, to Fausta, the Daughter of Gracchus, at Palmyra* (1838), later known as *Aurelian;* and *Julian; or, Scenes in Judea* (1841). In these books the principal characters tell the stories, but the subtlety of analysis which would rescue the epistolary form from a charge of artificiality, such a subtlety as, for instance, is present in Richardson's work, is here lacking. Furthermore, the expression here used is somewhat too theatrical for the stories told. The stories are interesting, on the other hand, for their portrayal of background, and Ware may be said to point to Lew Wallace in this respect. Just why the author should have chosen to use the epistolary form is not quite ascertainable, but if one is seeking earlier parallels, the *Letters from Julia, the Daughter of Augustus, to Ovid,* supposedly taken from a manuscript unearthed at Herculaneum, published in London in 1753, furnishes one. The use in England of the epistolary form for a novel dealing with the ancient world is rather rare, more so than in America, where, too, it is hardly common.

Following in the footsteps of the Reverend William Ware is the Reverend J. H. Ingraham, who has written three historical novels of Israel and Egypt, all of which are in the form of letters. They are: *The Prince of the House of David; or, Three Years in the Holy City* (1855); *The Pillar of Fire; or, Israel in Bondage* (1859); and *The Throne of David. From the Consecration of the Shepherd of Bethlehem to the Rebellion of Prince Absalom* (1860). Recently, Ingraham has been coming into his own and there are many readers, some discriminating, who feel that for a picture of Israel in full scope and view *The Prince of the House of David* far surpasses *Ben Hur.* Suffice it to say that the letters which compose the books teem with admirable description and are full of narrative that is of a most moving quality. The pictures that they give us of Egypt and Israel allow them to take a not undistinguished place in the company of historical novels.

Somewhat in the mode of the Ware and Ingraham epistolary novels is *Shahmah In Pursuit of Freedom; or, The Branded Hand* (1858). Particularly interesting is the subtitle, *Translated from the Original Showian and Edited by An American Citizen,* which is reminiscent of Horace Walpole's subtitle to his *Castle Of Otranto.* The entire tone of the book is allegoric; the letters are vigorous but lengthy and essay-like and, in the respect that they are written by a traveling prince, suggest Marat's *Lettres Polonaises.* The effect of the whole is that of an anti-slavery tract.

In a different vein from these historical novels of Ware and Ingraham is a book which was published in London in 1844, the work of an American author. It was *High Life in*

New York by Mrs. Anne Stephens, who wrote under the nom de guerre of "Jonathan Slick, Esq." The book contains about thirty letters to a friend in Connecticut and is written in the Yankee dialect. It reminds us at times of a diluted and earlier form of Mark Twain's Yankee wit and stands in line with that particular sort of humor with which the stage Yankee has been equipped all the way from *The Contrast* (1790) to Will Rogers.

C. M. Sedgwick, a prolific sentimental authoress, wrote a curious novel called *Married or Single?* published in 1857, which is largely in the epistolary spirit. The book presents the story of two young girls who find the letters of their immediate ancestors in an old family trunk. The letters found are presented along with the story of the girls and, while the invention is an ingenious one, the execution is burdened with excessive and unwrung sentimentality.

The William Henry Letters (1870), by Mrs. A. M. Diaz, is a particularly delightful and lively series of letters from an American schoolboy. Most of the letters are introduced by a brief prose explanation, which succeeds in placing the following epistle. The letters are further augmented by answers from grandmother and sister, but those of William Henry himself are the most completely diverting of the lot.

In 1873 was published in Boston Thomas Bailey Aldrich's epistolary work, *Marjorie Daw and other People. Marjorie Daw* is a particularly witty epistolary bit and incorporates in its letters humor, excitement, romance, and psychological shrewdness. It is a composition of the most delightful and surprising sort. Comparable to it is "The Love Letters of Smith," by H. C. Bunner in *Short Sixes. Stories to be Read While the Candle Burns* (1890), a story comprising scraps of paper of an epistolary nature, witty and novel, and a single love letter that is a very gem of its kind.

In 1882 Augustus M. Swift published, *Cupid, M.D.,* a novel made up chiefly of the correspondence of John Wykeham and Eliot Blake. Eliot is a young victim of the drug habit and is in the sanitarium in which he hopes to be cured of his desire for morphine. He finally succeeds with the help of Lily Pattison, and their love affair fills the bulk of the letters. The letters are interrupted every now and then in order to give opportunity for the appearance of Lily's diary. The story is rather slow moving but not without that sympathy created by the human equation of a man willing to fight for his own good. One of the most important of the American novelists, Henry James, has contributed two short pieces in letters, *A Bundle of Letters* and *The Point of View* (1879-1882), both of which are concerned with the experiences of Americans abroad and neither of which is of prime importance. James adds verisimilitude by following the occasional method of dating a letter.

The Familiar Letters of Peppermint Perkins (1886), is especially interesting, not only in its own right, but also because it is a direct forerunner of such a work as A. P. Herbert's *Topsy*. Like the later English book, it presents the letters of a modern girl of its period, a girl who is made up of equal parts of naïveté and cunning. Her reactions to life and people form the extremely amusing substance of the entire book. The individual letters which form the bulk of the book were originally published in the Boston *Saturday Evening Gazette*.

His Letters (1892), by Julien Gordon, is a collection of 115 letters from Hubert Thornton to Mrs. Moncrieff. The one-sidedness of the correspondence makes the whole book rather tiresome. The story is introduced by a chapter of narrative in which we are given a picture of the protagonist who falls in love with Mrs. Moncrieff after he has seen her portrait at an exhibition. The letters are a simple progressive record of the man's love. As presented they are but fragments, the "editor" having seen fit to destroy many of them. They are full, however, of the poetry of worship which true love must necessarily catch. In 1893 Kate Douglas Wiggin published *A Cathedral Courtship*, in letters, a little romance of two who meet while touring in England. The letters are written by "She" and "He," each to close friends "back home." A particularly delightful squib in the epistolary mode is *The Documents in Evidence* (1893), by Henry M. Blossom, Jr. This is a triangular business romance arising from the fact that a young man chances to save a girl from falling from a carriage, and is motivated by the theory that "He who has no patrimony, must get his wealth by matrimony." In a single volume by Conover Duff, published in 1895, are to be found two long epistolary stories, "The Master-Knot" and "Another Story." The former of these is a sentimental romance done with a sort of sophistication and ending on a note of tragedy in death. The latter is a slight story of high society of the period, presented largely in letters from women of fashion. The story is rather negligible; the letters are accurate in expression, especially in their combination of the affectation and pseudo-daring of the late nineties. In 1896 was published *'Twixt Cupid and Croesus; or, the Exhibits in an Attachment Suit,* by Charles Peale Didier, again a triangular romance in which Cupid conquers all. To the following year belongs *The Story of an Untold Love,* by Paul Leicester Ford. The author tells us that he does not know what to call this, for it is neither diary nor letter. The various "parts" are dated and cover a period of five years. The love story contained, that of Don Maitland and Maizie Walton, is a delightful one, and this narrative of the career of an historian and his perfect helpmate is unfolded in a series of letters (at least from their tone, signatures, and so on, they seem to be letters) which are written down for the sake of the example they offer the children. In 1898 came *The Sins of a Widow,* "confessed" by Amelie L'Oiseau, a mild work in which a widow finds her ideal. In the last year of the decade William L. Kountz published his *Billy Baxter's Letters,* six letters of Billy to his "pal," Jim, full of infectious humor and written in a language that is made to fit the character of the writer, who makes use of a great deal of the up-to-the-minute slang of his period.

The revival of novels in letters in the first decade of the twentieth century, which was previously noted in English literature, may be seen here paralleled in America. That really excellent sentimental novelist, Myrtle Reed, has given us two pieces of epistolary fiction in *Love Letters of a Musician* (1898), and *Later Love Letters of a Musician* (1900). Both are fair and fragrant works and are filled with a knowledge and appreciation of music that place them not only among epistolary novels, but among the better musical novels as well. They have much sentimentality in them; but they have, also, much grace.

Less sentimental in tone than is the revival of the period in England are most of these American epistolary novels from 1900 to 1909. The chief virtue of *Mrs. Sinclair's Experiments* (1900), by Mrs. Wilson, is that its letters are brief and convincing and are exchanged among several correspondents. Otherwise, this is a rather mediocre story of love and trial, equal in the excessiveness of its sentimentality to anything produced in England at the same time. In 1901 Gertrude Franklin Atherton published anonymously a novel entitled *The Aristocrats*. The social satire here is brilliant, and the letters written by Lady Helen Pole to her friend in England are full of pointed criticisms of the Americans among whom she is situated in the Adirondacks. In the same year was published *Lauriel. The Love Letters of an American Girl*, edited by A. H. These "love letters" are the epistles of Laura Livingston to her friend, later lover, then husband, Rex Strong. The "editor" says of her that she is "the type of womanhood that makes men noble, and may make them great" (p. VI). Laura's letters from various spots in America and from abroad are thoroughly in keeping with this definition of her. *While Charlie Was Away,* an epistolary novel by Mrs. Poultney Bigelow, published in 1901, presents the letters of Mrs. March to Lord Darraway, her faithful and devoted cousin, and his answers to her. Mrs. March's letters are impetuous, indiscreet, and delightful; her cousin's are tenderly serious; the letters of both are entirely characteristic and extremely well written. For this reason alone, the novel is a pleasant and noteworthy minor work in the epistolary form. To 1902 belong *The Price Inevitable; or, the Confessions of Irene. An Autobiography,* by Aurelia I. Sidner, and *Some Letters of an American Woman concerning Love and Other Things,* by Sarah Biddle. The mere fact that the former was published by the Popular Publishing Company seems to set its type. It is a "scandal romance" of the deepest dye. The author attempts to lay bare the soul of a woman that another woman may profit thereby, by taking a sordid page or two from her life and giving it to the world. The narrative, a series of letters from Irene to her friend Grace, tells the love story of Irene, which ends by her being made "an honest woman" at last. The latter novel is a rather rambling little work, a sort of American counterpart of Laurence Housman's *An Englishwoman's Love Letters.* In the same year was published *Our Lady of the Beeches,* by Bettina, Baroness Van Hutten, a rambling and philosophic romance, the first half of which is written in letters. To 1902 likewise belongs, *The Letters from a Self-Made Merchant to His Son,* by the present editor of the *Saturday Evening Post,* George Horace Lorimer. The book which is the sequel to this, *Old Gorgon Graham* was published in 1904 and is likewise in letters, the subtitle being, *More Letters from a Self-Made Merchant to His Son.*

In 1903 Jack London published *The Kempton-Wace Letters,* a story of love in a series of letters, the scene of which shifts from London to California; and in the same year William Dean Howells likewise published *Letters Home.* The letters are written by a set of people who are well differentiated and characterized. They are always, too, "in character." The fascination of New York for the stranger is well brought out in this work. The book is in Howells' most delightful comic vein, and few excel him at his best in the field of social satire. The year 1903 brought, too, *A Parish of Two,* by Henry Goelet McVickar and Price Collier (Percy Collins). The book contains the letters from Douglas Dayton to his friend Percy Dashiel. The dual authorship, a popular form, is present as in *A Fellowe and His Wife* and *Farthing Hall.*

The literary quality of these letters would seem to be their chief claim to attention.

The year 1904 saw the appearance of at least six epistolary novels, more than had appeared in any year preceding. *A Country Interlude* by Hildegarde Hawthorne is a rather static story in which little happens. As is usual with these novels (the author calls the work a novelette) the plot is concerned with love. *Daphne and Her Lad,* another collaboration, is by M. J. Lagen and Cally Ryland, and presents the love letters of two newspaper people: the editor of a woman's page of the *Evening Star* (a masculine editor at that), and Daphne, who is in the office of the *Globe*. The narrative is slow but interesting. *The Jessica Letters, An Editor's Romance* (1904), is a lengthy, half-humorous, half-sentimental novel composed of convincing letters which are interspersed with snatches from a diary. The *Letters of a Self-Made Merchant* and its sequel, by George Horace Lorimer, gave rise, as popular successes so frequently do, to a number of imitations. Two of these are, *Letters from a Son to his Self-Made Father. Being the Replies to Letters from a Self-Made Merchant to His Son* (1904) by Charles Eustace Merriman and *Letters of a Self-Made Failure* (1914) by Maurice Switzer. The first is an excellent satire of the Lorimer book. It is dedicated to Mark Twain, "A ready-made wit," whom it attempts to imitate in tone and tempo throughout; but it is chiefly of interest only to those who know the Lorimer book well. As a parody, it has little ability to stand alone because, unlike Fielding's literary attempts on *Pamela*, it never succeeds in becoming anything more than a mere parody. The second work owes little to the Lorimer work. Jim writes to his brother Bob, and gives an account of himself and his adventures as he pursues his business career. A sort of pseudo-philosophy is apparent at times and a distant humor permeates the entire book. It may likewise be conjectured that *Letters of a Business Woman to her Daughter, and Letters of a Business Girl to her Mother* (1923), by Zora Putnam Wilkins, sugar-coated pills of precept and moral instruction, were suggested to the author by the Lorimer work. The book is relieved by the fact that the letters of the daughter are filled with a zealous youth, although the girl is too easily successful.

In 1904 likewise came a curious epistolary collaboration, the work of four authors: Kate Douglas Wiggin; Mary Findlater; Jane Findlater; and Allan McAulay. This book, *The Affair at the Inn,* contains "an account of certain events which are supposed to have occurred in the Month of May, 19—, at a quiet country inn on Dartmoor, in Devonshire; the events being recorded by the persons most interested in the unfolding of the little international comedy." The story is written by four authors, each author being responsible for one character as follows:—Miss Virginia Pomeroy, of Richmond, Virginia, U. S. A., by Kate Douglas Wiggin; Mr. Mac-Gill of Tunbridge Wells, England, by Mary Findlater, author of *The Rose of Joy;* Miss Cecilia Evesham, Mrs. Mac-Gill's English companion, by Jane Helen Findlater, author of *The Green Graves of Balgourie;* Sir Archibald Maxwell Mackenzie, of Kindaroch, N. B., by Allan McAulay, author of *The Rhymer.* The part written by Kate Douglas Wiggin is as whimsical and delightful as anything she has done. Virginia feels that because she is on Dartmoor she must follow the ways of Hardy, Blackmore, Baring Gould, and Phillpotts, since they "play the pipes of misty moorlands." It is interesting to note that Hardy and Phillpotts are disapproved of.

To 1905 belongs *Lady Bobs, Her Brother and I. A Romance of the Azores,* by Jean Chamblin. Here the letters are written by Kate, a young, obscure actress to her friend Nora. She meets Lady Bobs and her brother George in the Azores, and the inevitable courtship follows. The letters are vivacious, amusing, and natural. The struggles of a young writer in pursuit of fame are admirably recorded in *The Letters of Theodora,* (1905), by Adelaide L. Rouse. The relation of the upward rise is accomplished in sprightly fashion and the letters are lively and convincing. In the same year came Irene Osgood's *To a Nun Confess'd. Letters from Yolande to Sister Mary,* a book not only eighteenth century in its title, but in the high abandon of its sentimentality as well.

A title, surely long enough to belong to the eighteenth century is that of *Her Brother's Letters. Wherein Miss Christine Carson, of Cincinnati, is shown how the affairs of Girls and Women are regarded by Men in general and, in particular, by her Brother, Burt Carson, Lawyer, of New York City* (1906), a book of Charles Dana Gibson's period of American society, by an anonymous author. This is full of women's strictures on men and of men's strictures on women, and in it a brother finally succeeds in getting his sister married. *Letters to Women in Love,* by Mrs. John Van Vorst, was likewise published in 1906, and the book contains the letters written to four women in love. They are not love letters; they treat of love. The author tells us that love letters "are interesting only for the person to whom they are addressed. But letters to people in love—are they not addressed more or less to the world at large?" (Foreword, p. 5). The author further finds that "indifference, ambition, egoism and jealousy" are the influences, the effects of which she wishes to study. The four "cases" are typical, each one being representative of discordant impulses.

The author of *John Henry* wrote an epistolary work in *Ikey's Letters to His Father* (1907). This is, of course, George V. Hobart, (Hugh McHugh). The book is a series of letters written by Ikey Hohenstein to his father David Hohenstein, while Ikey is on his first tour as a traveling salesman for his father. The father's answers are included. The year 1907 provides two epistolary works of an Oriental trend. The first, *The Lady of the Decoration* by Frances Little, tells of the experiences of an American woman who works in a foreign mission in the Orient. This book is a curious combination of sentiment and humor. A sequel to this, *The Lady and Sada San,* continuing the letters of the first work, appeared in 1912. The second Oriental epistolary work of this year, more famous than the first, is Wallace Irwin's pseudo-philosophical *Letters of a Japanese Schoolboy,* in which straight humor stands shoulder to shoulder with some remarkably strained and unamusing writing.

Grace Donworth's *Letters of Jennie Allen* (1908), is a story in letters that attempts to reproduce dialect with but mediocre results.

Helen Reimensnyder Martin chose a sort of eighteenth-century title for her epistolary romance, *When Half-Gods Go. Being the Story of a Brief Wedded Life as Told in Intimate and Confidential Letters written by a Bride to a Former College Mate* (1911). The title is based on Emerson's line, "When half-gods go, the gods arrive." The love story, here coming after sorrow, is exquisitely introduced.

In 1912 was published what is in all probability the most widely known of all these American novels in letters, Jean Webster's *Daddy-Long-Legs*. In many respects this has a saccharine quality especially beloved of a preceding generation, but it displays likewise a continuous and scrutinizing sense of humor. The letters themselves are too self-conscious, but are, none the less, plausible. *Dear Enemy* (1916) is a novel in letters by the same author and uses much the same material as the earlier work. It carries the "Pollyanna" tradition established in *Daddy-Long-Legs* even farther than did that book. The year 1912 likewise marked the publication of *The Unofficial Secretary*, by Mary Ridpath Mann. This belongs to the travel-letter type of novel. The letters are written from a young woman on her way to and during her stay in South America and are both natural in tone and pleasing in their presentation of local scenes.

The Confessions of a Débutante (1913), is another epistolary work with a sort of Charles Dana Gibson young woman for a heroine. The letters are natural but not particularly amusing or unusual. *The Quest of the Dream,* by Edna Kingsley Wallace, was likewise published in this year. This is a rather dull and uninspired sentimental novel in letters, in which the author attempts to be fanciful and imaginative and merely succeeds in being "cute." The letters are all soliloquies one fails to overhear. At least five epistolary novels belong to 1914. The first is *Letters of an Old Farmer to His Son*, a particularly American volume by William R. Lighton, in which all the letters seem to exist for the express purpose of presenting homely wisdom and wit. The second is *Letters of a Woman Homesteader*, by Elinore Praitt Stewart. The letters unfold the story of Elinore Rupert in her fight to establish life anew after the death of her husband. They are eighteenth-century-like in that they purport to be "genuine letters" and contain several "histories." The narrative told is both smooth in its progression and human in its appeal. A graceful and delicate romance published in this year is *My Lady of the Chinese Courtyard*, by Elizabeth Cooper, author of *Living Up to Billy*, both in letters. The amazing difference between these two works is sufficient to indicate that this author was able to use the letter as a distinctly pliable and expressive medium for the telling of a story. There is a sustained loveliness in the letters of *My Lady of the Chinese Courtyard*, and the author, in attempting to fill them with Chinese atmosphere, does not make herself ridiculous. The fourth epistolary novel of this year is *Via P and O*, by Jane Stocking, a book written very much in the manner of Frances Little. Here are letters from China and the East, the chief interest in which is descriptive. The last, *The Wooing of a Recluse*, by Gregory Marwood, represents the Western novel in letters and is unusual chiefly for the fact that the same name is used by the writer of the letters (Gregory Marwood) as is used by the author of the book. The letters themselves tell a sentimental story of what seems to be a hopeless love and tells that story in a manner that is rather incongruously bookish.

The year 1915 offers at least three epistolary novels. A very sprightly story in letters is *The Cocoon*, by Ruth McEnery Stuart, a publication of this year. The book tells, in letters, of a young woman who is taking a rest cure in a Virginia sanitarium. There is here an occasional insertion of diary, but most of the book is in letters. The *raison d'être* of the letters is logical; but the situation is artificial, and the style varies between the affected and the humorous. Reminiscent of the epistolary method of Ingraham is *The Hope of Glory. Being Part of a Correspondence written in the Roman Empire between the Years 52 and 66 A.D.*, by William Schuyler. The author is referred to in Mary Fisher's introduction to the work (p. XV) as a Socratic gadfly. The book, itself a sort of sequel to the same author's historical novel *Under Pontius Pilate*, gives a representative picture of the Roman Empire at the time when paganism was overthrown by Christianity. The letters, written chiefly by Lucius Domitius Ahenobarbus to his friend Caius Claudius Proculus, are both informative and "in character" at all times. A very convincing work in letters, *Living Up to Billy*, by Elizabeth Cooper, published in 1915, tells of the struggle of a woman to make herself over as a suitable mother to the baby she adores. It is touchingly and realistically done in more or less New York English, that captures the vernacular with considerable accuracy. The letters are short and succeed in revealing the character of the showgirl, Nan, who is Billy's mother, with a degree of patent reality that might be envied by even greater authors who have used the epistolary mode as a creative medium.

In 1916 comes the first of a series of epistolary works written completely in the slang idiom. This is headed by *You Know Me, Al* of that year, the work of Ring Lardner, and the best of the lot; and this is followed by an abject series of *Dere Mable* (1918); *Same Old Bill* (1919); and *That's Me All Over, Mable* (1919), all the work of Edward Streeter. A sequel to *Dere Mable* was written by Florence Elizabeth Summers in 1918 and called *Dere Bill. Mable's Love Letters to Her Rookie.*

Very much like *The Letters from a Self-Made Merchant to His Son* are *Uncle Bill's Letters to His Niece*, by Ray Brown (1917), another of those collections of letters giving sound advice from elder to younger that seem to be so popular in American epistolary literature.

James Lane Allen has given us an epistolary novel in *The Emblems of Fidelity* (1918), which he subtitles, *A Comedy*

in Letters (it is to be remembered that Thomas Hardy subtitles *The Hand of Ethelberta "a comedy in chapters"*). In
this book a list of characters, dramatis personae, is set forth at
the beginning in true Richardsonian fashion. Allen himself
figures in the correspondence as Beverly Sands, "rising young
American novelist." His diary appears, from time to time,
alongside the large number of letters which he and all the
other people write. In 1921 came *The Pipes of Yesterday.
A Novel,* by Frederick Arnold Kummer and Mary Christian.
This is another collaboration in letters. Interestingly enough,
the end is not the happy one of the 80's, 90's and 1900's, but
the rather resignatory one of the early 20's, where the young
woman, unable to share her lover with his work as an author, becomes merely "a friend."

To the year 1922 belongs *Letters to a Djinn,* by Grace
Zaring Stone, a very casual novel in letters in which an American girl tells of her adventures on the way to, and in, Aus-
tralia. The letters are pleasant and chatty; the action is slow;
the atmosphere is accurately and picturesquely captured.

Letters to a Lady in the Country (1925), is a very intelligent and animated epistolary work of fiction by the late
Stuart Sherman, and the letters contained therein sound entirely like letters. The year 1927 brought *Love Letters, A Romance in Correspondence,* by Harold R. Vynne. This is a
story of misunderstanding and reunion told in letters with
carefully explanatory narrative interludes. The work is chiefly
interesting for its format rather than its content, though there
is in it a vein of humor which relieves what might otherwise
prove to be a much too sentimental tale. *Footprints* (1929),
by Kay Cleaver Strahan, is a murder-mystery story in which
the murder is solved by means of a packet of letters which
comprise most of the book. The letters are preceded by two
chapters of straight narrative, which present the situation the
letters ultimately solve, and there is likewise a conclusion of
straight narrative. The epistolary mystery story is, of course,
by no means a novelty. *Dracula* is in letters; *Desperate Reme-
dies* by Thomas Hardy, and *The Moonstone* by Wilkie Col-

lins are both written in journal form. In *Footprints* the letters are all from two different people to a third person, and they present a fascinating story in an absorbing and baffling fashion. In 1929 was likewise published *Promise Not to Tell*, full of very natural letters from Lucinda to Christopher and from Christopher to Lucinda. The loose morality of a certain type of American abroad is well set down, but the endless round of riotous parties becomes extremely tiresome by the time the overlong story reaches its conclusion. A story of prison life, written in letters, *The Crooked Vein* (1930), is the work of Brewster Kane. Gerald Lorraine is put in prison for misusing the mails, and while he is there he writes his amusing commentary. "In the bright lexicon of youth there's no such word as fail—or jail. . . ." The book presents a natural, humorous, and moderately sympathetic study of prison life, free of sentimentality. An even more recent epistolary effort is *The Dublin Letters*, by Lee Harriman (1931), in which the letters take on all the frenzy of the "jazz age." A further indication of this same sort of thing is to be found in that evolution of the letter form, the novel in telegrams, chiefly exemplified by such a book as *Show Girl* (1928).

While no outstanding book, no greatest American novel has been written in letters, yet the strain is a fairly continuous one in American fiction from its inception in 1789 to the present century. Just as it has cropped up periodically in England and in France, so it has here. Just as it spread through all sorts of fiction in those countries, so it has here, and there is even one of Ornum and Co.'s fifteen-cent romances, *Three-Fingered Jack*, the full title of which is, *Obi; or, Three-Fingered Jack. The Famous Black Robber of the West Indian Islands*, written in letters. As in England all the work of Richardson was in letters, so the work of the Reverend William Ware was here, too, although, of course, the comparison between them ends there. Thus, while the strain has been minor in American literature, and while it never emerged into great prominence as a form into which fiction was cast, it is present and worth chronicling from the comparative point of view.

Indeed, the epistolary form achieved a majority nowhere save in England. It was always distinctly a minor thing in France, in Italy, and on the Continent in general. But no great literature, with the possible exception of the Spanish, seems to have escaped completely from the impulse. Its tendencies, its manifestations, its uses are everywhere analogous, and thus established for fiction the universality of the letter as a literary and personal accessory of immense worth and palpable convenience.

CONCLUSION

IT HAS been the attempt of the preceding chapters to trace, in a more or less chronological fashion, a history of the epistolary impulse as an aid to story telling from the earliest literary period to the immediate present. In attempting to span so considerable a stretch of time there has been the ever-present necessity for being eclectic. The selections in the earlier chapters were made because it was felt that they were integrally representative of the literatures of which they are part. The guiding aim has, however, at all times been the presentation of the continuity of the epistolary impulse.

It has been interesting to note that the growth of the literary epistle and the introduction of the letter as a part of the mechanism of fiction have been such that they could be observed side by side and cheek by jowl. The two strains have each been continuous and, at certain times, coincident.

The gradual emergence in the sixteenth century of the letter as a formal, model type has been noted and discussed, and its importance, not only in that century, but also throughout the span of later literary production in that field, has been analyzed and, it is hoped, carefully recorded. It has been seen that, from the formal letter-writers, the letter itself passed through a period of vitalization and later through another of fictionalization. The use of the letter for fictional purposes has been seen to be, in its early stages, casual, hesitant, almost uncertain of effect. Later it gathered certainty and with more frequent use became, after the livening influence of Richardson, an almost indispensable literary device.

Samuel Richardson's work stands as a definite monument of the power of the man, firm, great, unflinching, and unfading. If there seems to be too much of Richardson here, it can only be said that this man's work is the greatest, in exclusively epistolary form, in English literature. The many successors and imitators serve but to emphasize this fact for us. The great impulse which the use that Richardson made of the epistolary novel in achieving popularity has been recorded in detail. We have traced the gradual upward trend of the novel in letters from 1742 to its brilliant peak in 1785, from which it suddenly and, in some ways unjustly, was allowed to decline. No type of novel, however, no school of literature, has been of more concentrated growth, of more conscious adoption by its users, of more determined and set habit than the epistolary; no type of fiction has drawn into its folds more names famous in the history of literature itself. Finally, and perhaps most importantly, no type of writing has had a more sincere place in the affection of the public than has the epistolary.

The neglect which the minor novelists have endured, as a group, must perhaps be laid to the lack of critical interest; to one who has read to some degree the work of these people the lack of attention seems somewhat inexcusable. It is hoped, then, that they have not here been so neglected, as far as goes their contribution to the novel in letter form. In the forty years during which the epistolary novel flourished these novelists played a considerable role. Nor did the novel of this sort die at the end of its popularity of forty years' standing; rather has it had a practically continuous, if not always robust, life since 1785. The very fact that so many individual authors have turned to it since that time and that there was a sort of epistolary revival in the 1890's, are ample proofs of its enduring influence and positive worth.

BIBLIOGRAPHY

PART I

Works of Reference

The American Novel. By Carl Van Doren. New York, 1929

L'Anglomania e L'Influsso Inglese in Italia nel Secolo XVIII. Di Arturo Graf. Torino, 1911

The Annual Register; or, a View of History, Politics and Literature, Dodsley, London, N. D.

The Collected Essays and Addresses of Augustine Birrell. Three Volumes. Vol. I. New York, 1923

British Novelists and Their Styles, Being a Critical Sketch of the History of Prose Fiction. By David Masson. Boston, 1889

The Cambridge History of American Literature (in Four Volumes). Ed. by Trent, Erskine, Sherman and Van Doren. New York, 1917

The Cambridge History of English Literature. Ed. by Ward and Waller. New York, 1907

The Dictionary of National Biography. Ed. by Stephen and Lee. Oxford, 1917

Early American Fiction, 1774-1830. A Compilation of the Titles of Works of Fiction, by Writers Born or Residing in North America, North of the Mexican Border, and Printed Previous to 1831. By Oscar Wegelin. New York, 1929

The Early American Novel. By Lillie Demming Loshe, Ph.D. New York, 1907

The Eighteenth Century Novel in Theory and Practise. By Charles Herbert Huffman. Dayton, Virginia, N. D.

English Biography in the Eighteenth Century. By Mark Longaker. Philadelphia, 1931

English Literature and Society in the Eighteenth Century. Ford Lectures, 1903. By Leslie Stephen. London, 1904

The English Novel. By George Saintsbury. London, 1913

A List of English Tales and Prose Romances Printed Before 1740. By Arundell Esdaile. London, 1912

English Thought in the Eighteenth Century. By Leslie Stephen. New York, 1927

French Novelists. Manners and Ideas from the Renaissance to the Revolution. By Frederick C. Green. New York, 1929

Franklin's Bagatelles. Ed. by Joseph George Rosengarten. Philadelphia, N. D.

The Gentleman's Magazine. Newbery, London, 1731-1800.

The Georgian Era: Memoirs of the Most Eminent Persons who have Flourished in Great Britain. From the Accession of George the First to the Demise of George the Fourth. Four Volumes. Vol. III. London, 1834

Geschichte Der Deutchsen Literatur. Von Wilhelm Seherer. Berlin, 1883

Histoire de la Littérature francaise. Par Gustave Lanson. Paris, 1896

A History of American Literature. By William B. Cairns, Ph.D. Revised Edition. New York, 1930

A History of English Literature, 1780-1880. By Oliver Elton. New York, 1920

The History of the English Novel. Vols. I to IV. By Ernest A. Baker. London, 1928-30

History of French Literature from the Earliest Times to the Present. By Wm. A. Nitze and E. Preston Dargan. New York, 1927

A History of the French Novel. By George Saintsbury. London, 1917

A History of Modern English Literature. By Sir Edmund Gosse. New York, 1928

Hours in a Library. By Leslie Stephen. London, 1892

The Life and Works of Francis Hopkinson. By George E. Hastings. Chicago, 1926

The Light Reading of Our Ancestors. By Lord Ernle. New York, 1927

The Literature of Roguery. By Frank Wadleigh Chandler. New York, 1907

Manly Anniversary Studies, The. "English Epistolary Fiction before *Pamela*." By Helen Sard Hughes. Chicago, 1923

Medieval Rhetoric and Poetic. By Charles Sears Baldwin. New York, 1928

The Monthly Review. Griffiths, London, 1749-1800

La Nouvelle Héloise de Jean-Jacques Rousseau. Par Philippe Van Tieghem. Paris, 1929

Novels and Novelists from Elizabeth to Victoria. By J. Cordy Jeaffreson. Vol. I. London, 1895

The Novels and Novelists of the Eighteenth Century in Illustration of the Manners and Morals of the Age. By William Forsythe. London, 1871

The Oriental Tale in England in the Eighteenth Century. By Martha Pike Conant. New York, 1908

L'Ottocento. Di Guido Mazzoni. In Storia Letteraria D'Italia. Scritta da una società di Professori. Milan, 1913

Polly Honeycombe: A Dramatick Novel in One Act. By George Colman. Becket & Davis, London, 1760

The Popular Novel in England, 1770-1800. By J. M. S. Tompkins. London, 1932

Prejudice and Promise in XVth Century England. By C. L. Kingsford. Clarendon Press, 1925

Richardson. By Brian W. Downs. London, New York, 1928

Samuel Richardson. By Sheila Kaye-Smith. London, N. D.

Samuel Richardson—A Biographical and Critical Study. By Clara Linklater Thomson. London, 1900

The Rise of the Novel of Manners. By Charlotte E. Morgan. New York, 1911

Le Roman en France. Depuis 1610 jusqu'à nos jours. Par Paul Morillot. Paris, N. D.

Le Roman personnel. Par Joachim Merlant. Paris, N. D.

Romanzieri e romanzi del cinquecento e del siecento. Di Alfonso Albertazzi. Bologna, 1891

Romanzieri e romanzi del Settecento. Di G. B. Marchesi. Bergamo, 1903

Il Settecento. Di Tullio Concari. In Storia Letteraria D'Italia. Scritta da una Società di Professori. Milan, N. D.

Il Settecento. Di Guilio Natali. In Storia Letteraria D'Italia. Scritta da una Società di Professori. Milan, 1929

Sir Thomas Malory, His Turbulent Career. A Biography. By Edward Hicks. Cambridge, 1928

The Tale of Terror. A Study of the Gothic Romance. By Edith Birkhead. New York, N. D.

CHAPTER I

Texts

Alciphron. Letters from the Country and the Towns. Trans. by
 F. A. Wright. London, N. D.
Alcuin. By Andrew F. West. New York, 1916
Bible, The. Oxford University Press
Egyptian Literature. (World's Great Classics) Intro. by Epi-
 phanius Wilson. Colonial Press, 1901
Epistles of Pliny, The. William Melmoth-Clifford H. Moore.
 The Bibliophile Society, Boston, 1925
Epistolae de rebus familiaribus et varie di Francisci Petrachae.
 Ed. by Giuseppe Fracasseti. Florence, 1859
Epistolae Ho-Elianae: Familiar Letters, Domestic and Foreign.
 By James Howell. Bell, London, 1737
Iliad of Homer. Trans. by Theodore A. Budsley. London, 1874
Letters of Marcus Tullius Cicero, The. Oxford, 1783
Letters of Sidonius, The. By O. M. Dalton. Clarendon Press,
 1915
Paston Letters, The. Ed. by James Gairdner. London, 1872
Roundabout Papers. By Wm. Thackeray. London, 1879
The Works of John Lyly. Ed. by R. W. Bond. Oxford, 1902

CHAPTER II

Texts

Daphnis and Chloe, The Shepheards Holidae. By Angell Daye.
 Ed. by Joseph Jacobs. London, 1890
Familiar Letters on Important Occasions. By Samuel Richard-
 son. Intro. by Brian W. Downs. (First edition, 1741) New
 York, 1928

CHAPTER III

Familiar Letters on Important Occasions. By Samuel Richardson. Intro. by Brian W. Downs. New York, 1928
The Works of Alexander Pope, Esq. Nine Volumes Complete.
 Ed. by Joseph Wharton, D.D. Vols. VII, VIII, IX. London,
 1797

The Works in Verse and Prose of Nicholas Breton. Ed. by the
Rev. Alexander B. Grosart. Two Volumes, Vol. II, Chertsey
Worthies Library. (Printed for Private Circulation.) Lon-
don, 1879

CHAPTER IV

Account of the Secret Services of M. De Vernay to Count Tech-
ley. Trans. from the French. Revised by T. Brown, London,
1685

Adventures of Lindamira, The; A Lady of Quality. R. Wellington, 1702

Amorous History of the Gauls, The. By Roger de Ralubin. Osborn, 1727

Amours Between Philander and Sylvia, or, Love-Letters Between A Nobleman and His Sister. For D. Brown. J. Tonson, B. Tooke, G. Straham, S. Ballard, W. Mears, F. Clay,
1749

Bath Intrigues. By Eliza Haywood. J. Roberts, 1725

Constant Lovers, The. London, 1731

Continuation of Letters Written by a Turkish Spy at Paris.
By Daniel Defoe. London, 1718

Country Gentleman's Companion for the Town. London, 1702

Court Intrigues. By Mrs. Mary de la Rivière Manley. London,
1711

Double Captive, The. By a Young Gentleman. London, 1718

Familiar Epistles of Col. Henry Martin. London, 1685

Familiar Letters of Love and Gallantry. By T. Brown. London,
1719

Fatal Amour Between a Beautiful Lady and a Young Nobleman,
The. For J. Moore, 1719

Five Love-Letters from a Nun to a Cavalier. By Marianna
D'Alcoforado. For H. Brown, 1678

Five Love-Letters Written by a Cavalier. For R. Bentley and M.
Magnes, 1683

Friendship in Death. By Mrs. Elizabeth Rowe. H. Lintot, 1728

Gentleman Apothecary, The. By J. DeVilliers. For H. Brown,
1670

Historical Account of the Amours of the Emperor of Morocco.
By the Count of ———. E. Mallet, 1702

King of the Pirates, The. By Daniel Defoe. London, 1719

Letters from a Lady at Paris to a Lady at Avignon. Mears and Browne, 1716

Letters from a Lady of Quality to a Chevalier. Trans. by Mrs. Eliza Haywood. London, 1721

Letters from the Marchioness De M— to the Count De R—. Trans. from the original French, by Mr. Humphreys. Wilford, 1735

Letters from a Persian in England to His Friends in Ispahan. By George Lyttleton. London, 1735

Letters from the Palace of Fame. By Mrs. Eliza Haywood. H. Lintot, 1727

Letters Moral and Entertaining. By Mrs. Elizabeth Rowe. London, 1729

Letters of Abelard and Eloise. London, 1722

Letters of a Lady of Quality to a Chevalier. By Mrs. Eliza Haywood. London, 1724

Letters Written by Mrs. Manley. London, 1696

Letters Writ by a Turkish Spy. For G. Strahan; W. Mears, 1687

Life of the Countess De Gondez. By Mrs. P. Aubin. J. and J. Knapton, J. Darby, A. Bettesworth, F. Fayraw, J. Osborn and T. Longman, J. Pemberton, C. Rivington, F. Clay, J. Batley, and A. Ward, 1729

Lining of the Patch-Work Screen, The. By Mrs. Jane Barker. London, 1726

London Spy, The. By Edward Ward. J. How, 1703-09

Love-Letters Between a Certain Nobleman and The Famous Mr. Wilson. London, 1723

Love-Letters Between a Nobleman and His Sister. By Mrs. Aphra Behn. For J. Hindmarsh, 1683

Love-Letters Between a Nobleman and His Sister. D. Brown, J. Tonson, J. Nicholson, B. Tooke and G. Strahan, 1707

Love-Letters Between Polydorus and Messalina. London, 1689

Love-Letters from Henry VIII to Anne Boleyn. For J. Churchill, 1714

Love-Letters on All Occasions. By Mrs. Haywood. London, 1730

Love in Excess; or, The Fatal Enquiry. By Mrs. Haywood. Chetwood, 1721

Lover's Secretary, The. London, 1692

Lover's Secretary, The. (v. The Adventures of Lindamira.) Re-

vised and Corrected by Mr. T. Brown. 3rd ed. For W.
Fealer; R. Wellington, J. Wellington, A. Bettesworth, F.
Clay, in trust for B. Wellington, 1734
Lover's Sighs, The. (v. The Post Man Robb'd of His Mail.) By
Gonsalvo de Mendoza. London, 1719
Love's Poesie. For J. Hindmarsh, 1686
Memoires of the Court of France. By Madam Daunois. For E.
Whitlock, 1697
Memoirs of the Adventures of a French Lady of Quality. Lon-
don, 1705
Memoirs of the Dutchess Mazarine. By Cesar Kischard de Saints
Réal. W. Cademan, 1676
Memoirs of the Dutchess Mazarine. London, 1713
New Version of the Lady Gr——S. London, 1682
Perfidious P—, The. London, 1702
Perplex'd Duchess, The. S. Powell; for G. Rich and W. Smith,
Dublin, 1727
Persian Letters. By C. de Sécondat. Trans. by Mr. Ozell. (v.
Letters from a Persian.) J. Millar, 1730
Post-Man Robb'd of His Mail, The. London, ca. 1693
Pylades and Corinna. London, 1731
Reform'd Coquet, The. By Mrs. Davys. A. Stephens, 1724
Secret History of the Court of Caramania. By Mrs. Eliza Hay-
wood. London, 1728
Seven Portuguese Letters. For H. Brome, 1781
CCXI Sociable Letters. By the Duchess of Newcastle. London,
1718
Spanish Politician, The. London, 1718
Stage-Coach Journey to Exeter, A. By Mrs. Manley. For J.
Roberts, 1725
Turkish Spy, The. London, 1698
Letters of an Italian Nun and an English Gentleman. Translated
from the French of J. J. Rousseau. 6th ed. For Sherwood,
Neely, and Jones, 1817

CHAPTER V

Texts

The Spectator. Ed. by Robert Bisset. Vol. V. London, N. D.
The Works of Samuel Richardson. Nineteen volumes.

Pamela. Four volumes.
Clarissa. Eight volumes.
Sir Charles Grandison. Seven volumes.
With Introductions by William Lyon Phelps. New York, 1902.

CHAPTER VI

Texts

Adolphus de Biron. A Novel founded on the French Revolution.
Plymouth, Nettleton, N. D.
Adventures Underground. A letter from a Gentleman swallowed
up in the late Earthquake. Falstaff, 1750
Aerostatic Spy, The; or, Excursions with A Balloon. By An
Aerial Traveller. Symonds, 1785
Affecting Story of Lionel and Arabella, The. A Republication of
the Historical account of the Discovery of the Island of
Madeira. Payne & Bouquet, 1750; Griffiths, 1756
Agnes de Courci, A Domestic Tale. By Mrs. Bennett. Hookham,
1789
Albina; A Novel in a Series of Letters. Lane, 1786
Alethia; or, Letters from Selima, Empress of the Turks, to her
Daughter Isabella, of Grand Cairo. Noble, 1771
All's Right at Last, or, the History of Miss West. Noble, 1773
Alwyn; or, the Gentleman Comedian. By Thomas Holcroft.
Fielding and Walker, 1780
Anchoret, The. A Moral Tale. In A Series of Letters. Newbery,
1773
Anecdotes of a Convent. By the author of Memoirs of Mrs. Wil-
liams (Helen-Maria Williams). Becket & Dehondt, 1771
Anecdotes of the Russian Empire. In a series of letters, written a
few years ago, from St. Petersburg. Cadell, 1784
Anna: A Sentimental Novel, in a Series of Letters. Hookham, 1782
Anna St. Ives. A Novel. By Thomas Holcroft. Shepperson &
Reynolds, 1792
Anti-Pamela. Huggonson, 1741
Anti-Pamela, or Feign'd Innocence Detected: In a series of
Syrena's Adventures. (Mrs. Haywood.) London, 1741
Apology for the Life of Mrs. Shamela Andrews, An. By Henry
Fielding. Dodd, 1741
Argus; the House-Dog at Eadlip. Memoirs in a Family Corre-

spondence. By the Author of Constance and the Pharos.
Hookham, 1789

Artless Lovers, The: A Novel, in a Series of Letters. From Miss
Lucy Wheatly in town, to Miss Annabel Grierson in the
Country. Wilkie, 1768

Arundel. By the author of The Observer. (Richard Cumberland)
Dilly, 1789

Assignation, The; A sentimental novel, in a Series of Letters.
Noble, 1774

Barford Abbey: A novel in a Series of Letters. By Miss Minifie.
Cadell, 1768

Barham Downs. A novel. By Robert Bage. Wilkie, 1784

Belleville Lodge, a Novel. Dublin; Wogan, Byrne, Moore, Jones
and Rice, 1793

Belmont Grove; or, the Discovery. By a Lady. Lane, 1785

Blossoms of Virtue, The. London, 1770

Budget of Love, The; or, Letters Between Florizel and Perdita.
To which are prefixed Some Interesting Accounts of the
Fair Heroine. Bew, 1781

Camilla; or, the Correspondence of a Deceased Friend. Cass, 1785

Camp Guide, The; in a Series of Letters from Ensign Tommy
Toothpick to Lady Sarah Toothpick, and from Miss Nelly
Brisk to Miss Gadabout. Fielding & Walker, 1778

Card, The. By John Kidgell. Newbery, 1755

Cardiphonia; or, the Utterances of the Heart, in the course of
Real Correspondence. By the author of Omicron's Letters.
Buckland, 1781

Cautious Lover, The; or, the History of Lord Woburn. By a
Young Gentleman of Oxford. Cadell, 1772

Centaur Not Fabulous, The; In Six Letters to a Friend, on the
Life in Vogue. Millar & Dodsley, 1755

Charles; or, the History of a Young Baronet and a Lady of
Quality. A Novel. Bew, 1779

Child of Woe, The. A Novel. By Mrs. Elizabeth Norman.
Symonds, 1789

Clandestine Lovers, The. In a Series of Letters. Noble, 1789

Clara Lennox; or, The Distressed Widow. A Novel, founded on
facts. Interspersed with an historical description of The
Isle of Man. By Mrs. Harriet Lee. Adlard, 1797

Clarentine. A Novel. Robinsons, 1796

Clementina Bedford. In Letters and Narrative. By J. J. Cambar. Symonds, 1796

Clio; or, a Secret History of the Life and Amours of the late celebrated Mrs. S—N—M. Written by herself in a letter to Hillarius. Cooper, 1752

Colonel Ormsby; or, the Genuine History of an Irish Nobleman in the French Service. Macgowan, 1782

Confessions of a Coquet, The. In a Series of Letters. Lane, 1785

Confidential Letters of Albert, The; from his First Attachment to Charlotte to her Death; from the Sorrows of Werter. Robinsons, 1790

Conflict, The; a Sentimental tale, in a Series of Letters. By Mr. Heron, Newcastle. Deighton, 1793

Constantia; or, the Distressed Friend. Johnston, 1770

Continuation of the Life of Marianna, The. To which is added, the History of Ernistina; with Letters, and other Miscellaneous pieces. Becket & Dehondt, 1768

Coombe Wood. By the author of Barford Abbey, and The Cottage. (Miss Minifie.) Baldwin, 1783

Correspondence of Theodosius and Constantia, The; from their First Acquaintance to the Departure of Theodosius. Now first published from original MSS. By the Editor of the Letters that Passed Between Theodosius and Constantia, After She Had taken the Veil. By John Langhorne. Becket & Dehondt, 1765

Correspondence of Two Lovers, The; Inhabitants of Lyons. Published from the French originals. Hookham, 1789

Correspondents, The. An original novel; in a Series of Letters. Dublin; Exshaw, 1775

Cottage, The; a novel; in a Series of Letters. By Miss Minifie. Durham & Co., 1769

Count de Poland, The; by Miss M. Minifie, one of the authors of Lady Frances A— and Lady Caroline S—. Dodsley, 1780

Country Curate, The; or, Letters from Clericus to Benevolus. Longman & Co., 1788

Coxheath. A Novel. In a Series of Letters. By a Lady. Fielding & Walker, 1779

Dangerous Connections; or, Letters collected in a Society and Published for the Instruction of other Societies. By Choderlos de Laclos. Hookham, 1784

D'Arcy. A novel by Charlotte Smith. Philadelphia; Carey, 1796

Daughter, The; or, the History of Miss Emilia Royston, and Miss Harriet Ayres. In a Series of Letters. By the authoress of the Exemplary Mother. (Maria Susanna Cooper) Dodsley, 1775

Death's A Friend. A Novel, by the Author of The Bastard. Bew, 1788

Delicate Crimes. In a Series of Letters. (Previous Edition under the Title: Fatal Effects of Inconstancy) Hooper, 1777

Delicate Distress, The. By "Frances" (Mrs. Griffith). Becket, 1769

Délices du Sentiment, Les; or, the Passionate Lovers, in a Series of Letters, which have recently Passed between two celebrated characters, well-known in polite Life for their Virtues, Talents, and Accomplishments, with a Translation from the Originals. Written in Cypher. Macgowan, 1787

Denial, The; or, the Happy Retreat. By the Rev. James Thomson. Sewell, 1790

Derwent Priory; or, Memoirs of an Orphan, in a Series of Letters. First published Periodically; now republished with Additions, by the Author of The Castle on the Rock. Symonds, 1798

Description of Millenium Hall, A, and the Country Adjacent: together with the characters of the inhabitants; and such historical anecdotes and reflections as may excite in the Reader Proper Sentiments of Humanity and Lead the Maid to the Love of Virtue. By Mrs. Sarah Scott. Carnan & Newbery, Jr., 1762

Desmond, A Novel. By Charlotte Smith. Robinsons, 1792

Disguise, The: A Dramatic Novel. Dodsley, 1771

Disinterested Love; or, the History of Sir Charles Royston and Emily Lesley. In a Series of Letters. Wilkie, 1776

Disinterested Love; or, the Modern Robin Grey; in a Series of Letters Founded on Facts. By a Widow Lady. Hookham, 1788

Disinterested Nabob, The; a novel interspersed with Genuine Descriptions of India, its manners and customs. Robinsons, 1787

Distressed Lovers, The; or, the History of Edward and Eliza. In a Series of Letters. Dublin; Watson & Colles, 1768

Distressed Virtue; or, the History of Miss Harriet Nelson; in which is included the Unhappy Story of Miss Caroline Lennox. In a Series of Letters. Noble, 1781

Divorce, The. In a Series of Letters to and from Persons of High Rank. Baldwin, 1771

Doncaster Races; or, the History of Miss Maitland; a Tale of Truth, in a Series of Letters, published from the originals, with interesting Additions. By Alexander Bicknell, Author of the History of Lady Anne Neville; Isabella, or the Rewards of Good Nature, Etc. Stalker, 1790

Double Disappointment; The; or, the History of Charles Marlow. In a Series of Letters. Hookham, 1774

Double Surprise, The. In a Series of Letters. Hookham, 1783

Doubtful Marriage, The. A Narration Drawn from Characters in Real Life. By Wm. Hutchinson. Dublin; Wogan, 1793

Duped Guardian, The; or the Amant Malade. In a Series of Letters. By Mrs. Cartwright. Cass, 1786

Edwin and Julia; a novel, in a Series of Letters. By a Lady. London, 1774

Ela; or, the Delusions of the Heart. A Tale, founded on facts. By Mrs. Burke. Robinsons, 1787

Elegant Tales, Histories and Epistles of a Moral Tendency; on Love, Friendship, Matrimony, Conjugal Felicity, Jealousy, Constancy, Magnanimity, Chearfulness, and other Important Subjects. By the author of Woman; or, Historical Sketches of the Fair Sex. Kearsley, 1791

Eleonora, in a Series of Letters, written by a Female Inhabitant of Leeds in Yorkshire. (Mrs. Gomersall). Walter, 1789

Elisa Powell; or Trials and Sensibility: A Series of Original Letters collected by a Welsh Curate. Robinsons, 1795

Eliza Cleland. Lane, 1788

Emma; or the Unfortunate Attachment. A Sentimental Tale. Hookham, 1773

Emma Corbet; or, the Miseries of Civil War. By (Courtney Melmoth) S. J. Pratt. Bath, Pratt & Church; London, Baldwin, 1780

Emily Herbert; or, Perfidy Punished. Jones, 1786

Errors of Innocence, The. By Harriet Lee. Robinsons, 1786

Errors of Nature; The; or, The History of Charles Manley, in a Series of Letters. By Mr. B. Walwyn. Cownal, 1783

Euphemia. By Mrs. Charlotte Lennox. Cadell, 1790

Evelina; or, the History of a Young Lady's Entrance Into the World. By Frances Burney. Lowndes, 1778

Excursion, The; a Novel. By Mrs. Brooke. Cadell, 1777

Exemplary Mother, The; or Letters between Miss Villars and Her Family. Published by a Lady from the originals in her Possession (Maria Susanna Cooper). Becket, 1769

Exiles, The; or, Memoirs of the Count de Cronstadt. By Clara Reeve. Hookham, 1788

Expedition of Humphrey Clinker, The. By Tobias Smollett. Johnston, 1771

Fair Imposter, The. A Novel. By a Lady. Hookham & Carpenter, 1792

Fair Syrian, The; a Novel. By the author of Barham Downs (Robert Bage). Walter, 1787

Faithful Fugitive, The; or, Adventures of Miss Teresa M. In a Series of Letters to a Friend. Vernon, 1766

False Friend, The; a Domestic Story. By Mary Robinson. Longman & Rees, 1799

False Friends, The. By the author of The Ring. Barker, 1785

Family Pictures. A Novel, containing curious and interesting memoirs of several persons of fashion in W—re. By a Lady. Nicoll, 1764

Fanny, a Novel in a Series of Letters. By a Lady. Richardson, 1786

Fanny; or, the Amours of a West Country Young Lady. In a Series of Letters. Manby, 1775

Fashionable Friend, The; a Novel. Becket & Dehondt, 1773

Fatal Compliance, The; or, The History of Miss Constantia Pembroke. Jones, 1771

Fatal Effects of Deception. Jones, 1773

Fatal Effects of Inconstancy, The; or, Letters of the Marchioness de Syrcé, the Count de Mirbelle, and others. Trans. from the French. Bew, 1774

Fatal Friendship, a Novel. By a Lady. Lowndes, 1770

Fate of Velina De Guidova, The. By Mrs. Ann Radcliffe (?). Lane, 1790

Fault Was All Her Own, The. In a Series of Letters. By a Lady. Riley, 1771

Favorites of Felicity, The. In a Series of Letters. By John Potter. M. B. Becket & Co., 1785

Feelings of the Heart, The; or, the History of a Country Girl. Written by Herself and addressed to a Lady of Quality. Noble, 1772

Felicia to Charlotte; or, Letters from a Young Lady in the Country, to a Friend in Town. (Vol. II, Payne & Bouquet, 1750) Robinson, Vol. 1, 1744

Female Frailty; or, the History of Miss Wroughton. Noble, 1772

Female Stability; or, the History of Miss Belville. In a Series of Letters. By the late Miss Palmer. Newbery, 1780

Female Werter, The. Trans. from the French of M. Perrin. Robinsons, 1792

Force of Love, The. In a Series of Letters. By John Dent, author of Too Civil By Half. Cass, 1786

Fortunate Orphan, The; or, Memoirs of the Countess of Marlow. Penn'd by Herself and revis'd by the Chevalier de Mouhy. Needham, 1745

Frederica Risberg, a German Story. Lane, 1793

Friends, The; or, Original Letters of a Person deceased. Now first published from the MSS. in his Correspondent's Hands. Bell, 1773

Fruitless Repentance; or, the History of Miss Kitty Lefever. Newbery, 1769

Gamesters, The. By the author of Burton Wood (Mrs. A. M. Johnson). Baldwin, 1786

Generous Attachment, The; a Novel in a Series of Letters. Bew, 1787

Generous Sister, The. In a Series of Letters. By Mrs. Cartwright. Bew, 1779

Genuine Copies of the Love-Letters and Cards which have Passed between an Illustrious Personage and a Noble Lady, during the Course of a Late Amour. Published by a Proctor of Doctors Commons. Brown, 1770

Genuine Distresses of Damon and Celia. In a Series of Letters, between the late General Crawford, Sir John Huffey Delaval, Bart., Sir Francis Blake Delaval, K.B., and two Unfortunate Lovers. By William Renwick. Dodsley, 1772

Genuine Letters to a Young Lady of Family, Figure, and Fortune. Wilkie, 1761

Genuine Memoirs of Miss Harriet Melvin, and Miss Leonora

Stanway. In a Series of Letters. By a Young Lady of Glocester. Fuller, 1772

Geraldina, a Novel, founded on a Recent Event. Robinsons, 1798

Gipsy Countess, The. By Miss Gunning. Longman & Rees, 1799

Gordian Knot, The. By "Henry" (Richard Griffith). Becket, 1769

Guide to Domestic Happiness, The. In a Series of Letters. Buckland, 1776

Happy Release, The; or, the History of Charles Wharton and Sophia Harley. In a Series of Letters. Noble, 1787

Harcourt; a Sentimental Novel. In a Series of Letters. By the Authoress of Evelina. Dublin; Bryne, 1780

Hartley-House, Calcutta. Dodsley, 1789

Henrietta, Countess Osenvor; a Sentimental Novel, in a Series of Letters. By Mr. Treysac de Vergy, Counsellor in the Parliament of Paris, and Editor of the "Lovers." Roson, 1770

Hermione; or, the Orphan Sisters. Dublin; Exshaw, 1791

History of a Young Married Lady of Distinction: in a Series of Letters between Madame du Montier and the Marchioness * * *, her daughter. Noble, 1773

History of Alicia Montague, The. By Mrs. Jane Marishall. Robinson & Roberts, 1767

History of Charles Mandeville, The. A Sequel to Lady Julia. By Mrs. Brooke. Lane, 1790

History of Charles Wentworth, Esq.; in a Series of Letters, The. By the author of A National History of Guiana. (Mr. Bancroft). Becket, 1770

History of Eliza Musgrove, The. Johnston, 1769

History of Eliza Warwick, The. Bew, 1777

History of Emily Montague, The. By Mrs. Frances Brooke. Dodsley, 1769

History of the Honourable Mrs. Rosemont and Sir Henry Cardigan, in a Series of Letters, The. Hookham, 1781

History of Jemmy and Jenny Jessamy, The. By Eliza Haywood. London, 1753

History of Lady Barton. In a Series of Letters. By Mrs. Griffith. David, 1772

History of Lady Bettesworth and Captain Hastings, The. In a Series of Letters. Noble, 1780

History of Lady Caroline Rivers, The. By Mrs. Elizabeth Todd.
(Printed for the authoress.) London, 1788

Histories of Lady Frances A—— and Lady Caroline S——. By the
Miss Minifies. Dodsley, 1763

History of Lady Julia Mandeville, The. By Frances Brooke.
Dodsley, 1763

History of Lady Louisa Stroud; and the Honourable Miss
Caroline Stretton, The. Noble, 1764

History of Lord Ainworth and the Hon. Charles Hartford, Esq.,
in a Series of Letters, The. Roson, 1773

History of Lord Belford and Miss Sylvia Woodley, The. In a
Series of Letters. Noble, 1784

History of Lord Stanton, The. By a Gentleman of the Middle
Temple, author of The Trial. Vernon, 1774

History of the Marquis de Roselle, The. In a Series of Letters.
By Madame de Beaumont. Becket, 1765

History of Melinda Harley, Yorkshire, The. Robinsons, 1778

History of the Miss Baltimores, The; in a Series of Letters. Hookham, 1783

History of Miss Caroline Manners, The. In a Series of Genuine
Letters to a Friend. T. Evans, 1772

History of Miss Clarinda Cathcart and Miss Fanny Renton,
The. By Jane Marishall. Noble, 1765

History of Miss Delia Stanhope, The. In a Series of Letters to
Miss Dorinda Boothby. Lowndes, 1766

History of Miss Dorinda Catsby and Miss Emilia Faulkner, The.
In a Series of Letters. Bladon, 1772

History of Miss Emilia Belville, The. Noble, 1767

History of Miss Greville, The. By Mrs. James Keir. Cadell, 1787

History of Miss Indiana Danby, The. Dodsley, 1765

History of Miss Lucinda Courtney, The. In a Series of Original
Letters, written by Herself to her Friend Miss Constantia
Bellmour. Noble, 1764

History of Miss Maria Barlow, The; in a Series of Letters. Fielding & Walker, 1777

History of Miss Meredith, The; Dedicated by Permission, to the
Most Noble Marchioness of Salisbury. By Mrs. Parsons.
Hookham, 1790

History of Miss Pittborough, The. In a Series of Letters. By a
Lady. Millar, 1767

History of Miss Sommerville, The. Written by a Lady. Newbery & Carnan, 1769

History of Miss Temple, The. By a Lady (Miss Rogers). Wallis, 1777

History of Mr. Cecil and Miss Grey, The. In a Series of Letters. Richardson & Urquhart, 1771

History of Mr. Stanly and Miss Temple, a Rural Novel, The. Johnson, 1773

History of Pamela Howard, The. By the author of Indiana Danby. Lowndes, 1773

History of Sir William Harrington, The. Written some Years Since, and revised and corrected by the *late* Mr. Richardson; now first published. By Thomas Hull. Bell, 1771

History of a Young Lady of Distinction, The. Translated from the French of Madam de Beaumont. (Originally published in 1754) Noble, 1766

Ill Effects of a Rash Vow, The. In a Series of Letters. Lane, 1789

Illicit Love: a Novel. By Mrs. Morris, author of the Rival Brothers, a Novel; etc. Symonds, 1791

Indiscreet Marriage, The; or, Henry and Sophia Sommerville. In a Series of Letters. By Miss Nugent and Miss Taylor of Twickenham. Dodsley, 1779

Interesting Story of Edwin and Julia, The; being a Rational and Philosophical Enquiry into the Nature of Things. In a Series of Letters. By a Doctor of Physic, M.A., etc. Kearsley, 1790

Irish Guardian, The; a Pathetic Story. Johnson, 1775

Italian Letters; or, the History of the Count de St. Julian. Robinsons, 1784

James Wallace, a Novel. By Robert Bage. Lane, 1788

Jemima and Louisa. In which is contained several remarkable incidents relating to two Ladies of Distinguished Families and Fortunes. In a Series of Letters. (By a Lady.) Owen, 1759

Jessy; or, the Bridal Day. Written by a Lady, after the Manner of the late Mr. Richardson, but *not* revised by that celebrated writer. Noble, 1771

John Buncle, Jr. By Thos. Cogan. Johnson, 1778

Julia de Roubigné: a Tale. In a Series of Letters. By Henry Mackenzie. Cadell, 1777

Juliana, a Novel. By the author of Francis the Philanthropist. Lane, 1786

Juliana Ormeston: or, the Fraternal Victim. By Mrs. Harley, author of The Countess of Henebon, Castle Mowbray, St. Bernard's Priory, etc. Dublin; Wogan, Byrne, Stone, Jones and Rice, 1793

Juliet; or, the Cottager: in a Series of Letters. By a Lady. Lane, 1791

Labyrinths of Life, The. By the author of Excessive Sensibility, Fatal Follies. Robinsons, 1791

Lady Almira Grantham, in a Series of Letters, interspersed with Several Interesting Stories, written in the year MDCCLXXIX. Printed at Bath by Hazard, 1792

Laura; or, Letters from Persons in Switzerland. By the author of Camille. Hookham, 1788

Laura and Augustus; an Authentic Story, in a Series of Letters. By a Young Lady. Cass, 1784

Letters between Clara and Antonia: In which are Interspersed the Interesting Memoirs of Lord des Lunettes, a Character in Real Life. Bew, 1779

Letters between Emilia and Harriet. Dodsley, 1762

Letters Between an English Lady and her Friend at Paris. In which are contained the Memoirs of Mrs. Williams. By a Lady. Becket, 1770

Letters between Henry and Frances. Johnston, 1757

Letters between an Illustrious Personage and a Lady of Honour at B——. Walter, 1785

Letters Between two Lovers and their Friends. By the author of Letters Supposed to Have Been Written by Yorick and Eliza. By William Combe. Bew, 1781

Letters from Clara; or, the Effusions of the Heart. Wilkie, 1771

Letters from Elizabeth Sophia de Valière to her Friend Louisa Hortensia de Carteleu. By Madam Riccoboni. Trans. from the French by M. Maceuen. Dublin; Potts, Williams, Walker and Jenkins, 1772

Letters from Emerance to Lucy. Translated from the French of Mme. la Princesse de Beaumont. Nourse, 1766

Letters from an English Traveller, Martin Sherlock, Esq. Cadell, 1780

Letters from Henrietta to Morvina. Founded on Facts. Bew, 1778

Letters from Julia, the Daughter of Augustus, to Ovid. A MS. Discovered at Herculaneum. L. Davis, 1753

Letters from Lady Julia Catesby, to her Friend Lady Henrietta Campley. By Frances Brooke. Dodsley, 1760

Letters from a Lady, who Resided Some Years in Russia, to her Friend in England. With Historical Notes. Dodsley, 1775

Letters from Lothario to Penelope. Becket, 1770

Letters from an Old Man to a Young Prince. London, 1750

Letters from An Old Man to a Young Prince, with the Answers. Translated from the Swedish. To which are prefixed those of Her Present Majesty to Her Son, with the Translations. Griffiths, 1756

Letters from Perdita to a Certain Israelite, and his Answers to Them. Fielding, Stockdale & Co., 1781

Letters Moral and Entertaining. By Mrs. Cartwright. Macgowan, 1781

Letters of Charlotte During her Connection with Werter, The. Cadell, 1786

Letters of An English Lady, written to one of Her Female Friends. Robinson & Roberts, 1769

Letters of a Hindoo Rajah; written Previous to, and during the Period of His Residence in England. To which is prefixed a Preliminary Dissertation on the History, Religion, and Manners of the Hindoos. By Eliza Hamilton. Robinsons, 1796

Letters of Julia and Caroline, The. By Maria Edgeworth. (Written 1787) London, 1795

Letters of the Late Ignatius Sancho, an African, to which are prefixed Memoirs of His Life. Dodsley, 1782

Letters of Princess Zilia to Prince Aza of Peru. From the French. By James Seguin. Wilde, 1755

Letters of a Solitary Wanderer, The: Containing narratives of Various Description. By Charlotte Smith. Dublin; Burnet, Wogan, Brown, Porter, Colbert, Folingsby, Rice, Jones, Stockdale, Jackson, Mercier & Co., Kelly and Pary, 1801

Letters Supposed to have been Written by Yorick and Eliza. (William Combe.) Bew, 1779

Letters to Alcander. Written between the Years 1777 and 1783. Becket, 1795

Letters to Eleonora. Becket, 1771

Letters to a Friend in the Country Upon the News of the Town, A. Raymond, 1755

Letters to a Young Prince from his Governor. Trans. into English. Linde, 1755

Letters Written from Lausanne. Trans. from the French. Dilly, 1799

Letters Written in France in the Summer of 1790, to a Friend in England; containing Various Anecdotes relative to the French Revolution, and the Memoirs of Mons. and Madame De F—. By Helen-Maria Williams. Cadell, 1790-2

Liberal American, The. A Novel. By a Lady. Lane, 1785

Life of Miss Catlane, The; or, the Ill Effects of a Hasty Marriage. In a Series of Letters. (Printed for the author.) London, 1788

Light Summer Reading for Ladies; or the History of Lady Lucy Fenton. Robinson & Roberts, 1768

Love and Madness. A Story too True. In a Series of Letters between Parties Whose Names would Perhaps be Mentioned were they less known or less lamented. By Sir Herbert Croft. Kearsley, 1780

Love Fragments. A Series of Letters. By Mr. Robinson. Wallace, 1782

Lovers, The; or, the Memoirs of Lady Mary Sc— and the Hon. Miss Amelia B—. By M. Treysac de Vergy. (Printed for the Editor and Sold by the Booksellers.) London, 1772

Loves of Calisto and Emira, The; or, the Fatal Legacy. Published from the Originals, by John Seally, Gent. Becket, 1776

Magdalen, The; or, the History of the First Penitent Received into that Charitable Asylum. In a Series of Letters to a Lady. With Anecdotes of the Other Penitents, by the late Dr. Dodd. Lane, 1784

Maid of Quality, The; or, the History of Lady Lucy Layton. Vernor, 1770

Maiden Aunt, The. Written by a Lady, Menella Bute Smedley. Bew, 1776

Marcus Flaminius; or, a View of the Military, Political, and Social Life of the Romans. In a Series of Letters from a Patrician to his Friend, in the Year 762 from the Foundation of Rome to the Year 769. By E. Cornelia Knight. Dilly, 1792

Margaretta, Countess of Rainsford. A Sentimental Novel. Johnston & Payne, 1769

Masqued Weddings, The. In a Series of Letters. Hookham, 1781

Masquerades; or, What You Will. By the author of Eliza Warwick. Bew, 1780

Matilda; or, the Efforts of Virtue. In a Series of Letters. By a Lady. Lane, 1785

Melwin Dale. In a Series of Letters. By a Lady. Lane, 1786

Memoirs of a Scots Heiress. Addressed to the Rt. Hon. Lady Catherine . . . By the Author of Constance. Hookham, 1791

Memoirs of An Unfortunate Queen. Interspersed with Letters Written by Herself to Several of her Illustrious Relations. Bew, 1776

Memoirs of An Unfortunate Young Nobleman. Freeman, 1743

Memoirs of Colonel Digby and Miss Stanley. A Narrative Founded on Facts. In a Series of Letters. By Mrs. Fogerty. Swagg, 1773

Memoirs of Fanny Hill. By John Cleland. London, 1749

Memoirs of Francis Dillon, Esq. In a Series of Letters written by himself. Hookham, 1772

Memoirs of Lady Harriet Butler. Now First Published from Authentic Papers in the Lady's own Hand. Freeman, 1761

Memoirs of Lady Woodford. Written by Herself and addressed to a Friend. Noble, 1771

Memoirs of Magdalen; or, the History of Louisa Mildmay. Now First Published from a Series of Original Letters. By Hugh Kelly. Griffin, 1767

Memoirs of Mary. A Novel. By Mrs. Gunning. Bell, 1793

Memoirs of Miss Sidney Bidulph. Extracted from Her Own Journal, and Now First Published. By Mrs. Frances Sheridan. Dodsley, 1761-1767

Memoirs of Mr. Charles Guildford. In a Series of Letters wrote by himself to a Friend. The whole founded on real facts. Withy, 1761

Memoirs of Several Ladies of Great Britain. Interspersed with Literary Reflections, and accounts of Antiquities and Curious Things. In Several Letters. Noon, 1755

Memoirs of the Marchioness de Louvoi. By a Lady. (Lady Mary Walker, author of Letters from the Duchess de Crui and others.) Robson, 1777

Memoirs of the Marquis de St. Forlaix. Trans. from the French by Mrs. Brooke. Dodsley, 1770

Memoirs of the Marquis de Villebon. In a Series of Letters, founded on Facts. Cadell, jun. & Davies, 1796

Mentoria; or, The Young Lady's Friend. By Mrs. Rowson. Dublin; Wogan, 1791

Midnight the Signal. In Six Letters to a Lady of Quality. Dodsley, 1780

Miss Melmoth; or, the New Clarissa. Lowndes, 1771

Mistakes of the Heart, The; or, the Memoirs of Lady Caroline Pelham and Lady Victoria Nevil. In a Series of Letters. Published by M. Treysac de Vergy. Shatwell, 1769-1772

Modern Couple, The; or, the History of Miss Davers. In a Series of Letters. Noble, 1770

Modern Fine Gentleman, The. Lowndes, 1774

Modern Wife, The; a Novel. Lowndes, 1768

Monimia, a Novel. Lane, 1791

Modern Manners. In a Series of Familiar Epistles. Faulder, 1781

Mount Henneth, A Novel in a Series of Letters. By Robert Bage. Lowndes, 1782

Munster Village. By Lady Mary Walker. Robson, 1778

Mutability of Human Life, The; or, Memoirs of Adelaide, Marchioness of Melville. By a Lady. Dublin; Price, Slater, Whitestone, Watson, Chamberlaine, Hoey, Williams, Potts, Coller, Burnet, Walker, Jenkin, Cross, White, Exshaw, Beatty, 1777

Myrtle, The; or, the Effects of Love. In a Series of Letters. By a Lady. Lane, 1785

Nabob, The. In a Series of Letters. By a Lady. Lane, 1785

Nature: a novel, in a Series of Letters. Murdoch, 1770

New Clarissa, The; a True History. By Madame de Beaumont. Nourse, 1768

News-Paper Wedding, The; or, An Advertisement for a Husband. Snagg, 1774

Noble Family, The. In a Series of Letters. By Mrs. Austin. Pearch, 1771

Nunnery, The; or, the History of Miss Sophia Howard. Noble, 1767

Old Maid, The; or, the History of Miss Ravensworth. In a

Series of Letters. By Mrs. Skinn, late Miss Masterman, of York. Bell, 1770

Omen, The; or, Memoirs of Sir Henry Melville and Miss Julia Eastbrook. Lowndes, 1785

Original Letters, etc., of Sir John Falstaff and his Friends; now first made public by a Gentleman, a Descendant of Dame Quickly, from Genuine MSS. which have been in the Possession of the Quickly Family Near Four Hundred Years. Robinsons, 1796

Original Love Letters, between a Lady of Quality, and a Person of Inferior Station. By Wm. Combe. Bew, 1784

Orlando and Seraphina: a Turkish Story. Lane, 1787

Palinode, The; or the Triumphs of Virtue over Love. A Sentimental Novel. By Treysac de Vergy. Woodfall & Evans, 1771

Pamela Censured. Roberts, 1741

Pamela's Conduct in High Life. By Hugh Kelly. Chandler, 1741

Parsonage House, The. By a Young Lady. In a Series of Letters. Macgowan, 1780

Patty and Peggy; or, the Sisters of Ashdale. Dodsley, 1783

Perfidious Guardian, The; or, Vicissitudes of Fortune exemplified in the History of Meretia Lawson. Wilkins, 1790

Peruvian Letters, trans. from the French, with an additional original volume, The. By R. Roberts. Cadell, 1775

Petticoat-Pensioners, The; Being the Memoirs of the Most remarkable of these Gentlemen in and about London and Westminster. (S. F. Philomath.) Horner, 1749

Philosophical Quixote, The; or, Memoirs of Mr. David Wilkins. In a Series of Letters. Johnson, 1782

Picture, The; a Novel. By Miss Minifies of Fairwater in Somersetshire. Johnson & Co., 1766

Pilgrim, The; or, a Picture of Life, in a Series of Letters, written mostly from London by a Chinese Philosopher to his Friend at Chang-Tong, containing Remarks upon the Laws, Customs, and Manners of the English and Other Nations. By Charles Johnstone. Cadell, 1775

Platonic Marriage, The. In a Series of Letters. By Mrs. Cartwright. Hookham, 1786

Precipitate Choice, The; or, the History of Lord Ossory and Miss Rivers. By a Lady. Jones, 1772

Predestined Wife, The; or the Force of Prejudice. A novel in a

Series of Letters. By the author of Edward and Sopnia, Powis Castle and Eliza Cleland. Kerby, 1789

Private Letters from an American in England to his Friends in America. Almon, 1769

Pupil of Pleasure, The. By Courtney Melmoth. (S. J. Pratt). Robinsons, 1777

Quaker, The; in a Series of Letters. Lane, 1786

Radzivil, a Romance. Trans. from the Russ of the celebrated M. Wocklow. By Mrs. Ann Radcliffe (?). Lane, 1790

Rambles of Fancy, The: or, Moral and Interesting Tales. By Miss Lucy Peacock. Containing:
    (1) The Laplander
    (2) The Ambitious Mother
    (3) Letters from Lindamira to Olivia
    (4) Letters from Miranda to Elvira
    (5) Letters from Felicia to Celia
    (6) The American Indian
    (7) The Fatal Resolution
    (8) The Creole.   Buckland, 1786

Rattle, The. In a Series of Letters. Noble, 1787.

Recess, The. By Sophia Lee. Cadell, 1785

Reclaimed Libertine, The; or, the History of the Honourable Charles Belmont, Esq., and Miss Melvill. In a Series of Letters. Noble, 1769

Relapse, The: a Novel. Lowndes, 1779

Relapse, The, or, Myrtle Bank. Stalker, 1791

Rencontre, The; or, Transition of a Moment, in a Series of Letters. By a Lady. Lane, 1785

Retaliation; or, the History of Sir Edward Oswald and Lady Frances Seymour. A Novel. By Mrs. Cartwright. Noble, 1787

Reuben, or the Suicide. Swift, 1787

Reveries of the Heart; during a tour through a Part of England and France. In a Series of Letters to a Friend. Johnson, 1781

Ring, The. In a Series of Letters. By a Young Lady. Stockdale, 1783

Rival Brothers, The; a Novel. In a Series of Letters founded on Facts. By a Lady. Printed for the authoress and Sold by Symonds, 1784

Robert and Adela; or, the Rights of Women best Maintained by the Sentiments of Nature. Robinsons, 1795

Rudiments of Taste; in a Series of Letters from a Mother to her Daughter. Dilly, 1789

Saint Julian's Abbey; in a Series of Letters. Lane, 1788

School, The; being a Series of Letters between a Young Lady and her Mother. Flexney, 1772

School for Fathers, or, The Victims of a Curse. A Novel. Robinsons, 1788

School for Husbands. Written by a Lady. Dublin; Price, 1776

School for Tutors, The; consisting of a Series of Correspondence chiefly between a Young Gentleman and his Tutor. Flexney, 1788

School for Widows, The; a Novel. By Clara Reeve. Hookham, 1791

School for Wives, The. In a Series of Letters. Dodsley, 1763

Self-Deceived, The; or, the History of Lord Byron. Noble, 1773

Sempronia. Lane, 1790

Sentimental Deceiver, The; or, the History of Miss Hammond. In a Series of Letters. By a Lady. Lane, 1784

Sentimental Journey Through Greece, A. By M. De Guys. Cadell, 1772

Sentimental Memoirs. By a Lady. Hookham, 1785

Sephallisa to Sylvius. A Letter from a Lady in the Country to her Lover in Town. Bickerton, 1743

Series of Genuine Letters between Henry and Frances, A. Richardson & Urquhart, 1770

Series of Letters, A. By the author of Clarinda Cathcart, Alicia Montague, and the Comedy of Sir Harry Gaylove (Jane Marishau). Elliot, 1788

Shrine of Bertha, The; in a Series of Letters. By Miss M. E. Robinson. Lane, 1794

Sketch of Happiness in Rural Life, and the Misery that Attended an Indiscreet Passion, A. Millar, 1769

Slave of Passion; or, Fruits of Werter. Philadelphia, 1802

Small Talker, The; a Series of Letters from a Lady in the West of England, to Lady Ann D——, abroad. Johnson & Payne, 1769

Solicitudes of Absence, The. A genuine Tale. By Wm. Renwick. Forster, 1788

Sophronia; or, Letters to the Ladies. Johnston & Co., 1761

Sorrows of the Heart, The. By John Heriot. Murray, 1787

Spanish Memoirs, in a Series of Original Letters, containing the History of Donna Isabella della Villarea, niece to Don John, Twentieth and Last Duke of Arandina. Elliot, 1787

Stellins; or, the New Werter. Lane, 1793

Story of Lady Juliana Harley, The. A Novel, in letters. By Mrs. Griffiths. Cadell, 1776

Subterranean Cavern, The; or Memoirs of Antoinette Monflorance. By the author of Delia and Rosina. Lane, 1798

Suspicious Lovers, The. By the author of Woodbury. Wilkie, 1777 .

Sutton Abbey; a Novel. In a Series of Letters founded on Facts. Richardson & Urquhart, 1779

Sydney St. Aubyn. In a Series of Letters. By Mr. Robinson, author of Love Fragments, etc. Herbert, 1794

Sylph, The. A Novel. By Georgiana Cavendish, Duchess of Devonshire. Lowndes, 1779

Test of Filial Duty, The. In a Series of Letters between Miss Emilia Leonard and Miss Charlotte Arlington. By Sarah Scott. Carnan, 1772

Theodosius and Arabella. A Novel in a Series of Letters, by the late Mrs. Hampden Pye. Lane, 1786

Theron and Aspasio; or, a Series of Dialogues and Letters upon the Most Important and Interesting Subjects. Rivington, 1755

Tour to Milford Haven, in the Year 1791, A. By Mrs. Morgan. Stockdale, 1795

Triomphe de la Raison, Le; or Lettres de deux jeunes Dames de Qualité, dedié par permission à Madame la Duchess de Devonshire. Par Mlle. Cacouault de la Mimardière. Dilly, 1785

True Anti-Pamela, The; or, Memoirs of Mr. James Parry, Late Organist of Ross in Herefordshire. In which are inserted his Amours with the Celebrated Miss Powell of Monmouthshire. Printed for the Author. London, 1742

True Narrative of an Unfortunate Elopement, in a Series of Letters. A. Holdsworth, 1770

Tutor of Truth, The. By the author of the Pupil of Pleasure. Courtney Melmoth. (S. J. Pratt). Richardson & Urquhart, 1779

Twin Sisters, The; or, the Effects of Education. A Novel by a Lady. Hookham, 1788

Two Mentors. The; a Modern Story. By the author of The Old
     English Baron (Clara Reeve). Dilly, 1783
Undutiful Daughter, The; or, the History of Miss Goodwin.
     Noble, 1770
Unexpected Wedding, The; in a Series of Letters. Becket, 1768
Unfortunate Lovers, The; or, the Genuine Distress of Damon
     and Clelia. In a Series of Letters. Dodsley, 1771
Unfortunate Sensibility; or, the Life of Mrs. L——. Written by
     Herself. In a Series of Sentimental Letters, addressed to
     Mr. Yorick in the Elysian Fields. Richardson & Urquhart,
     1784
Unfortunate Union, The; or, the Test of Virtue. A Story founded
     on Facts and Calculated to promote the Causes of Virtue in
     Younger Minds. By a Lady. Richardson & Urquhart, 1778
Unhappy Wife, The. A Series of Letters. By a Lady. Newbery,
     1770
Vale of Felicity, The; or, Sylvan Happiness. Portrayed in a Series
     of Letters, Moral and Entertaining. By a Lady. Hamilton,
     1791
Vicissitudes of Fortune, The; or, the History of Miss Sedley.
     Jones, 1773
Victim of Passion, or Memoirs of the Comte de Saint Julien.
     Lane, 1795
Village Memoirs. By Joseph Cradock. London, 1775
Virtue in Distress; or, the History of Miss Sally Pruen and Miss
     Laura Spencer. By a Farmer's Daughter in Glocestershire.
     Fuller, 1772
Virtuous Villagers; in a Series of Letters. By John Potter, M.B.
     Cass, 1784
Visiting Day, The. Lowndes, 1768
Wedding Ring, The; or, the History of Miss Sidney. In a Series
     of Letters. Noble, 1779
Widow, The; or, A Picture of Modern Times. A Novel. In a
     Series of Letters. By Mrs. Mary Robinson. Hookham, 1794
Woman of Honour, The. Lowndes, 1768
Woman of Letters, The; or, the History of Miss Fanny Bolton.
     Noble, 1783
Young Widow, The; or, the History of Cornelia Sedley. By Wil-
     liam Hayley. Robinsons, 1789
Young Widow, The; or, the History of Mrs. Ledwich. Written by

Herself, in a Series of Letters to James Lewis, Esq. Noble, 1785

CHAPTER VII

Texts

Ayrshire Legatees, The. By John Galt. Edinburgh and London, 1821

Aunt Sarah and the War. A Tale of Transformations. London, 1915

Christina, Princess of Wolfenbuttel. By the author of Caroline of Lichtfield (Thomas Holcroft). London, Second Ed., 1809

Christine. By Alice Cholmondeley. London, 1912

Confessions of a Well-Meaning Woman, The. By Stephen McKenna. London, 1922

Delphine: A Novel. By Madame de Staël-Holstein. Trans. from the French. London, 1805

Dodd Family Abroad, The. By Charles James Lever. London, 1853-4

Dracula. By Bram Stoker. London, 1897

Elizabeth Visits America. By Elinor Clayton Glyn. London, 1909

Englishwoman's Love-Letters, An. By Laurence Housman. London, 1900

Etchingham Letters, The. By Mrs. Ella Fuller Maitland, to the Rt. Hon. Sir Frederick Pollock. London, 1899

Falkland. By Edward Bulwer-Lytton. London, 1827

Farthing Hall. By Hugh Walpole and J. B. Priestley. London, 1929

Fellowe and his Wife, A. By Blanche Willis Howard and William Sharp. Boston, 1892

Feudal Tyrants; or, the Counts of Carlsheim and Sargans. A Romance taken from the German. By Matthew Gregory Lewis. London, 1806

Fräulein Schmidt and Mr. Anstruther. By Mary Annette, Gräfin von Arnim. London, 1907

Gwenda. By Mabel Barnes-Grundy. New York, 1910

Hauntings. Fantastic Stories. By Vernon Lee. 2nd ed., London, 1906

Helen; or, Domestic Occurrences, a Tale. Printed for the authors, London, 1807

Heroine, The; or, Adventures of Cherubina. By Eaton Stannard
Barrett, Esq. London, 1813

Indian Voyage, The. By Mrs. H. Lefanu. London, 1804

Jamsie. By Ethel Sidgwick. (Amer. Ed.) Boston, 1918

Lady Susan. By Jane Austen. (Written *ca.* 1805.) Oxford, 1871,
1925

Lake, The. By George Moore. (In letters and narrative.) London, 1905

Leonora. By Maria Edgeworth. Dublin, 1805

Leòntina. A Novel. By Augustus Von Kotzebue. Trans. from the
German. London, 1809

Lesley Castle. An Unfinished Novel in Letters. By Jane Austen.
New York. First pub. from orig. MSS. in 1922

Letters between Amelia in London and her Mother in the Country. By William Combe. London, 1824

Letters from An Ocean Tramp. By William McFee. London,
1908

Letters from Mrs. Palmerstone to Her Daughter. By Mrs. Hunter.
London, 1810

Letters of an Actress. London, 1902

Letters of Her Mother to Elizabeth, The. By William Rutherford Hayes Trowbridge. London, 1901

Letters (from Senhouse) to Sanchia Upon Things as they are.
By Maurice Henry Hewlett. London, N. D.

Letters Which Never Reached Him, The. By Elizabeth A. Heyking. London, 1900

Life of a Lover, The. In a Series of Letters. By Sophia Lee.
London, 1804

Life, Treason, and Death of James Blount of Breckenhow. Compiled from the Rowlestone Papers by Beulah Marie Dix.
New York, 1903

Like Another Helen. By "Sydney Carlyn Grier" (Hilda Gregg).
London, 1899

Listener's Lure: an Oblique Narration. By Edward Verral Lucas.
London, 1906

Love and Freindship. By Jane Austen. New York, First Pub.
from orig. MSS.—1922

Love Letters of a Husband. London, 1928

Love-Letters of a Worldly Woman. By Mrs. W. K. Clifford.
London, 1891

Love's Cross-Currents: a Year's Letters. By Algernon Charles Swinburne. London, 1905

Mariage de Convenance, A. By Charles Francis Keary. London, 1890

Matilda's Mabel. By Neil Lyons. London, 1903

Memoirs of a Princess: or, First Love. An Historical Romance. By Olivia W. S. London, 1812

Missing Answers to an Englishwoman's Love Letters, The. London, 1901

Mohammed Benani. London, 1887

Mr. Brown's Letters to a Young Man About Town. By W. M. Thackeray. New York, 1853

Mordaunt. Sketches of Life, Characters, and Manners, in Various Countries; including the Memoirs of a French Lady of Quality. By Dr. John Moore, author of Zeluco and Edward. London, 1800

Oakwood Hall. By Catherine Hutton. London, 1819

Pericles and Aspasia. By Walter Savage Landor. London, 1835-6

Picture of the Age, The. A Novel. London, 1800

Ramsbottom Letters, The. By Edward Theodore Hook. London, 1872

Redgauntlet: A Tale of the Eighteenth Century. By Sir Walter Scott. Edinburgh, 1824

Rich Man, A; or, He Has Great Merit. Being the Autobiography of Archibald Plack, Esq., Late Lord Mayor of London. In a Series of Letters to his Grandson, The Honourable George Spend. By John Galt. (Originally published in Tait's Edinburgh Magazine, June to August, 1836). Edinburgh, 1925

Rosa Amorosa. By "George Egerton" (Mrs. Goldring Bright). London, 1901

Saltonstall Gazette, The. By Mrs. Ella Fuller Maitland. London, 1896

Set in Silver. By C. N. and A. M. Williamson. London, 1909

Stark Munro Letters, The. By Sir Arthur Conan Doyle. London, 1894

St. Clair; or, the Heiress of Desmond. By S. Owenson (Lady Sidney Morgan). London, 1804

Tenant of Wildfell Hall. By Anne Brontë. London, 1848

Topsy. By A. P. Herbert. New York, 1931

Uncle's Advice. A Novel in Letters. By William Hewlett. London, N.D.

Undelivered Letters, from an American Girl to Her English
   Husband. By Cosmo Hamilton. London, 1926
Upton Letters, The. By Arthur Christopher Benson. London,
   1905
Verena in the Midst. A Kind of Story. By Edward Verrall Lucas.
   New York, 1920
Wandering Heath. (Contains "Letters from Troy".) By Sir
   Arthur Thomas Quiller-Couch. London, 1895
When All the World is Young. By Reginald Lucas. London,
   1908
Visits of Elizabeth, The. By Elinor Clayton Glyn. London, 1901
Welsh Mountaineer. By Catharine Hutton, author of The Miser
   Married. London, 1817
Wild Irish Girl, The; a National Tale. By Miss Owenson, au-
   thor of The Novice of St. Dominick, Patriotic Sketches.
   London, 1806
Year and a Day, A. By Mme. Panache. London, 1818
Your Affectionate Godmother. (Letters to Caroline.) By Elinor
   Glyn. New York, 1914

CHAPTER VIII

Texts

1. FRENCH

Adelaide de Meran. Par Pigault-Lebrun. Paris, 1815
Adele de Senanges; ou, Lettres de Lord Sydenham. Par Mme.
   de Souza (Adelaide-Marie Emilie Filleul) . Paris, 1794
Amours; ou, Lettres d'Alexis et Justine. Paris, 1786
Caliste; ou, Lettres écrites de Lausanne. Par Mme. de Charrière.
   Paris, 1786
Comte de Comminge, Le. Par Mme. de Tencin (Claudine Alex-
   andrine Guerin) . Paris, 1735
Delphine. Par Madame de Staël. Paris, 1802
La Dernière Héloise; ou, Lettres de Junie Salisbury, recueillies
   et publiées par M. Dauphin, citoyen de Verdun. Paris, 1784
Henriette de Wolmar; ou, La Mère jalouse de sa Fille pour
   servir de suite a la Nouvelle Héloise. Paris, 1768
Histoire du Marquis de Cressy. Par Mme. Riccoboni (Marie
   Jeanne Laboras de Mezieres) . Paris, 1758
L'Histoire d'Atrée. Par Honoré d'Urfé. Paris, 1607-19

Julie; ou, La Nouvelle Héloise. Par Jean-Jacques Rousseau. Paris, 1761

Letters of an Italian Nun and an English Gentleman. Par Jean-Jacques Rousseau. Paris, 1781

Lettres à Mlle. Voland. Par Denis Diderot. Paris, N.D.

Lettres à Une Innconnue. Par Prosper Merimée. Trans. N. Y., 1897

Lettres Angloises; ou, Histoire de Clarissa Harlove. Par Samuel Richardson (traduites par Abbé Prévost?). Paris, 1751

Lettres Athéniennes. Par Claude Prosper Jolyot de Crébillon (Crébillon fils). Paris, 1732

Lettres de deux Amants habitants de Lyons. Publiées par M. Léonard. Paris, 1783

Lettres de Fanny Butler. Par Mme. Riccoboni. Paris, N.D.

Lettres de Julie Catesby. Par Mme. Riccoboni. Paris, 1759

Lettres de la Marquise de M—au Comte de P—. Par Claude Prosper Jolyot de Crébillon (Crébillon fils). Paris, 1732

Lettres de mon Moulin. Par Alphonse Daudet. Paris, 1869

Lettres du Marquis de Roselle. Par Mme. Elie de Beaumont. Paris, 1769

Lettres neuchateloises. Par Mme. de Saint-Hyacinthe Charrière (Isabella Agnes Elizabeth Van Tuyll). Paris, 1784

Les Lettres d'Amabard, traduites par l'Abbe Tamponet. Par Francois-Marie Arouet de Voltaire. Paris, 1769

Lettres Persanes. Par Charles Louis de Sécondat, Baron de la Brède et de Montesquieu. Paris, 1721

Lettres Peruviennes. Par Madame de Graffigny. Paris, 1747

Lettres Polonaises. Par Jean Paul Marat. (Pub. for the Bibliophile Society.) Boston, 1904

Lettres Portugaises. Paris, 1668

Liaisons Dangereuses. Par Choderlos de Laclos. Paris, 1782

Malheurs de L'Amour. Par Mme. de Tencin. Paris, 1747

Marie; ou les Peines de l'Amour. By Louis Buonaparte. Gratz, 1812

Mémoirs de deux jeunes Mariées. Par Honoré de Balzac. Paris, 1842

Miss Rovel. Par Victor Cherbuliez. Paris, 1875

Mitsou; ou, Comment l'Esprit vient au Filles. Par "Colette" (Colette Willy). Paris, 1929

Mon Oncle Barbassou. By Mario Uchard. London, 1888

La Morte. Par Octave Feuillet. Paris, 1886

Le Nouvel Abailard; ou, Lettres de deux Amants qui ne se sont jamais vus. Par Réstif de la Bretonne. Paris, 1778

Nouvelles Lettres Angloises; ou, Histoire de Chevalier Grandisson. Par Samuel Richardson. (Abbe Prévost?) Paris, 1755-56

Obermann. Par Étienne Pivert de Sénancour. Paris, 1804

Le Paysan Parvenu. Par Pierre Carlet de Chamblain de Marivaux. Paris, 1735-36

Le Paysan Perverti; ou, les Dangers de la Ville-histoire recente mise au jour d'après les veritables lettres des personnages. Par Réstif de la Bretonne. Paris, 1775

Le Philosophe par Amour; ou, Lettres de deux Amants passionés et vertueux. Paris, 1765

La Réligieuse. Par Denis Diderot. Paris, 1796

Sophie; ou, Lettres de deux Amies recueillies et publiées par un Citoyen de Genève. Paris, 1779

Tolla la Courtisane; ésquisse de la Vie privée a Rome en l'an de Jubilé 1700. Par Emmanuel Pierre Rodocanachi. Paris, 1897

La Vie de Marianne; ou les Aventures de la Comtesse de. . . . Par Pierre Carlet de Chamblain de Marivaux. Paris, 1731-1741

2. ITALIAN

La Cantatrice per disgrazia. Di Pietro Chiari. Venezia. N.D.

La Donna che non si trove. Di Pietro Chiari. Venezia, 1762

L'Esploratore turco e le diliu relazioni segrete alla Porte Ottoman. Di Giovanni Paolo Marana. Paris, 1684

La filosofessa italiana. Di Pietro Chiari. Venezia, N.D.

Francese in Italia. Di Pietro Chiari. Venezia, N.D.

Lettere Amorose. Di Aloise Pasqualigo. N. P., 1569

Lettere di Alphonso d'Este ed Isabella de Savoia. Di Cesare Balbo. N. P., N.D.

Lettere di Guilia Willet. Della Marchesa Orintia Romagnoli Sacrati di Cesena. N. P., 1818

Lettere di una Italiana. Della Baronessa Carolina Decio Coscenza di Napoli. N. P., 1825

Lo Spione Italiano; ossia, Corrispondenza segreta e familiare fra il Marchese di Licciocara e il Conte Piefiela, tutti e due Viaggiatori incogniti, per i diverse Corti d'Europa. N. P., 1782

Storia di Clarice Visconti Duchessa di Milano. Di Giovanni Agrati. N. P., 1817

Le Ultime Lettere di Jacopo Ortis. Di Ugo Foscolo. Bologna, 1799

La Viaggiatrice; ossia Le Avventure di Madamigella E. B. Di Pietro Chiari. Venezia, 1760

3. GERMAN

Die Leiden des Jungen Werthers. Von Johann Wolfgang von Goethe. Weimar, 1774

CHAPTER IX

Texts

Adelaide. A New and original Novel. By a Lady of Philadelphia (Margaret Botsford). Phila., 1816

Affair at the Inn, The. By Kate Douglas Wiggin, Mary Findlater. Jane Findlater, Allan McAulay. Boston and New York, 1904

Aristocrats, The. By Gertrude Franklin Atherton. New York, 1901

Art of Courting, The—displayed in Eight different Scenes; the principal of which are taken from Actual Life, and published for the Amusement of The American Youth. By Ebenezer Bradford. Newburyport, 1795

Billy Baxter's Letters. By William J. Kountz, Jr. Harmarville, Pa., 1899

Bundle of Letters, A. By Henry James. The Parisian, 1897

Castle of Serrein, The; or, Abode of Perpetual Pleasures: in a Series of Letters by Seignora R. Interwoven with her own Memoirs, Etc. Portsmouth, 1800

Cathedral Courtship, A. By Kate Douglas Wiggin. New York, 1893

Clara Howard; or, the Enthusiasm of Love, in a Series of Letters. By Charles Brockden Brown. Phila., 1801

Cocoon, The. By Ruth McEnery Stuart. New York, 1915

Collection of the Familiar Letters and Miscellaneous Papers of Benjamin Franklin. Boston, 1833

Confessions of a Débutante. New York, 1930

Coquette, The; or, the History of Eliza Wharton. A novel founded on Fact. By Hannah Webster Foster. Boston, 1797

Country Interlude, A. By Hildegarde Hawthorne. New York, 1904

Crooked Vein, The. By Brewster Kane. Boston, 1930

Cupid, M. D. A Story. By Augustus M. Swift. New York, 1882

Daddy-Long-Legs. By Jean Webster. New York, 1912

Dangerous Friendship; or, the Letters of Clara D'Albe. Translated from the French by a Lady of Baltimore. Baltimore, 1807

Daphne and Her Lad. By M. J. Lagen and Cally Ryland. New York, 1904

Dear Enemy. By Jean Webster. New York, 1912

Dere Bill. Mable's Love Letters to Her Rookie. By Florence Elizabeth Summers. New York, 1918

Dere Mable. Love Letters of a Rookie. By Edward Streeter. New York, 1918

Documents in Evidence, The. By Henry M. Blossom, Jr. St. Louis, 1894

Dublin Letters, The. By John Harriman, Jr. New York, 1930

Emblems of Fidelity, The. A Comedy in Letters. By James Lane Allen. New York, 1919

Emigrants, The; or, the History of an Expatriated Family, being the delineation of English Character and Manners written in America. By Gilbert Imlay. London, 1793

Emily Hamilton, a novel founded on incidents in real life. By a Young Lady of Worcester County (Eliza Vicery). Worcester, 1803

Familiar Letters of Peppermint Perkins. Boston, 1886

Footprints. By Kay Cleaver Strahan. New York, 1929

Foresters, The. An American Tale: being a sequel to the History of John Bull, the Clothier. In a Series of Letters to a Friend. By Jeremy Belknap. Boston, 1792

Hapless Orphan, The; or, the Innocent Victims of Revenge. A Novel, founded on Incidents in real life. In a Series of Letters from Caroline Francis to Marie B. . . . By an American Lady. Boston, 1793

Her Brother's Letters. Wherein Miss Christine Carson, of Cincinnati, is shown how the Affairs of Girls and Women are regarded by Men in General and, in Particular, by her

Brother, Lent Carson, Lawyer, of New York City. Anonymous. New York, 1906

High Life in New York. By Jonathan Slick, Esq., of Weathersfield, Conn. A series of Letters to Mr. Zephariah Slick, Justice of the Peace, and Deacon of the Church over to Weathersfield, in the State of Connecticut. By Anne Stephens. London, 1844, II Vols.

Hints to My Countrymen. By an American. By Theodore Sedgwick. New York, 1826

His Letters. By Julien Gordon. New York, 1892

History of Maria Kittle, The. In a Letter to Miss Ten Eyke. By Ann Eliza Bleecker. New York, 1793

Hope of Glory, The. Being a Part of A Correspondence written in the Roman Empire between the Years 52 and 66 A.D. By William Schuyler. Boston, 1915

Ikey's Letters to His Father. By George V. Hobart (Hugh McHugh, author of "John Henry"). New York, 1907

Infidelity; or, the Victims of Sentiment. A Novel in a Series of Letters. By Samuel Relf. Phila., 1797

Jane Talbot. By Charles Brockden Brown. Phila., 1801

Jessica Letters, The; An Editor's Romance. New York, 1904

Julian; or, Scenes in Judea. By William Ware. New York, 1841

Kempton-Wace Letters, The. By Jack London. New York, 1903

Lady and Sada San, The. A Sequel to The Lady of the Decoration. By Frances Little. New York, 1912

Lady Bobs, Her Brother and I. A Romance of the Azores. By Jean Chamblin. New York, 1905

Lady of the Decoration, The. By Frances Little. New York, 1907

Later Love-Letters of a Musician. By Myrtle Reed. New York, 1900

Lauriel. The Love-Letters of an American Girl. Edited by A. H. Boston, 1901

Letter-Bag of the Great Western, The. By Thomas Chandler Haliburton. "Sam Slick." New York, 1840

Letters found in the Ruins of Fort Braddock, including an Interesting American Tale, originally published in the Connecticut Mirror. By John Gardiner Calkins Brainard. New York, 1832

Letters from a Self-Made Merchant to his Son. By George Horace Lorimer. Boston, 1902

Letters from a Son to his Self-Made Father. Being the Replies to Letters from a Self-Made Merchant to his Son. By Charles Eustace Merriman. Boston, 1904

Letters from Palmyra. By William Ware. (Later edited under title of "Zenobia; or, the Fall of Palmyra".) New York, 1832

Letters Home. By William Dean Howells. New York, 1903

Letters of a Business Woman to her Daughter and Letters of a Business Girl to her Mother. By Zora Putnam Wilkins. Boston, 1923

Letters of a Japanese Schoolboy. By Hashimura Togo (Wallace Irwin). New York, 1907

Letters of an Old Farmer to His Son. By William R. Lighton. New York, 1914

Letters of a Self-Made Failure. By Maurice Switzer. Boston, 1914

Letters of a Woman Homesteader. By Elinore Praitt Stewart. New York, 1914

Letters of Jennie Allen to Her Friend Miss Musgrove. By Grace Donworth. Boston, 1908

Letters of Theodora, The. By Adelaide L. Rouse. New York, 1905

Letters to a Djinn. By Grace Zaring Stone. New York, 1922

Letters to a Lady in the Country. By Stuart P. Sherman. New York, 1925

Letters to Women in Love. By Mrs. John Van Vorst. New York, 1906

Living Up to Billy. By Elizabeth Cooper. New York, 1915

Love Letters, A Romance in Correspondence. By Harold R. Vynne. New York, 1927

Love Letters of a Musician. By Myrtle Reed. New York, 1898

Marjorie Daw and other people. By Thomas Bailey Aldrich. Boston, 1873

Married or Single? By C. M. Sedgwick. New York, 1857

Master-Knot a "Another Story", The. By Conover Duff. New York, 1895

Memoirs of the Bloomsgrove Family. In a Series of Letters to a Respectable Citizen of Philadelphia. By Enos Hitchcock, D.D. Boston, 1790

Mrs. Sinclair's Experiments. By Mrs. Wilson. Kansas City, Mo., 1900

My Lady of the Chinese Courtyard. By Elizabeth Cooper. New York, 1914

Old Gorgon Graham. More Letters from a Self-Made Merchant to his Son. By George Horace Lorimer. New York, 1904

Original Letters of Ferdinand and Elizabeth, The. By John Davis. New York, 1798

Our Lady of the Beeches. By Baroness Von Hutten. New York, 1902

A Parish of Two. By Henry Goelet McVickar and Price Collier (Percy Collins). Boston, 1903

Pillar of Fire, The; or, Israel in Bondage. By Rev. J. H. Ingraham. New York, 1895

Pipes of Yesterday, The. A Novel. By Frederic Arnold Kummer and Mary Christian. New York, 1921

Point of View, The. By Henry James. Century Magazine, December, 1882

Price Inevitable; or, the Confessions of Irene. An Autobiography. By Aurelia I. Sidner. New York, 1902

Power of Sympathy, The. By Sarah Wentworth Morton (?). Boston, 1789

Prince of the House of David, The; or, Three Years in the Holy City. By Rev. J. H. Ingraham. New York, 1855

Probus; or, Rome in the Third Century. In Letters from Lucius M. Piso from Rome, to Fausta, the Daughter, of Gracchus, at Palmyra. By William Ware, later known as "Aurelian". New York, 1838

Promise Not to Tell. New York, 1929

Quest of the Dream, The. By Edna Kingsley Wallace. New York, 1913

Randolph. A Novel. By John Neal. Phila., 1823

Rebecca; or, the Fille de Chambre. By Mrs. Susannah Rowson. ("Fille de Chambre", title of first edition.) London, 1792; 2nd Ed., Boston, 1814

Same Old Bill, Eh Mable? By Edward Streeter. New York, 1919

Sarah; or, the Exemplary Wife; or, Sincerity. By Mrs. Susannah Rowson. Boston, 1813

Secret History; or, the Horrors of St. Domingo, in a Series of Letters, written by a Lady at Cape Francis to Colonel Burr, late Vice-President of the United States. Principally during the command of General Rocheambeau. By Miss Hassall. Phila., 1808

Shamah in Pursuit of Freedom; or, The Branded Hand. Trans. from the Original Showian and Edited by an American Citizen. New York, 1858

Short Sixes. Stories to be Read While the Candle Burns. By H. C. Bunner. New York, 1890

Sins of a Widow, The. Confessed by Amélie L'Oiseau. New York, 1898

Some Letters of an American Woman concerning Love and other Things. By Sarah Biddle. Phila., 1902

Story of an Untold Love, The. By Paul Leicester Ford. New York, 1897

That's Me All Over, Mable. By Edward Streeter. New York, 1919

Three-Fingered Jack. (Obi; or, Three-Fingered Jack. The Famous Black Robber of the West Indian Islands.) New York, N.D.

Throne of David, The. From the Consecration of the Shepherd of Bethlehem to the Rebellion of Prince Absalom. By Rev. J. H. Ingraham. New York, 1860

To a Nun Confess'd; Letters from Yolande to Sister Mary. By Irene Osgood. Boston, 1905

Trials of the Human Heart, The. A Novel, in four Volumes. By Mrs. Susannah Rowson. Phila., 1795

'Twixt Cupid and Croesus; or, the Exhibits of an Attachment Suit. By Charles Peale Didier. New York, 1896

Uncle Bill's Letters to His Niece. By Ray Brown. New York, 1917

Unofficial Secretary, The. By Mary Ridpath Mann. Chicago, 1912

Venture in Identity, A. By Lucile G. Houghton. New York, 1911

Via P. and O. By Jane Stocking. New York, 1914

When Half-gods Go. Being the Story of a Brief Wedded Life as Told in Intimate and Confidential Letters written by a Bride to a Former College Mate. By Helen Reimensnyder Martin. New York, 1911

While Charlie Was Away. By Mrs. Poultney Bigelow. London, 1901

William Henry Letters. By Mrs. H. M. Diaz. Boston, 1870

Wooing of a Recluse, The. By Gregory Marwood. New York, 1914

INDEX